Turn Right at the Fountain

Turn RIGHT at the Fountain

GEORGE W. OAKES

at the Fountain

New and Enlarged Edition

WALKING TOURS OF

London
Oxford
Cambridge
Edinburgh
Copenhagen
Amsterdam
Bruges
Brussels
Paris
Rome
Florence   Vienna
Venice   Munich
Geneva
Athens
Madrid Barcelona
Toledo
Segovia

Illustrated with Maps

Holt, Rinehart and Winston · New York · Chicago · San Francisco

To Joanna, Diana, and James,

who walked with me

ACKNOWLEDGMENTS

I wish to express my gratitude to many friends whom I have consulted in organizing the walks recommended in these pages. They have been most generous, not only by contributing considerable time and effort, but also by taking an unusual degree of personal interest in this book.

The New York *Times* was good enough to grant me permission to republish a few chapters that, in whole or in part, have appeared in its Travel Section. In particular, I wish to thank Paul J. C. Friedlander, Travel Editor of the New York *Times,* whose enthusiastic and imaginative development of the idea of these articles and keen editorial judgment have been major factors in their success. I am also deeply indebted to him for important suggestions in the preparation of this book.

My friends Charles B. Seib, Assistant Managing Editor of the Washington *Star,* and Edwin Tribble, Sunday Editor of the Washington *Star,* have kindly assisted me with both encouragement and valuable editorial suggestions.

I wish to acknowledge the assistance I received in preparing the chapters on Rome from the following friends: Mrs. Yolanda Alfaro Maddux for sharing with me her extensive knowledge; Mrs. Gabriella Mellen for her extremely useful and stimulating ideas; Dr. Marcello Guidi, for his advice; Mr. and Mrs. Richard K. Irons for their constructive comments; and Miss Mary Cavaletti for the benefit of her experience in guiding Americans through Rome.

In preparing the chapters on Madrid and Toledo, I received considerable help and useful advice from Miss Helen Lemley, an American who is highly experienced as a well-known professional guide in Madrid. I wish to thank Mrs. Maxine Hitchcock for her kindness in advising me about Spain. I am also deeply indebted to Mrs. Peggy Donovan whose knowledge and years of residence in Spain contributed so much to the chapters on Madrid and Segovia. Miss Mari de Oliva helped me considerably with the chapters on Madrid and Barcelona.

Mrs. Henry S. Reuss kindly prepared for me valuable material which contributed greatly to the chapter on Vienna. Mme. Edith Platzer, wife of the Austrian Ambassador, generously offered helpful comments based on her knowledge of Vienna. Our old friend Svend Steenberg provided great assistance in the preparation of the chapter of his native Copenhagen. I also desire to thank the extremely competent guides of the Centre d'Information de Bruxelles for their aid in preparing the chapter on Brussels. Mrs. Heather Brigstocke kindly assisted me with the chapter on Athens.

Carroll R. Guest, who drafted so well the maps for some of these walks, played an essential role in the preparation of the book. I particularly wish to thank Samuel Surovell of Federal Graphics, Washington, D.C., for the care and attention he devoted to preparing the maps of Spain, Athens, Brussels and other walks in this revised edition. The following map publishers have generously permitted me to use their maps as a basis for the preparation of the maps in this book: Geographia Ltd., London; Alden and Co. Ltd., Oxford; W. Heffer and Sons Ltd., Cambridge; Scottish Tourist Board, Edinburgh; Politikens Forlag A/S, Copenhagen; N. V. Cartografisch Instituut Bootsma, Amsterdam; Tourist Office, Bruges; Blondel La Rougery, Paris; E. Verdesi, Rome; Vincitorio, Milan; Kartographische Anstalt Freytag-Berndt und Artaria, Vienna; Hotel Vier Jahreszeiten, Munich; Kompass-Verlag, Munich; Association Des Intérêts de Genève; R. de Rouck, Brussels; and Direction-General del Turismo, Spain.

Without the excellent typing of Miss B. Lieberman of Select Stenographic Service, the manuscript hardly could have been prepared.

Finally, I assume full responsibility for all errors that, despite my best efforts, have appeared in this volume.

FOREWORD

In the course of many years of European travel I have discovered a secret—the only way to get to know a city is by walking through it. Whether you have a few hours or more than a week, you will discover that by strolling you'll absorb much more of the special appeal of each city you visit. You will have a chance to explore the hidden byways and unusual places which give every city its own character. You can set your own pace, spend as much time as you like in the spots that interest you, and altogether enjoy yourself more.

Unless you walk you are bound to miss much. You have to go on foot to find the out-of-the-way corners, the hidden courtyards or tiny squares that often are so close to a great art gallery, for example, yet which so many tourists fail to see. To dash from a monumental cathedral to a famous museum is often too exhausting and concentrated to make for pleasant sightseeing. You will appreciate what you see much more if you travel in leisure, and experience variety along the way.

Aimless strolling—just wandering wherever your fancy suggests—can be a delight. But if you wish to visit the main places of interest, it will take weeks or even months to get to know a European city this way. The stroller who would see all that is great and beautiful and interesting in a reasonable length of time must follow a carefully planned route.

With this in mind, I decided to share my secret and wrote a series of "walking-tour" articles for the travel section of the

New York *Times*. This book came about as a result of the popularity of that series, which was started in the *Times* Travel Section in the spring of 1961. The response was so great and so many readers suggested that this series should be expanded into a book that I decided to rewrite the articles, add new walks, and include more cities to make the present volume.

In order that the information be as up-to-date as possible, I spent three months in Europe in the summer of 1962 and two months during the autumn of 1963 going over these walks. One experience on this trip made me realize how useful many visitors had found the articles in the *Times*. In London, the proprietor of "The Grenadier," a pub located off Hyde Park Corner that I included in one walk, told me that during the previous summer several hundred people had stopped in carrying the newspaper article describing this walk.

The countries chosen are those which most tourists visit, and the cities are the ones that visitors primarily interested in European history, art, and culture will want to see. In my view they represent the best of Europe.

The routes suggested do not include every important church, museum, art gallery, and historic building that you will want to visit. What I have done is to select routes that lead you to places of historic and artistic interest in the course of a walk through the more fascinating and delightful sections of each city. It so happens that these strolls do pass most of the places you'd want to see anyway. By following these walks, you will get a good over-all impression of what's considered most worthwhile and unusual in each city.

No specific time schedule is given for the completion of each stroll; that's a matter each reader or walker will want to decide for himself. The time you take depends on how long you want to linger at any one spot. When you feel you have done enough, stop and resume another time. The idea is to offer enjoyable walks that the average sightseer will find convenient to take in a morning or afternoon. Some will want to do more, some less. Your European trip will be more enjoyable if you plan your daily program as you feel inclined.

There is no particular order in which the walks should be done. Just select those that appeal to you. Every walk is accompanied by a map which clarifies the route you will follow.

Each walk begins at a well-known place—often in the center of the city. The concierge at your hotel will tell you the best way to get there. As many of the walks are not circular, you should inquire for return directions at the same time. Most cities have either subways or buses that run to or from a point not far from the start and finish of each route. The London and Paris maps show the underground or Metro stations near each route.

All of the cities described in this book are gradually changing—some more than others—to keep pace with the needs of the day. So, here and there, some places may be slightly different from what they were in the summer of 1962 and autumn of 1963.

If this book helps you either to anticipate the pleasure you will have in these fourteen cities or to enjoy their attractions more while you are there, it will have served its purpose.

G.W.O.

CONTENTS

CONTENTS

Britain

Britain

I LONDON

"THE CITY"—WEST

The Temple to Guildhall

The City of London, consisting of one square mile, is the oldest and original part of the present great metropolis. Because of its great age, you should approach it gradually, and with an awareness of due respect. You will get a better feel of this ancient community—believed to have been founded by the Romans shortly after they invaded Britain in A.D. 43—if you start your walk at the City's western limits.

Although small in area (677 acres) the City teems during the working week with 400,000 office workers, who pour into this commercial, financial, and legal hub of Britain from all parts of London and its suburbs. The uniform of most businessmen is bowler hat, black suit, and umbrella, although some stockbrokers wear top hats.

If the City has lost a good deal of its former world-wide influence on trade and finance, it is still very much an international business center. True to its tradition, it continues to be governed by the Lord Mayor and the Corporation. The City is in many ways a distinct community, as you will observe during your stroll. Even its policemen wear a special badge to set them apart from ordinary "bobbies."

Begin your walk at **Lincoln's Inn Fields,** one of London's largest squares (a couple of blocks from the **Holborn station** on the Central and Piccadilly underground lines). Designed in 1618 by the great architect and landscape gardener Inigo Jones, Lincoln's Inn Fields counts John Milton and Nell Gwyn among the famous historical figures who lived here. Today, most of the old houses are solicitors' offices, and the

3

START

HIGH HOLBORN

HOLBORN

HOLBORN

GRAYS INN ROAD

LINCOLNS INN

LINCOLN'S

INN

SILVER VAULTS

CHANCERY LANE

ST. ANDREW ST.

HOLBORN

KINGSWAY

FIELDS

PUBLIC RECORD OFFICE

FETTER LA.

WINE OFFICE CT.

ROYAL COURTS OF JUSTICE

FLEET

ST.

ST. BRID: CH.

ALDWYCH

ST. CLEMENT DANE: CH.

MID: TEMPLE

THE TEMPLE

STRAND

TEMPLE LANE

VICTORIA

EMBANKMENT

LONDON
'THE CITY'–WEST

ROUTE ->----->

UNDERGROUND STA. ●

100   50   0   100   YARDS   200

attractive gardens and wide lawns under the lofty old plane trees are frequented by office workers, especially at the noon hour.

On the north side of the square, at No. 13, is a little known but intensely interesting house, the **Soane Museum** (open Tuesday–Saturday, 10:00–5:00, except August; lecture tour on Saturday at 2:30). Sir John Soane was the distinguished architect of the late eighteenth and early nineteenth century who designed the Bank of England. His house is unusual because he provided in his will that the building and its furniture, as well as his art collection, should remain forever exactly as they had been during his lifetime. It is fascinating to see how mirrors have been used to give the impression of greater space. Sir John also had an extraordinary method of hanging pictures on shutters—be sure to see the amusing Hogarth paintings, *The Rake's Progress* and *The Election*.

At the east end of the square stands Lincoln's Inn, one of the four **Inns of Court,** whose records date from 1424 (open weekdays, 8:00–7:00; Sunday and holidays, 8:00–3:00). The Inns of Court—Lincoln's Inn, Gray's Inn, the Middle Temple, and the Inner Temple—dating from the reign of Edward I, make up a university of the law, exceeded only in age by the universities of Oxford and Cambridge, with which they have a centuries-old association. Go through the entrance into the delightful gardens with lawns as well manicured as putting greens, and ask at the old red brick gatehouse for permission to see the fine Tudor Old Hall, built in 1492 and noted for its linenfold paneling and splendid roof. The vaulting under the Inigo Jones chapel nearby is most attractive.

Now return to the gatehouse and step through the archway into **Chancery Lane.** To the left, about fifty yards along on the opposite side of the street, are the fascinating **Silver Vaults,** which provide a unique experience for the tourist and shopper.

Next to the Bank of England, the silver vaults and strong-rooms in this safe-deposit building are considered the most secure in Britain. The entrance is in a street called Southampton Buildings, just to the right off Chancery Lane. You go down about thirty-five feet below ground to the building's sub-basement, built in London blue rock under the **Holborn,** an ancient stream that ran from the village of Holborn to the Thames. Behind a three-ton steel door you will find thirty-five small shops along long corridors. Here you can browse for old silver, fine antiques, porcelain, etc. Londoners who are connoisseurs of old silver usually look here first for what they want. (Vaults are open Monday–Friday, 9:00–5:30; Saturday, 9:00–12:30.)

When you leave the silver vaults and return to Chancery Lane, turn left. A few hundred yards farther, beyond Lincoln's Inn, on the left side of the street you will come to the **Public Record Office** (open Monday–Friday, 1:00–4:00), the repository of Britain's historic documents. Among the outstanding exhibits here are two volumes of William the Conqueror's *Domesday Book,* an original copy of the Magna Charta, a letter from George Washington to his "great and good friend" George III (1795), and Nelson's logbook kept during the Battle of Trafalgar. If you enjoy looking at historic documents, you will find the Public Record Office a mine of information about Britain from its earliest days to the present.

At the end of Chancery Lane, turn right into Fleet Street, the heart of London's newspaper world. In a moment you will pass **Temple Bar,** which, since the twelfth century, has marked the western boundary of the City. Formerly, tolls were collected from all those passing the Bar.

Today, before entering the City, the Sovereign still goes through the formality of requesting permission to do so from the Lord Mayor, who signifies his approval by surrendering the City sword, point downward. When the sword is returned, the Lord Mayor bears it before Her Majesty as a symbol that he will protect her during her visit.

A few steps farther on are the **Law Courts.** Inquire at the porter's lodge to learn whether you can attend court to see the wigged judges and barristers in session.

Fleet Street, named for the stream which formerly flowed alongside (the water is now carried in a sewer), was at one time a Roman road. The spired church to the west, in the middle of the Strand, is Sir Christopher Wren's beautiful **St. Clement Danes.** Almost completely destroyed by bombing during World War II, the building has been extraordinarily well restored and is now the headquarters church of the RAF. In the section designated as a memorial to all airmen who lost their lives in the war, there is a special shrine consecrated to the U.S. Air Force.

Cross over to the other side of Fleet Street and stop in for coffee and a bun at the tiny 250-year-old shop of **Twining Bros.,** the tea merchants. Inside, the walls are covered with prints of old London.

A few yards farther on is the Wren gatehouse to the **Middle Temple.** The Middle and Inner Temples are so named because they occupy property that once belonged to the Order of Knights Templars, founded in 1118, during the Crusades. The Templars were a religious military order, dedicated to assisting pilgrims to the Holy Land. In Jerusalem, they made their headquarters near the church on the site of Solomon's Temple, from which they derived their name.

It is not clear just when during the early Middle Ages the lawyers occupied the Temple as tenants of the Knights, but it was prior to 1381, the year Wat Tyler led his unsuccessful revolt against serfdom.

Walk under the archway into ancient **Middle Temple Lane.** The overhanging seventeenth-century building above the footwalk is one of the few surviving examples of London housing before the Great Fire of 1666. Just down the sloping lane on the right is **Middle Temple Hall,** one of England's magnificent Elizabethan halls, built about 1570 (open Monday–Friday, 10:00–12:00, 3:00–4:30; Saturday, 10:00–1:00, 2:00–4:30). Severely bombed during World War II, it has been remarkably restored with much of its original material. You will marvel at the famous double hammerbeam, black oak roof. The twenty-nine-foot-high table in the hall was made from a single oak tree from Windsor Forest. The tree was a gift of Queen Elizabeth I, and was floated down the Thames. Below the dais is the "cupboard," a serving table made from timber of the *Golden Hind* and given to the inn by Sir Francis Drake, a member of the Templars. *Twelfth Night* was staged here in 1601 by the theatrical company in which Shakespeare was a partner. On request, the porter will usually be able to show you the panel rooms of the benchers' private apartments, which overlook the river. It is interesting to recall that five members of the Middle Temple signed the Declaration of Independence.

In the Temple buildings hereabout lived Dr. Johnson, Charles Lamb, Oliver Goldsmith, Sir William Blackstone, and William Makepeace Thackeray. Just below Middle Temple Hall are the delightful gardens where, during term time, barristers often stroll, wearing their traditional gowns. It was in these gardens, it is said, that the red and white roses which gave their names to the Wars of the Roses were plucked. As you wander along these old walks and through the ancient arches, you will sense the historic atmosphere of the Temple. There, during hundreds of years, the English legal system developed.

Go through the archway from Middle Temple Lane into the Inner Temple's Pump Court. On your right is **Inner Temple Hall,** recently rebuilt in Georgian style, and just beyond, toward the river, is Inner Temple Gardens.

Turn left to visit **Temple Church,** the finest of only four round churches that remain in England. It dates from the twelfth century and was built in the style of the Holy Sepulcher in Jerusalem (open daily, except Monday and Thursday, 10:00–1:00, 2:00–5:00). Go through the archway from Temple Church to **King's Bench Walk** with its fine seventeenth-century houses.

Turn into Inner Temple Lane and you will come to Fleet Street through a gate below a timbered building with large bow windows. Look sharply for the entrance to No. 17 so you can visit **Prince Henry's Room.** This is an interesting example of a seventeenth-century timber-constructed city house. The large paneled room on the first floor, with its Jacobean plastered ceiling, gives you a good idea of the ornate interior decoration of the period (open 1:45–5:00).

As you return to Fleet Street, cross over at Fetter Lane and turn right a few yards to No. 145, the entrance to the well-known restaurant, **"The Cheshire Cheese,"** established in 1667. It is pleasant to have lunch in this small old tavern with sawdust on the floor which is believed to have been a favorite of Dr. Samuel Johnson's (a reservation is advisable). It still has a great deal of atmosphere, although frequented largely by tourists. Just down Wine Office Court (a few yards from the tavern) is **Dr. Johnson's house,** built in the seventeenth century, at 17 Gough Square, where you can visit the old garret in which he compiled his famous dictionary. Several mementos of the great lexicographer are on view, including two first editions of the dictionary, published in 1755. (The house is open weekdays, 10:30–5:00, except from October through April when it closes at 4:30.)

Cross Fleet Street again and walk past the imposing buildings of some of London's major newspapers. Just beyond Salisbury Court is the entrance to **St. Bride's Church,** one of Sir Christopher Wren's famous City churches, largely rebuilt after World War II. Fortunately, the lovely steeple, the City's tallest, survived the bombing attacks.

In a moment you will be at busy Ludgate Circus. Cross the circus, and a little farther along on Ludgate Hill, turn left and enter **Old Bailey.** Before you, on the right, you will find the noted Old Bailey Criminal Court, built on the site of **Newgate Gaol,** which was used as a prison as early as the eleventh century. Here, among countless others, William Penn and Daniel Defoe were jailed.

Cross Newgate Street and walk along Giltspur Street past "Bart's" (**St. Bartholomew's Hospital,** London's oldest) to West Smithfield, once the scene of medieval tournaments and now known for the adjacent **Smithfield Central Markets,** which cover ten acres and deal mainly in dressed meat, poultry, and dairy produce. It is the largest market of its kind in the world, where 400,000 tons of foodstuffs are sold yearly. The best time to visit the busy markets is between 5:00 and 9:00 A.M., so perhaps you will want to return on another occasion. Right now may be the moment to explore some of the colorful market pubs hereabout.

At the eastern end of the market, turn left on Lindsey Street, and walk through Charterhouse Square to visit **Charterhouse,** originally a fourteenth-century priory but later, in 1611, a hospital which accommodated eighty poor brethren and forty poor students. From this foundation grew the well-known public school of the same name, but the school was moved, almost a hundred years ago, to Surrey, and now the old brick and timbered buildings are the residence of only a few elderly bachelors and widowers. Ask the porter at the gate to show you the original monastery gates and the outlines of the monks' cells, as well as the Great Hall dating from the sixteenth century and the splendid Elizabethan Great Chamber above the library.

Return to West Smithfield, and at the beginning of Little Britain you will find on the left the Norman **Church of St. Bartholomew the Great,** London's oldest parish church. It is well worth visiting as an interesting example of a London church erected before the Great Fire of 1666. Also, you will enjoy its charming, although tiny, cloisters and shaded churchyard with ancient tombstones. Benjamin Franklin worked as a printer in what is now the **Lady Chapel,** a site that has had a checkered history through the centuries, being first a chapel, then a private house, a printing works, a public house, a dance hall, a factory, and in the 1890's restored to its original state.

Walk down Little Britain and King Edward Street, then turn left at Angel Street, opposite London's main post office and cross St. Martin's le Grand. Turn left and walk a half block to Gresham Street. Turn right, and a block farther along will bring you to Foster Lane and the **Goldsmiths' Hall.** You can see this palatial hall—one of the leading City livery companies, where lovely gold plate and antique silver are exhibited on special occasions—if you write in advance to the Clerk of the Goldsmiths' Company, Cheapside, London E.C. 2 (the hall is closed in August and September).

These City livery companies, of which eighty-one still exist, have a membership of about ten thousand. Their members, which include leading professional men and businessmen in the City, maintain the age-old traditions and customs of the companies. Originally medieval craft guilds, the livery companies became closely associated with the municipal affairs of the City. The liverymen of the companies nominate the candidate for Lord Mayor. Aside from their role in the governing of the City, the companies are concerned with charitable and philanthropic activities and are associated with thirty famous schools. Several are responsible for important technical-training schools and colleges. For example, the Goldsmiths, one of the wealthiest and oldest (founded in 1327), established a school at London University. The company also still conducts the London Assay Office for hallmarking gold and silver plate.

Leaving Goldsmiths' Hall, walk down Foster Lane to **Cheapside.**

Cross the busy thoroughfare and enter the churchyard of Wren's masterpiece, **St. Paul's Cathedral,** the architectural and spiritual glory of the City. Stroll around the gardens on your way to the front of the cathedral and look up at the huge dome outlined against the sky. This is a peaceful oasis in the City, with flower beds and birds singing in the shrubbery. St. Paul's was built between 1675 and 1710 and is the largest cathedral in Britain. You will want to make a leisurely visit, either now or at another time, to see the cathedral proper, the crypt with the tombs of Nelson and Wellington, and, if you are energetic, the whispering gallery and the stone gallery, which commands a superb view of London.

At this point you should take a slight diversion to visit the **College of Arms,** the official headquarters for the determination of armorial bearings and pedigrees. It was chartered in 1555.

As you leave St. Paul's, cross the main road and stop in at the information center of the City of London before entering Godliman Street. At the corner of Queen Victoria Street you will find an old red brick building where the College of Arms, or Heralds' Office, is located. Here is the office of the Earl Marshal, the chief ceremonial officer of the Kingdom and the head of the college. The other officials of the college are the three kings of arms, the six heralds, and the four pursuivants. These functionaries have important and colorful duties to perform at the time of the coronation of the British Sovereign or at the annual opening of Parliament. The kings of arms have the legal right to trace, establish, and record pedigrees. The college library and collection maintain the most complete heraldic and genealogical records in the world. Visitors may inquire at the college for heraldic data. For a fee and on submission of proper documentary evidence that your family has been authorized to display arms, you can be granted your armorial bearings. (The college is open Monday–Friday, 10:00–4:00; Saturday, 10:00–1:00.)

Now retrace your steps to the information center. Ahead of you is a large new building, the extension of the Bank of England. Cross over to **Watling Street,** one of the main roads built by the Romans. You can either go through the bank building to see the sunken gardens or turn left on Bread Street to reach Cheapside. After a few yards you will pass Wren's famous **Bow Church.** Tradition has it that anyone born within the sound of Bow Bells is a "cockney," a true Londoner. The proverbial bells of Dick Whittington's time were destroyed in 1666. Their replacements were ruined during the bombing of the church in World War II, but new bells were installed in 1962 and are rung on various occasions.

Turning left at King Street, you will see before you the ancient and impressive **Guildhall,** the Hall of the Corporation of the City of London, dating from the early fifteenth century.

As you enter the Great Hall, the seat of government of the City, you will note its coat of arms over the Gothic porch, bearing the words *"Domine dirige nos"* ("Lord, direct us"). The hall is often the scene of presentations of "the freedom of the City of London" to distinguished citizens of Britain and foreign countries. Here, too, are held the annual Lord Mayor's banquets as well as state dinners. You will be fascinated by the shields and embroidered banners of the city livery companies, as well as the wooden figures of Gog and Magog, the famed giants of English mythology who are traditionally associated with the Guildhall. The originals of these famous statues were destroyed in the 1940 air-raid fire and replaced a few years ago. An impressive statue of Sir Winston Churchill is probably the best work of art in the Hall. During your tour of the Guildhall, be sure to use the radio tour instrument, available without cost, to listen to a twenty-minute talk on the Guildhall. Both the Queen's and Churchill's voices can be heard in excerpts from their Guildhall speeches.

You should stop in at the **Guildhall Library,** which contains many instructive exhibits about the City and its famous residents.

As you wander about Guildhall, so intimately bound up with past centuries of old London, you will share the feeling of long tradition that is characteristic of the City and which lives to some degree in the hearts of all Englishmen.

"THE CITY"—EAST

Guildhall to the Tower

If you have taken the first walk in the City, you will have ended up at the **Guildhall.** To resume your tour of the square mile of London's financial and business center from the Guildhall, you return to Cheapside, which leads into **Poultry** (named for the poultry dealers located there in medieval times). As you turn left into Poultry you pass the street named

Old Jewry, where the Jews lived prior to their expulsion from England in 1290. In another block you will reach the heart of the City, the busy square where the Bank of England, the Royal Exchange, and the Mansion House are located.

On the other hand, you may prefer to start this walk in the City at the **Mansion House,** the official residence of the Lord Mayor. The easiest way to get there from London's West End is to come by underground to the Bank Station.

At the corner of Poultry and Queen Victoria Street you will see the Corinthian portico of the eighteenth-century Mansion House to your right. This is the Lord Mayor's residence during his year of office—the last great town house in the City.

To view the interior of the Mansion House (it is open to the public every other Saturday afternoon at 2:00), you should phone the Lord Mayor's private secretary in advance (MAN 2500). The principal rooms are the Egyptian Hall, where large banquets and receptions are held; the salon, which displays a Waterford glass chandelier with 8,000 pieces; and the Court of Justice. The Lord Mayor presides over this court, which administers justice in the southern part of the City. Below the courtroom there are prison cells.

The classic building within the angle formed by Cornhill and Threadneedle Street is the **Royal Exchange.** Queen Elizabeth I ordered that the first building on this site be given its royal designation because it was the great meeting place for the city merchants. Part of the pavement from Sir Thomas Gresham's original building on this same site can be seen in the central court below the glass dome. The present structure dates from the mid-nineteenth century. Since 1955, it has housed the Guildhall museum, which contains not only Saxon and Roman antiquities, many connected with early London, but also relics of London's later periods. (Open weekdays, 10:00–5:00.)

The Royal Exchange chimes are rung at three hourly intervals beginning at 9:00 in the morning, and they play English, Scottish, Welsh, Canadian, and Australian airs to add notes of gaiety to the somber businesslike surroundings.

LONDON
'THE CITY'-EAST

ROUTE ->->->-

UNDERGROUND STA. ●

100   50   0   100   YARDS 200

As you stand on the steps of the Royal Exchange surveying the traffic jam of big red buses, taxis, and cars that converge here from seven main streets, you will see to your right the massive and imposing Bank of England. In the interests of security, a forbidding stone wall surrounds the bank's four acres. If you look carefully you will notice in the pediment facing you the statue of Britannia, referred to as "the Old Lady of Threadneedle Street."

The Bank of England, now a national institution, was chartered in 1694. Its best-known function today is the issuance of all paper money in the United Kingdom. As the government's banker, it establishes the official interest or bank rate, manages the national debt, handles exchange controls, and guards in its vaults the nation's gold reserves. It has been said of it that "no bank has played so large or so distinguished a part, not merely in the fortunes of a great nation, but in the general financial activities of the world."

Following a custom dating from 1780 when rioters threatened the Bank, each evening at 6:00 a detachment from the Brigade of Guards, consisting of one officer and sixteen rank and file, arrives to protect the famous edifice.

You can go into the entrance hall. There the gatekeepers and bank messengers dressed in red vests, pink tail-coats, long-tailed scarlet gowns, and tricorn hats after the fashion of the first governor's early-eighteenth-century gate porters, lend a historic air to the venerable institution. From the hall you have a glimpse of the charming courtyard with mulberry trees planted on its lawn.

Having set foot in the famous precincts of the bank, turn left along Threadneedle Street to the first cross street, Bartholomew Lane. Follow it a short block and then make a right on Throgmorton Street and walk to No. 8, known as "The House," the entrance to the **London Stock Exchange.** Until 1801, the exchange operated in the Royal Exchange and in coffee houses located in Change Alley and Threadneedle Street.

There is a special visitors' gallery where trading can be

observed taking place in the large galleries between 10:30 and 3:00. Guides explain not only the intense activity of the 2,500 brokers on the huge floor below, but even their sartorial garb (many customarily wear high silk hats). After watching the jobbers and brokers carrying out transactions by word of mouth, go downstairs to Throgmorton Street.

From here you wander around the byways of the City, crowded with black-coated workers. The hubbub in these tiny streets and alleys—many closed to motor traffic—gives the City its peculiar character and air of excitement. The buildings all around you are offices of banks, stock broker-ages, insurance companies, accountant firms, and all those intimately involved in finance and commerce. Stop at any one of them and read the names inscribed on plaques at the entrance. You will get a feel of the City's international char-acter by the number of foreign business houses listed on almost every building.

Opposite the Stock Exchange is Throgmorton Avenue. This takes you past **Drapers' Hall,** at No. 28, the home of the Drapers' Company, third-ranking livery company. Ask for the beadle, or custodian, in order to get permission to see the hall (closed in August). Turn right in Austin Friars to the modern **Dutch Church,** religious center of Dutch Protestants in London since 1550, except during the reign of Catholic Mary.

Opposite the church is Austin Friars passage, leading to Great Winchester Street. Turn right here and after a few yards you will be at Old Broad Street. The tall new stone building ahead is **Goodenough House,** home of Barclays Bank. Cross the street and to the right walk through Gresham House, which has a private lift right in the middle of the corridor that leads to Bishopsgate.

On the opposite side of this busy thoroughfare and a hun-dred yards to the left, you will find the smallest church in the city, **St. Ethelburga's** (60 by 30 feet), founded about the be-ginning of the fifteenth century. Inside are three stained-glass windows in memory of Henry Hudson, the discoverer of the Hudson River in New York.

Retracing your steps along Bishopsgate, just beyond St. Helen's Place (by a bus stop), you go through an archway to **St. Helen's Church,** one of the oldest in the City, dating from the early years of the thirteenth century (open 10:00–4:00). The courtyard in front of the church, with trees and a tiny lawn, is a charming spot. St. Helen's Church is particularly interesting because it is one of the few City churches that escaped the Great Fire. It is often known as the "Westminster Abbey of the City" for its fine early English architecture and many ancient tombs of prominent city figures, like Sir Thomas Gresham, founder of the Royal Exchange.

At this point you should wander down the winding alley of Great St. Helen's until you reach the street called St. Mary Axe. Turn left a few yards to the **Baltic Exchange,** at No. 26, the headquarters of merchants and brokers concerned with floating cargoes—grain, oil, timber, coal, etc. From the entrance, you can watch the exchange in operation. (Open Monday–Friday, 10:00–4:30.)

After visiting the Baltic, stop in at No. 24, **Cayzer House.** There is a fascinating world map on the wall in the reception hall that shows the movements of all the ships operated by the Union Castle and associated lines.

From here return along St. Mary Axe into Leadenhall Street. On the opposite side, along Lime Street, is **Lloyd's,** the world-renowned corporation of insurance underwriters. Its present membership of over four thousand has grown from a few merchants who met nearby in Edward Lloyd's coffee house about 1685, for whom Lloyd collected and posted shipping news. By 1769 the patrons of the coffee house set up their own establishment under the same name, and a few years later they obtained premises in the Royal Exchange. Lloyd's was incorporated by Act of Parliament in 1871 and has been engaged in all kinds of insurance (except life) since 1911.

Ask the waiter wearing a red cloak and top hat (his title

goes back to the coffee house days) for permission to look at "The Room," the huge Underwriting Room where the eighteenth-century **Lutine Bell** in the center is rung twice for good news and once for bad. During a busy period, three thousand people will be here. On exhibition in the Nelson Room is the Admiral's logbook containing his original message signaled to the Fleet at the Battle of Trafalgar: "England expects every man to do his duty."

Just past Lloyd's, down Leadenhall Place and on the left, you will have an amusing time wandering around the meat and provision stalls of **Leadenhall Market.** Fish, poultry, green vegetables, fruit, flowers, and cheese are sold in shops under the glass-covered arcade. Often well-dressed businessmen take a few minutes off from their work in August to dash in and purchase grouse flown down from Scottish moors as a special treat for their families.

You can leave the market on Gracechurch Street. Cross over and walk to the left under an arch, and turn right into Bell Inn Yard a bit down the street. This will lead you through archways and little passages into Castle Court and Birchin Lane. Here is a fascinating bit of the City; at times you think you are in a maze. If you feel like lunching in a well-known City chophouse, try **The George and Vulture** in St. Michael's Alley just before you reach Birchin Lane. It is said to have been founded in 1175 as "The George," but is mainly known because Charles Dickens was an habitué (ask to see Mr. Pickwick's bedroom). It may be noisy but, if you can seclude yourself in a booth, you will be entertained by the general bustle and perhaps even by snatches of conversation you may have with your table companions. Upon leaving, you come out on Lombard Street by following Birchin Lane just a few yards to the left.

Lombard Street, London's banking center since the Middle Ages, was named for the Lombard merchants of Italy who became moneylenders in the city during the twelfth century. Be sure to notice the banking signs still hung out, following the custom of medieval days, by Britain's largest commercial bank, **Martin's,** at No. 68, and one of the other "big five" banks, **Lloyd's,** at No. 71.

Cross Lombard Street and walk down Nicholas Lane to King William Street. After turning left you will shortly have a glimpse of the top of the **Monument,** which Sir Christopher Wren designed and erected between 1671 and 1677 as a memorial to the Great Fire. Its 202-foot height is said to be the exact distance from its base to the baker's shop in Pudding Lane where the Great Fire began. Keep to the left at the crossroads to the pedestrian island in Gracechurch Street. Then cross to Fish Street Hill and the column will be directly ahead of you. If you can face climbing 311 steps to the balcony below the golden ball, you will be rewarded by a fine view over the City, including the Tower and the Pool of London.

Many visitors will want to set foot on **London Bridge,** even though the present structure, built in 1831 and therefore the oldest in London, has none of the romance which is attached to the name. Approach the bridge by King William Street, a block from the monument. Near the site of London Bridge, the highest navigable point for shipping, stood earlier bridges going back to the tenth century. The **London Museum** in Kensington Gardens has some interesting reproductions of old London Bridge with its houses and shops.

If you walk over London Bridge you'll see the more publicized **Tower Bridge** downstream and the famous Tower along the embankment. Beyond the far end of London Bridge, on the right, stands **Southwark Cathedral,** well worth a visit on another occasion. On the Southwark bank, cranes and hoists may be loading freighters. Upstream there is a fine view of the dome of St. Paul's.

You descend a flight of stairs at the City end of the bridge to Lower Thames Street, turn right, and continue a couple of hundred yards to **Billingsgate Market.** Probably taking its name from Belin, a legendary king of the Britons, Billingsgate has been London's chief wholesale fish market since 1699, handling 350 to 400 tons of wet, dried, and shellfish daily. In fact, Billingsgate is the greatest inland wholesale fish market in the world. In Roman days this was a principal place for landing produce.

To see Billingsgate in action, you should be there around 8:00 in the morning. Nearly 200 firms and 2,500 individuals are engaged in buying and selling fish, which comes by truck and no longer by water. But the most colorful sight at Billingsgate, aside from all kinds of seafood on the stalls, are the 400-odd fish porters with their flat-topped leather hats on which each man can carry a hundredweight of fish. One porter carrying this amount won a mile race in the record time of seven minutes and thirteen seconds. These hats were orginally called "bobbing hats" because the act of carrying fish from the wholesaler to the retailer's vehicle was known as "bobbing." Many of the hats worn today have been handed down from father to son. You will have to mix around with the porters—perhaps in the adjacent Piscatorial Café—to decide whether their language still lives up to its reputation earned hundreds of years ago.

When you come out of the market, cross Lower Thames Street and, a few yards farther along, turn left into St. Dunstan's Hill, which leads to Great Tower Street. On the opposite side you will be in **Mincing Lane,** center of commodity markets in tea, sugar, coffee, cocoa, rubber, jute, tortoise shell, and ivory ever since the Genoese landed many of these goods here in the sixteenth century. Tea, long associated with Mincing Lane, is still the most important item of trade in this fascinating street of exotic commerce which the spice trade made famous. **Plantation House,** the large building on the left along Mincing Lane, has an elephant, symbol of the tea trade, over the entrance. Wander into "Hale & Son" just inside and you will see brokers handling such bizarre products as feathers or rhinoceros horns from India. There are also auction rooms for tea, coffee, sugar, and rubber in this building.

Returning to Great Tower Street, you walk along it a couple of short blocks to the open space of **Tower Hill.** Just before you get there, you will see **All Hallows' Church** on your right. This old church, built in the time of Cromwell, survived the Great Fire. Americans will be interested in the fact that President John Quincy Adams was married here. In front of you now stands the historic Tower of London, which has played such a prominent role in British history since William the Conqueror. (Open weekdays, 10:00–5:30; Sunday, 2:00–5:00.)

The Tower, Britain's most famous fortress, has been a royal palace, premier prison of the realm, execution site, repository of the crown jewels, treasure vault, mint, court of justice, arsenal, munitions factory, naval station, and garrison. It covers eighteen acres. To see it properly requires at least an hour, and to learn its fascinating history you should buy a special guide to the Tower.

After crossing the moat, now filled in with grass and flowers, you may want to start at the **Bell Tower** along whose ramparts Elizabeth I walked while a prisoner before becoming Queen. Now enter the **Wakefield Tower** where the royal jewels are on display. Here you will see **St. Edward's Crown,** the oldest in Britain. It was made for Charles II and last used in Queen Elizabeth II's coronation. Other royal regalia, including the Royal Sceptre, Orb, and Sword of State, are also on display.

Next to the Wakefield Tower is the **Bloody Tower** where the little princes were murdered in 1483 and where Sir Walter Raleigh was confined for thirteen years, while he wrote the *History of the World*.

On Tower Green, you will see the famous ravens. It is said that when they no longer appear, the end of Britain will occur. Note the brass plate that commemorates the site of the royal scaffold where Anne Boleyn and the Earl of Essex were executed.

The **White Tower,** dating from William the Conqueror, contains the oldest chapel in London and a large collection of armor and old weapons. Just nearby, sections of the old **Roman Wall** that surrounded London have been excavated.

While wandering around the Tower grounds you will encounter yeomen warders wearing their colorful blue uniform of Tudor days. Contrary to popular impression, they are not the "beefeaters," a term reserved for yeomen of the guard. To see the seven-hundred-year-old ceremony of the warders locking the gates at 10:00 in the evening and handing over the keys to the Governor, you must write the Governor for permission. The Governor commands the troops stationed in the Tower, which has been a military garrison for nine hundred years.

After touring the Tower, walk along **Tower Wharf** by the river, where ancient guns are on display and where today the Honourable Artillery Company of the City fires salutes on state occasions. As you turn back toward **Traitor's Gate** and contemplate the great personalities and events that have made the Tower probably the most storied spot in British history, you may be just in the mood for something out of the ordinary. After walking through the City and seeing it up close, why not view it from the water by taking one of the **sightseeing boats** from here to the **West End.** During the summer season, they leave from the Tower for **Westminster Bridge** every twenty minutes from 11:00 to 5:30. En route you will hear a very informative talk on all the points of interest you pass on both banks of the Thames.

WESTMINSTER

The Hub of Britain

Here is a walk in the heart of London that is particularly suited to visitors who wish to see some of the most interesting and accessible places but can spare only a couple of hours. In fact, if you have business or shopping to do in the West End, you can fit this pleasant stroll into those plans and visit some fascinating out-of-the-way spots.

Carrying a raincoat or umbrella, just in case the blue skies

THAMES

RIVER

HOUSES OF PARLIAMENT

VICTORIA TOWER GARDENS

LAMBETH BRIDGE

MILLBANK

MILLBANK

FINISH

PARLIAMENT

WESTMINSTER ABBEY

GREAT COLLEGE ST.

SMITH SQ.

WESTM. SCHOOL

TATE GALLERY

BULINGA ST.

ATTERBURY ST.

DEANS YARD

TUFTON ST.

MARSHAM ST.

HORSEFERRY RD.

JOHN ISLIP ST.

GREAT SMITH ST.

GREAT PETER ST.

BROADWAY

VAUXHALL BRIDGE RD.

PETTY

FRANCE

RINGHAM GATE

VICTORIA ST.

LONDON
WESTMINSTER

ROUTE ▸----▸

UNDERGROUND STA. ●

100 50 0 100 200 YARDS 300

disappear all of sudden (as they do too often in London) and a bit of rain descends, start at **Piccadilly Circus,** London's hub. Its name comes from "piccadill," a high collar with lace edges which was popular in the seventeenth century. In the center of the circus is the aluminum statue known as *Eros,* not intended by the sculptor to represent the God of Love, as generally believed, but rather the Angel of Christian Charity.

Walk west along Piccadilly for two blocks to **St. James's Church,** a charming red brick building, designed by Wren. Largely destroyed during the war, the church has since been restored. St. James's Church was very stylish in the eighteenth century, and society weddings are often held there still.

From the churchyard turn right into **Jermyn Street,** where you will be lured by the old-fashioned shops. On the left you will find an art-supply store over a hundred years old. A few doors away is a real pharmacy, not a drugstore. A bit farther along at No. 93, is a marvelous cheese shop, Paxton and Whitfield, boasting probably the most complete selection in London—with almost every variety you have ever heard of. Go inside and look at the huge slabs of English Stilton or Cheddar.

Return along Jermyn Street and turn right into Duke of York Street to **St. James's Square,** which was laid out by Charles II for fashionable mansions. As you enter the square, the building on the corner to your right is **Chatham House,** formerly the residence of three Prime Ministers, the Earl of Chatham, Lord Derby, and William E. Gladstone, but now the Royal Institute of International Affairs. As you walk around the square, be sure to notice the unusually fine plane trees in the gardens. At No. 14 you will pass the **London Library,** England's most famous subscription library, founded in 1841 and now possessing 600,000 volumes. The British Arts Council, which provides government grants for cultural institutions like the Royal Ballet and various symphony orchestras, is located at No. 4. Continuing around the patrician square, you come to a large building at the southwest corner,

Norfolk House, where General Eisenhower planned the invasions of North Africa and Europe during World War II.

At this end of the square a narrow street a few yards long leads into **Pall Mall,** the center of London's distinguished clubs. Pall Mall received its name from "pall-mall," an old French game similar to croquet, played in England at the time of Charles I. Immediately across the street, the large Italian *palazzo* houses the **Reform Club,** liberal in politics and including a large membership prominent in public affairs, journalism, economics, finance, and the law. For a look at the classic façade of the **Athenaeum,** London's leading literary and intellectual club, walk a few yards to the left beyond the Reform Club to the corner of Waterloo Place. There you may see a bishop, or a don on his way from his London home away from home, going back to Oxford or Cambridge.

Returning along Pall Mall you will pass several other clubs on your way to St. James's Street. Turning right into St. James's Street you will notice, in one of the oldest and smallest buildings in the area, the bow windows of Lock's, the well-known hatter, with plumed helmets from the days of the Duke of Wellington on display. A few doors away, at No. 3, there is a very narrow passageway, Pickering Place, cut between two houses and leading a scant hundred feet or so to one of London's charming courts—a secluded corner away from the noise of the city. This was London's last dueling ground, where Georgian gentlemen settled their disputes with rapiers. As you emerge from Pickering Place, directly opposite is the massive dark brick Tudor gatehouse of **St. James's Palace,** with its picturesque chimneys dominating the low buildings of the palace behind it. To appreciate fully the dramatic effect of the sixteenth-century clock tower and turrets, look at the palace from a block or so up St. James's Street.

St. James's Palace, built by Henry Vlll, was for several centuries the official London residence of the Sovereign, until Queen Victoria moved to Buckingham Palace. Major court functions were held at St. James's Palace; hence the present accreditation of foreign ambassadors "to the Court of St. James's."

When the Queen is not in residence at Buckingham Palace, a changing of the guard takes place here between October and March at 10:30 A.M. in Friary Court. At all times a unit of the Brigade of Guards stands sentry duty in front of the palace. Enter **Ambassadors Court** through the passageway west of the gatehouse. Strolling around the quiet courtyard, it is hard to realize you are within a stone's throw of traffic-jammed St. James's Street. **York House,** the residence of the Duke and Duchess of Gloucester, occupies the north side. From the southwest corner of the courtyard you can see silhouetted against the sky the dark red clock tower and its battlements. On a clear day, this is one of the most romantic scenes in central London. Wander leisurely through Stable Yard and on to **Clarence House,** the home of the Queen Mother. This imposing mansion, just beyond the palace and off the Mall, was built by the great architect John Nash.

The Mall, London's majestic boulevard between Buckingham Palace and Admiralty Arch, presents a stately vista. Lined with double rows of plane trees, it has a pinkish pavement, whose color comes out sharply in rainy weather. On ceremonial occasions, the flagstaffs along the avenue fly the standards of visiting dignitaries. Behind you and running along most of the Mall, the long classic façade of John Nash's Carlton House terrace—formerly mansions of the aristocracy—overlooks St. James's Park.

Cross over into **St. James's Park,** the most picturesque of London's public recreation areas. Named in the thirteenth century for a female leprosy hospital, the **Sisters of St. James in the Fields,** this oldest of the city's parks was taken over by Henry VIII in 1532 but not opened to the public until the reign of the Stuarts. Patterning his ideas after those of Versailles, the Stuart King Charles II cleaned up the swamps and underbrush and put in trees and new lawns. But as one sees it now, St. James's Park dates from the period of George IV.

Stroll down the walk, which cuts across the broad well-

kept lawns, filled on a fine summer day with Londoners re-
clining in beach chairs, toward the small suspension bridge.
Standing here, with your back to Buckingham Palace, you
may see the unusual landscaping of the park, with the somber
shades of the Foreign Office well to the right, over the weeping
willows. But the most striking view is toward the Horse
Guards Parade, with its pearl-gray stone buildings, behind
which rise the fantastic Victorian Gothic structures of **Whitehall Court.**

Across the little bridge, along the path to the left, is one of
London's more fascinating sights—**Duck Island,** a bird and
wildlife sanctuary. About 4:00 in the afternoon is probably
the best time to see the three species of pelicans (presented by
a Russian ambassador years ago) parading near the old Bird-
keeper's Lodge on the island, seeking their daily fish ration.
Twenty species of colorful wild ducks and geese also inhabit
the island and are usually swimming in the lake. Some of
the well-dressed men you will notice out for a bit of fresh
air may be MP's rehearsing a speech, or officials from the
Foreign Office.

After this excursion into what might be called a ducal
preserve, cross the road by the **Horse Guards Parade.** Here,
in the early summer every year, on the Queen's official birth-
day, the dramatic and stirring ceremony of Trooping the
Color takes place. In this magnificent spectacle, the Queen
on her charger leads a parade of the horse-and-foot Guards
Brigade, all resplendent in full-dress scarlet-and-blue uniforms, and some, like the mounted band, displaying silver and
gold as well.

Climb the few steps into **Downing Street** where, at No. 10,
the Prime Minister has resided since the days of Sir Robert
Walpole. The simple and dignified Georgian brick house was
designed by a Harvard graduate, Sir George Downing. A moment later, you are in **Whitehall.** If you happen to be there
just before 11:00 A.M., hurry along to the left a block or so
to the Horse Guards to see the changing of the guard—a
colorful ceremony.

From here, walk back along Whitehall past the **Cenotaph,** commemorating the dead in two world wars, to Parliament Square. Before you rises the lofty tower of **Big Ben,** Britain's timekeeper. On the right of the square there is an impressive **statue of Abraham Lincoln.** Cross the road and enter the courtyard just below Big Ben to visit Westminster Hall, the oldest and finest building in the **Houses of Parliament.** (Open weekdays from 10:00 until one hour before Parliament meets, and until 4:00 when Parliament is in recess.)

Westminster Hall, built by William Rufus in the eleventh century, is the only surviving part of the medieval **Palace of Westminster.** Today its noblest architectural feature is its magnificent hammerbeam oak roof, dating from 1399. The hall was the site of the Great Council, which preceded Parliament. Later, in the sixteenth century, it was Parliament's meeting place. The chief law courts also sat here from the end of the thirteenth century until 1825. The hall has been the scene of many famous state trials, and a brass marker on the south steps records the spot where Charles I was condemned to death. His successor, Oliver Cromwell, became Protector in Westminster Hall in 1653. His statue stands outside on Parliament Square, and, oddly enough, the statue of Charles I is only a few hundred yards away in Whitehall.

Foreign visitors can get permission to attend sessions of the House of Commons and House of Lords by applying to their Embassy or to the Admissions Office in St. Stephen's Hall, opposite Westminster Abbey. The best time to tour the Houses of Parliament with an official guide is on a Saturday or on any Monday in August between 10:00 and 4:30.

Opposite the Houses of Parliament is **Westminster Abbey.** Religious worship has been held on this site since 750 A.D., when a Benedictine abbey (the west monastery of the City of London, or Westminster) was built here. In the eleventh century, Edward the Confessor rebuilt the abbey, and in the thirteenth century Henry III enlarged it. Its architectural design is early English; its Gothic nave is the loftiest in England.

Every English sovereign from William the Conqueror

to Queen Elizabeth II has been crowned in the abbey. Be sure to see the coronation chair, made by the King's painter for Edward I; it contains the Stone of Scone, used as the coronation seat by kings of Scotland from 850 until Edward I captured it in 1296.

The Henry VII Chapel, a superb example of late Perpendicular Gothic style, with its lovely fan-tracery vaulting, is the abbey's architectural gem. Its nave is embellished by the carved stalls and the colorful overhanging banners of the Knights of the Bath.

Westminster Abbey is crowded with countless historic graves and memorials to Britain's great, but Americans should not miss the **tablet to President Franklin D. Roosevelt** just inside the great West Door near the **tomb of the Unknown Warrior.** It's a fascinating experience to wander around the abbey discovering the names of sovereigns, statesmen, poets, writers, and actors, on tombs and monuments, too numerous to mention. It seems as if every prominent figure in English history is either buried or commemorated by a memorial here.

If you have time, take a turn around the fourteenth-century **Cloisters** and then visit the **Chapter House,** called the "cradle of free Parliaments" because the House of Commons met here from 1352 to 1547. The original thirteenth-century pavement, the best-preserved in England, still retains its brilliant coloring.

Just beyond the Chapter House is one of the most extraordinary museums in London—the **Abbey Museum** in the Norman Undercroft, one of the few surviving parts of Edward the Confessor's church. At one time it was customary "at the funerals of Kings or Queens to represent them by a life-sized robed figure, either of wood or of wax, which lay on the coffin as it was borne through the streets." The Abbey Museum contains several remarkable examples of death masks, effigies, and wax figures.

The amazing wooden effigy, a death-mask portrait of Edward III, victor of the battle of Crécy, shows him as he died in 1377, with his mouth and left cheek affected by the muscular contraction that ended his life.

The remarkable death mask of Henry VII is so perfect in detail of bone structure and facial characteristics that it might have been made yesterday. The plaster around the ears has retained small tufts of red and gray hair that may have actually belonged to the dead king.

The full-size contemporary figure of Charles II dressed in his splendid robes of the Order of the Garter stands in a glass case, resplendent in all details. The effigy of Frances, Duchess of Richmond and Lennox, who died in 1702, represents one beautiful woman who supposedly succeeded in evading his advances. She was the model for the original figure of Britannia on the coinage of Great Britain.

There is also the effigy of Admiral Lord Nelson, commissioned in 1806, a year after his death, which provides the tourist a supplementary attraction to St. Paul's Cathedral, where he is buried. The figure of Nelson, dressed in his own clothing, was regarded by contemporaries as more lifelike than paintings for which he sat.

Farther along the cloisters' east walk, an obscure passageway to the left leads to the Little Cloisters. In this secluded garden, where the silence is broken only by the splashing of a fountain, you have a dramatic view of **Victoria Tower** of the Houses of Parliament, which stands higher than Big Ben.

Returning to the main Cloisters, you can stroll through a passageway into **Dean's Yard** and the grounds of **Westminster School,** founded by Queen Elizabeth I and one of the leading public schools in London. In term-time, students will be dashing in and out of the fourteenth-century dining hall, where the oak tables were fashioned from timber supposedly obtained from the remnants of the Spanish Armada. From a small garden just off the center quadrangle, there is another striking view of the Victoria Tower rising beyond the garden's old walls.

Making your way from Dean's Yard into Tufton Street, turn left at Great Peter Street, and walk right at Gayfer

Street, to **Smith Square.** This is one of those small London squares that add so much character to the city. Here you will find **Transport House,** headquarters of the Labour Party.

Leaving Smith Square by Dean Stanley Street, walk a few yards to Millbank. Across the road is **Victoria Tower Gardens,** a pleasant park along the river with some good views of the buildings up and down the Thames. A copy of Rodin's *The Burghers of Calais* dominates the gardens.

Follow Millbank for three or four blocks, past one of London's newest skyscrapers, the Vickers building, to the **Tate Gallery.** Its great collection of paintings and sculpture, second only to that of the **National Gallery in Trafalgar Square,** specializes in the British school since the seventeenth century, French impressionists and post-impressionists, as well as distinguished contemporary works. John Singer Sargent and James McNeill Whistler are two outstanding American painters exhibited here; each is represented by a full room. These artistic surroundings are a fitting place to end this stroll through the center of London.

CHELSEA AND KENSINGTON

The King's Road to Hyde Park

As a change from the intensity of sightseeing in historic and ancient London, you should visit two quite different sections of the **West End** that are residential and off the beaten track. What's more, they are delightful places to walk! Each exudes that peculiar quality of simple dignity and charm in its houses, squares, and quiet, narrow streets that is so characteristic of old London. Each reflects the intimacy of a small community—for London is really a mass of small towns—rather than the hectic air of a bustling world capital.

One is Chelsea, the traditional home of artists and writers, and the other is that part of Belgravia and Kensington just

HYDE PARK CORNER

HYDE PARK

HARRODS

LONDON
CHELSEA AND KENSINGTON

ROUTE 1 ->--->
ROUTE 2 >-•••->

UNDERGROUND STA. ●

100 50 0   100   200 YARDS 300

south of **Hyde Park.** Neither is usually more than a twenty-minute ride on one of the big red busses from Piccadilly Circus. Yet both are out of the way in the sense that you are not likely to go there in the course of an ordinary visit to London.

A few hours will be ample to wander around both districts, and to absorb the atmosphere of two of the most attractive parts of residential London.

Start at **Sloane Square** to explore the particularly delightful bits of **Chelsea.** (The **bus—No. 19 or 22**—provides the quickest and most direct transportation to Sloane Square from **Piccadilly Circus** or **Pall Mall.**)

Walk down the King's Road past the **Duke of York's Headquarters**. Turn left along Cheltenham Terrace to St. Leonard's Terrace; here you will find some of Chelsea's most distinguished Georgian houses. Across the open playing field of Burton's Court (a game of cricket between units of regiments of guards may be in progress), you will see the tower and cupola of **Chelsea Hospital's** red brick buildings.

Charles II founded the institution in 1682 for veteran and invalid soldiers and commissioned Sir Christopher Wren to design the buildings. Four hundred-odd pensioners live here. You should have a chat with these old men wandering around the grounds wearing dark blue coats and caps. Some in their nineties can recall vividly their experiences during the Boer War. In summer, on dress occasions, they are resplendent in scarlet uniforms and black three-cornered hats which date from the days of the Duke of Marlborough. Many display proudly their collection of campaign medals and decorations.

You should visit both **Wren's Chapel** with its oak carving and the Great Hall, festooned with battle flags and honors from 1698 to the Korean War. The **Governor's House** includes a fine council chamber built by Robert Adam. Pensioners will show you around the chapel and Great Hall daily from 10:00 to 12:00 and 2:00 to 6:00, and around the council chamber on Saturday from 2:00 to 4:00.

After strolling about spacious **Figure Court,** the main quadrangle with its Doric colonnade, you should wander on the south terrace overlooking the gardens where the **Chelsea Flower Show,** Britain's finest collection, is held every spring by the Royal Horticultural Society. The south grounds of the hospital and adjacent **Ranelagh Gardens** are quite extensive and beautifully landscaped with flower beds and shrubbery— a most enjoyable spot for a pleasant promenade under shaded alleys of tall trees.

As you leave the hospital, turn left along **Royal Hospital Road** and after two blocks you will come to Tite Street. You are now entering the Chelsea of literary and artistic tradition. Oscar Wilde lived at No. 34 in magnificent style. James McNeill Whistler built the famous studio, the White House, down on the left. John Singer Sargent resided at No. 31 for twenty-four years and died there. In recent years Augustus John had his studio at No. 33. Just beyond Tite Street, you pass on your left the **Physic Garden,** begun in 1673 by the Society of Apothecaries and still used for botany research. In 1732, the first cotton seed was shipped from here to the southern planters in the American colonies.

Royal Hospital Road runs into the **Embankment** just beyond the Physic Garden. Here you turn slightly to the right by the public gardens into **Cheyne Walk.** You will admire the wrought-iron gates and railings of the distinguished early Georgian houses that face the river. Pause for a moment in front of No. 16, where Dante Gabriel Rossetti and Algernon Charles Swinburne lived, and study these stately mansions, so pleasing architecturally. Several charming balconies overlook the gardens opposite. The popular eighteenth-century coffee house, **Don Saltero's,** used to be at No. 18. Now across Oakley Street and, after passing several eighteenth-century houses, you come to the **"King's Head and Eight Bells"** on the corner —one of the most delightful pubs in Chelsea. If you are in the mood for lunch, ask for one of the window tables upstairs with a view over the river. Or you can have a snack in the quaint bar downstairs. Artists and writers from the neighborhood frequently gather in the paneled bar and dining rooms, or outside along the street at midday Sunday. It is one of the liveliest "locals" in Chelsea. Leaving the pub, stroll to your left along Cheyne Row, an unusually charming street, shaded by trees, and one of the best-known in Chelsea. You can visit **Thomas Carlyle's house,** No. 24 (weekdays, 10:00–6:00) and see where the great historian lived for nearly fifty years and wrote his great works. His furniture and books remain as they were nearly a hundred years ago. At the end of Cheyne Row you will come into **Upper Cheyne Row,** a small, secluded street with many gaily painted, low houses. The Chelsea China Works used to be to the left on Lawrence Street, where Henry Fielding and Tobias Smollett lived. In the other direction, toward Oakley Street, there are several attractive modern houses with pleasant gardens.

Cheyne Row, after crossing Upper Cheyne Row, becomes Glebe Place. Continue up Glebe Place to the **King's Road,** so named because it was Charles II's route from Whitehall Palace to Hampton Court. On the right, you will find **Argyll House** at No. 211, regarded as one of the finest examples of eighteenth-century architecture in Chelsea.

The King's Road, Chelsea's main street, is a fascinating place for a promenade. As you wander along, window-shopping for everything from antiques and paintings to odd mementos and old stamps, you are likely to encounter, especially on a Saturday morning, some of Chelsea's colorful characters —actors, artists, writers, or just beatniks trying to be exotic. The King's Road is by no means merely an antiquarian's delight. Farther along are some of London's smartest dress shops. Take your time along the King's Road; it's one of the most interesting of the city's many "high streets."

Just beyond Sydney Street turn into **Burnsall Street,** the second on the left. Down here and in **Godfrey Street,** a continuation on the right, you will see some of the most enchanting little houses in Chelsea. Most of these are former cottages or coach houses that have been rebuilt in the past twenty-five years. Now they are painted in pastel shades—blues, pinks, and yellows—and usually belong to well-to-do professional men or businessmen, since Chelsea has become a highly fashionable residential area.

Returning to the King's Road, cross over into Radnor Walk. A few yards farther on the left is the **Chelsea Pottery,** where you can see potters at work producing modern ceramics for sale. Behind the pottery shop you will discover the **Chelsea Forge,** the only one left in the borough. Established in 1780, it makes wrought-iron gates today instead of the carriages it produced years ago.

You now follow the King's Road a short distance to **Sloane Square.** Before you reach the square, you will pass Gardner's, one of London's largest supermarkets. At Sloane Square you can hop on a bus to **Hyde Park Corner** for the start of the **Kensington** walk. Or if you have the time and inclination (it will take half an hour or so), stroll from Sloane Square through **Belgravia.**

Through Mews and Squares

If you decide to walk, cross Sloane Square to Cliveden Place, then turn left at Eaton Terrace. In a moment you will see **"The Antelope,"** a delightful pub and intimate restaurant. This is a favorite gathering place for the nearby residents in Eaton Square and the immediate neighborhood. The downstairs bar is very lively, and the small upstairs restaurant has a friendly quality stimulated by its gregarious patrons.

After pausing here for a bit, return to Eaton Gate and walk along the north side of **Eaton Square,** one of London's most elegant residential squares. In recent years these houses have been largely converted into stylish flats. When you reach Belgrave Place, turn left and walk three blocks to **Belgrave Square.** Before the last war the distinguished mansions in this square were among London's finest private dwellings. Now many of them are occupied by foreign embassies.

Continue around the square to the northern corner, where you enter Wilton Crescent, then turn right down **Wilton Row.**

As you saunter along here, you will be entranced by the pastel-colored cottages, formerly stables, that you will discover tucked away in little courtyards. In a moment you will come to **"The Grenadier,"** a celebrated old pub, once a billet and mess for the Duke of Wellington's First Regiment of Grenadier Guards. Outside the dark brick cottage you will see under a chestnut tree the remaining stone of the Duke's mounting block and, in summer, a grapevine that came from Hampton Court. With prints and trophies on its walls, the low-ceilinged interior preserves the atmosphere of the Duke's Grenadiers. The Duke himself is believed to have often played cards in one of the small dining rooms. His mansion, **Apsley House,** is nearby at Hyde Park Corner. The ghost of a grenadier officer flogged to death after being caught cheating at cards supposedly haunts the pub during September.

If you wish to visit **Hyde Park Corner,** walk through Old Barrack Yard and turn right in Knightsbridge. Otherwise, retrace your steps to Wilton Crescent and on to Motcomb Street.

If you have come by bus to Hyde Park Corner, you begin the walk through Belgravia and Kensington by following **Knightsbridge** for a few hundred yards past **St. George's Hospital,** through an archway on the left, Old Barrack Yard, and on to "The Grenadier."

Now make your way around to the right past the stone façades of Wilton Crescent to Motcomb Street. In a moment you will see a narrow entrance to **Kinnerton Street.** There are lots of tiny shops here that are worth exploring, as well as little alleyways and courtyards in **Kinnerton Yard** that reveal amusing pied-à-terres for the country-dwellers who keep a flat in town.

From **Motcomb Street,** with its art galleries, antique shops, and milliners, follow Cadogan Place one block to **Sloane Street,** the finest shopping street in this part of London. Walk on the other side of Sloane Street toward Knightsbridge to the first turning on the left, Hans Crescent. Then walk for a block or two until you come to **Harrods,** London's leading quality department store. One of Harrods' most exciting departments is the large food shop on the ground floor. Here you can spend lots of time in a serious gourmet-type investigation of all the varied and luxurious foods on sale. The poultry-and-game section offers grouse, venison, English *poussin,* wood pigeon, wild duck, and quail during the summer. The seafood display of kippers and lobsters is arranged most artistically. Even Scottish salmon, as well as Dover sole and other kinds of fish, are laid out on stone slabs.

After you have succeeded in tearing yourself away from these and other enticements, leave Harrods by the **Brompton Road** entrance and stroll along for three blocks to **Beauchamp Place.** This street will captivate you if you like wandering around attractive little shops, for there are all sorts here— shops selling antique silver and brass, shops dealing in old clocks, and china, as well as stores carrying the latest fashions. There is even one called "Dog's Baths Requisites," where poodles are shampooed and have their nails clipped.

Now cross Brompton Road and proceed back until you are opposite Harrods. Turn left, walk fifty yards, and you will be in **Trevor Square,** a pleasant rectangle of Georgian houses. From here it is just a step to one of London's smallest, most réscherché, and picturesque corners—tranquil **Montpelier Square.** The gardens and tastefully planted flower beds beneath large overhanging trees diffuse an air of restfulness that seems almost unbelievable only a few hundred yards from the throbbing noisy traffic of Knightsbridge and Brompton Road. This is one of the delights of residential London that will impress the apartment-dweller from New York, who can seldom escape from the din of the metropolis. If the square is open, go in, sit quietly on a garden bench, and read or just let your imagination dwell on the joys of living in such an atmosphere. Nearby you will notice a sign that has been there for years, forbidding street musicians from annoying the residents. Wander around the square and study the eighteenth-century houses, many with huge windows overlooking the gardens. Just off the square there is an old Georgian pub where you can have lunch, or simply bread, cheese, and a glass of bitter.

Montpelier Walk, a narrow street at the northwest end of the square, curves around to the left. Almost every house here has a charming front garden full of flowers that the residents have carefully cultivated. Some display equally attractive flower boxes.

You follow Montpelier Walk until you reach a turn to the right where you will spy a passage through a high brick wall, known to the residents as the "hole in the wall." Step through it and keep left a few yards until you come to a mews on the left. Pink, blue, russet, and yellow houses here provide an artistic setting more reminiscent of Provence than of London.

A few yards farther, on Ennismore Street, you approach one of Kensington's classic archways, which leads into **Ennismore Gardens Mews.** The row of pastel-colored cottages, once stables and now small town dwellings, is a picturesque sight facing the back gardens of **Brompton Oratory,** a baroque Roman Catholic Church. This is indeed one of those entrancing out-of-the-way corners of residential London that, when you discover it, grips you with its colorful and artistic atmosphere. Often, along here, photographers can be seen posing attractive models for fashion magazines, and artists are found working at their easels. Late in the day, the soft rays of the sun through the trees cast a golden glow over the mews. At this hour the high dome of the oratory silhouetted against the sky presents a dramatic sight.

In a moment you will be at **Prince's Gardens,** a well-planted square, from which you exit into Exhibition Road. Walk to the left a few hundred yards to the **Victoria and Albert Museum** (open daily, 10:00–6:00; Sunday, 2:30–6:00), which contains the nation's great collection of fine and applied art of all countries, styles, and periods. The museum is outstanding in many fields, especially sculpture, ceramics, furniture, costumes, textiles, engravings, and prints. There is a unique collection of Constable's paintings, as well as a fine group of the French Barbizon school. Across the street is the **Science**

Museum, illustrating the application of science to the various branches of technology and industry. Next to it stands the **Natural History Museum,** which houses a collection of animals, plants, and minerals (both museums are open daily, 10:00–6:00; Sunday, 2:30–6:00). Either now or on another occasion you should roam through the collections that interest you.

To return to Piccadilly Circus, just walk a block to the left to the **South Kensington** underground station, or take the **No. 9 bus** at the top of Exhibition Road by **Kensington Gardens.**

As you leave these two fascinating districts of residential London you will feel these walks have only introduced you to charms that you will want to savor more thoroughly at some future time.

Park, Palace, and Promenade

Here is a delightful walk in Kensington, London's fashionable residential section. You will find this route different and unusual. It will offer you lots of interest and variety—**Kensington Gardens** with its colorful herbaceous borders, **Kensington Palace,** and the **London Museum,** the quaint antique shops along **Church Street,** and the suburban type homes off Gloucester Road and on Campden Hill as well as the residence of **Sir Winston Churchill** and **Holland Park.** This stroll combines historic places, fascinating museums, restful parks, little out-of-the-way shops, and fine homes.

It is a very attractive part of London that many visitors never see because it's somewhat off the beaten track and yet it is very accessible. Not far from Hyde Park by underground or bus, it's the sort of a stroll you can easily do if you are in central London and have a couple of hours to spare. Should you have to return for an appointment, you're never far from public transport or a taxi. You can be back in Piccadilly Circus in about twenty minutes at most hours of the day. In short, this is one of the pleasantest walks you can take close to the center of London.

Kensington, through which you will be strolling, derives its name from the Kensings, a Saxon tribe. Queen Victoria was born in Kensington and created it a Royal Borough because of her affection for her birthplace.

If you have been following the suggested walk from **Hyde Park Corner** to **Exhibition Road,** you can continue, if you wish, along the route about to be described. Otherwise you should start at **Exhibition Road** by either taking a tube from Piccadilly Circus to **South Kensington Station** or a **No. 9 bus** to the top of **Exhibition Road** opposite the park.

Begin your stroll from **Exhibition Road** along **Imperial Institute Road** just opposite the thin golden spire of the modern Mormon Church. On either side of this road you pass the extensive complex of buildings that comprises the recently expanded **Imperial College of Science and Technology,** one of Britain's leading scientific institutions. The tower on your right was erected in honor of Queen Victoria's golden jubilee.

At the end of the road you will come into broad **Queen's Gate,** a stately avenue lined with tall town houses, mostly built at the end of the last century, that are characteristic of South Kensington. The **Gore Hotel,** famous for its Elizabethan dining room where food of the Elizabethan era is served in an appropriate setting, is at No. 189 Queen's Gate.

Now cross over and after going along Queen's Gate a block, turn left into Queen's Gate Terrace. In a couple of minutes you will come to **Gloucester Road,** the main shopping street for the neighboring residents.

Just on the other side you enter a corner of Kensington that has a village-like quality about it. Although one of London's characteristics is the number of small towns that make up this sprawling metropolis, few sections can boast of the charming suburban atmosphere that you encounter when you stroll in the neighborhood of narrow **Victoria Grove.** Take a look down **Launceston Place** at the low two-storied cottages. Or just a few yards further, on the right, turn into **Canning**

Place where you'll find delightful houses with big bay windows.

Victoria Road, just ahead, is one of the most pleasant and quiet residential streets in this part of London. Trees shade the walled gardens in front of the three-story family homes. It's hard to realize you are only minutes away from the noisy traffic on **Kensington Road** (which you reach by turning right into Victoria Road and continuing to the end). Along the way you might wander into one or two of the cul-de-sacs like Cambridge Place, on the other side of the street, to see the attractive houses.

When you reach Kensington Road you will be opposite **Kensington Gardens,** but don't cross over yet. Instead, turn right along this busy road for a couple of hundred yards past Palace Gate. The rather unobtrusive street you are looking for is on your right, **Hyde Park Gate,** named for an ancient tall gate to London once located on this site. A minute or two down it will bring you to a fine dark brick, impressive two-storied home with a large black door and shiny brass knocker, No. 28. This is the town residence of **Sir Winston and Lady Churchill.**

Now return to Kensington Road and cross over to the Gardens a bit on the right. Farther along you will see the ornate **Albert Memorial.** A few moments after entering the Gardens you will come to the beautifully landscaped **Flower Walk.** Its combination of trees, shrubbery and flower beds has been so artistically planned that most of the year you will see a fine horticultural display, usually one of the loveliest in London. This is just the place to sit for a while on one of the comfortable benches and enjoy the beauty of flowers as well as the chirping of the birds, for many varieties of bird life can be spotted in these trees. If you should stroll along the Flower Walk in the opposite direction from the Albert Memorial, you will come into the **Broad Walk**—a wide promenade planted with lime trees that runs from Kensington Road to Bayswater Road. At the top of the rise on the right is the famous **Round Pond** (dating from 1728)

where you often can be entertained watching boys and men sailing model yachts. The surrounding wide lawn is a popular spot for flying kites and exercising dogs.

Returning to the Broad Walk, you now are facing **Kensington Palace.** William III commissioned Sir Christopher Wren to rebuild and renovate it at the end of the seventeenth century in preparation for its use as his chief residence. The Court remained here until 1760. Since then various members of the Royal Family have resided here, and now it is the home of Princess Margaret and her family.

As you approach the Palace from the Broad Walk you will see on your left the **Sunken** or **Dutch Garden**—one of the most beautiful of its kind in England. Surrounded by lime trees, the garden can be viewed through various ornamental gates. From spring to late autumn the flower beds, planted around a rectangular pond, are a blaze of color. The borders are separated by long stretches of velvet-like lawn. To stand at the end of this artistic garden with the dark brick walls and chimney stacks of Wren's palace in the background is a memorable experience.

To your right you will see **Wren's Orangery** behind a formal lawn, an example of fine early eighteenth-century brickwork. The little terrace in front of the large glass windows catches whatever warm sunshine there may be.

The entrance to Kensington Palace (open 10:00–6:00 daily; 2:00–6:00 Sunday 1 March–30 September; closes at 4:00 1 October–28 February) is just opposite. You will want to visit the **State Apartments.** The paneled staircases, spacious galleries, fine furniture, and historic exhibits make the palace one of the most interesting in England. Queen Victoria's bedroom, furnished in the period by the late Queen Mary, is the room where the young Princess Victoria was told of her accession to the throne in 1837. There is an extraordinary clock in the cupola room known as the **Temple of the Four Great Monarchies.** The scenes on its sides represent Assyria, Persia, Greece and Rome. In **King William's Gallery** is an old wind dial made for William III. The pointer is operated by a weathervane on the roof. Be sure to see **Queen Victoria's doll house** and toys in the Anteroom. **Coronation robes** of King George V and Queen Mary as well as other items of regalia are on exhibit in the **King's Drawing Room.** You will also see **Princess Margaret's wedding dress** and costumes worn by Queen Victoria.

Normally you would not want to tour one museum right after another but Kensington Palace is unusual because the **London Museum** occupies the same set of buildings in which the State Apartments are located.

You will find the London Museum (open same hours as State Apartments) particularly fascinating because of its relics of prehistoric London, such as the **neolithic bowl** found on the site of London Airport. In addition to **Mithraic sculptures** of the Roman period, there is **a late first-century jug** inscribed "London at the Shrine of Isis," evidence of worship of the Egyptian goddess. This may be the earliest relic with the name of London on it. Some of the more unusual exhibits include the effigy of Queen Elizabeth I carried at her funeral in 1603, typical clothing of the Elizabethan era, a model of London Bridge about 1600 and St. Paul's before the fire of 1666, personal belongings of Charles I, children's games and toys, plus wedding dresses, robes and crowns worn by members of the Royal Family. In addition, there are fine collections of Bow and Chelsea porcelain, **Battersea enamelware,** paintings and prints of eighteenth-century London and later.

On leaving the Museum, keep to the right past the Sunken Garden, then around the corner of the Palace from the Broad Walk. Go through a gate and turn right to reach the official entrance of the Palace with its cupola overhead.

You now cross the wide private road called **Kensington Palace Gardens,** which is lined with many stately mansions with large gardens. Continue for a couple of hundred yards along a walk, York House Place, that leads to **Church Street,** one of London's ancient thoroughfares. On the other side of this busy shopping street you will be in **Holland Street.** The early Georgian houses and their little front gardens give this street a special character. Holland Street and **Gordon Place,** just a bit further on the left with its charming two-story cottages, are often painted by artists. The tiny houses on Gordon Place are said to have been used by ladies-in-waiting to Queen Anne when she resided in Kensington Palace.

Returning to Church Street, there's a pleasant little detour that takes you into a small garden behind the **Church of St. Mary Abbots** whose lofty spire is a Kensington landmark.

Church Street is an excellent place to buy antiques, so walk along to the left from Holland Street, around the wide bend and look in at the different shops. There's a great variety of antiques on sale here—old silver, china and glass, furniture, objets d'art, old jewelry, copper and brass, etc. You may feel like wandering along almost to **Notting Hill Gate** but if not, turn left a few hundred yards further along at **Campden Street.**

At the end of this street, which is lined with pleasant two-storied houses, you turn right on **Campden Hill,** a fashionable residential area since the seventeenth century. Many of the large houses that used to be here have now been replaced by well-designed modern ones, such as those you will pass on **Aubrey Walk,** the first turn to the left. Don't fail to note one of the gayest pubs in this part of London, the **Windsor Castle,** opposite the reservoir before you turn left on Aubrey Walk.

After a short stroll along this street with its attractive, vine-covered houses, you will come to **Aubrey House,** the site of Kensington Wells, an early eighteenth-century spa. Turn right into Aubrey Road and again right into **Campden Hill Square,** a delightful tree-shaded square. The comfortable homes that surround the square are much sought after.

A few steps down the hill will bring you to **Holland Park Avenue,** a main traffic artery. Turn left and, in a moment or two, sharply left again into Holland Walk, a pedestrian thoroughfare that skirts Holland Park at the top of the rise on your right. A bit further along the shaded footpath back in the trees you may see the rebuilt **Holland House.** This historic mansion became famous in the eighteenth century as the center of the gay Whig political and literary circle of which Charles James Fox was a distinguished member. If you stroll into **Holland Park** just past the new Holland Park School on your left, you can enjoy sitting at the outdoor café overlooking the grounds.

Continue along Holland Walk to **Kensington High Street.** Just to the right you will see a large modern building of original design with a tent-like roof. This is the **Commonwealth Institute.** Its galleries, built around a circular well, display interesting exhibits of the economic and cultural life of the Commonwealth countries. Documentary films are shown in the theater. There is also a library on Commonwealth affairs for students, as well as a restaurant overlooking the lawn. After touring this unusual building, you can catch a bus in Kensington High Street or a tube on **Earls Court Road** to take you back to Piccadilly Circus.

II OXFORD

THE SENIOR UNIVERSITY

North of the High

You should begin your walk through **Oxford** at a particularly scenic spot where you will at once sense the antiquity and beauty of this ancient university. In this way you will get yourself in the right mood to appreciate the history, tradition, and charm of Oxford's towers, cloisters, halls, and gardens.

The ideal place for such a start is **Magdalen Bridge** (pronounced Maudlen), where the London road enters Oxford, for there, before crossing the bridge, you behold that memorable vista—the graceful proportions of the slightly tapering **bell tower** (believed to be Cardinal Wolsey's design) with its pinnacled turrets soaring above **Magdalen College** and the tree-lined banks of the Cherwell. To your right, the lovely green meadows below Headington Hill lend a softness to the scene.

After glancing up and down the stream, and seeing students with their girls (often undergraduettes) renting punts, you pass the late-fifteenth-century tower and enter the grounds of Magdalen College through the main gate from **High Street** (known in Oxford as "The High"). During term, the college is open on weekdays from 2:00 to 5:00, on Sunday from 10:00 to 5:00; in the summer, from 10:00 to 7:00.

If you wish to view Oxford from its loftiest perch, ask the college porter at the entrance lodge to obtain permission from a Fellow of the college so you can climb the 144-foot bell tower. From its battlements the panorama of the university can be seen below, and it affords a unique sight of the varying patterns of the colleges and their gardens.

54

On the left of the gatehouse is the picturesque old seven-teenth-century **Grammar Hall** (built considerably later than the founding date of the college, 1458), and on the right the only open-air pulpit surviving in England. After looking around the chapel, a bit farther on the right, you should follow the passageway beneath the **Muniment Tower** to the cloisters. Ascending a flight of steps at the right-hand corner of the cloisters you will reach the distinguished **dining hall,** famed for its lovely linen-fold oak paneling, on which hang portraits of famous old members of the college, including a fine painting of Cardinal Wolsey. Note the woodcarving and coat of arms of Henry VIII over the high table.

As you saunter through the cloisters opposite the dining hall, look at the oak beams overhead and the crests of the famous old members of the colleges. Just beyond, to the right, past a fine herbaceous border you will come to a small stone bridge leading to **Addison's Walk,** named for the great essay-ist, a former member of the college. Beneath the bridge, perch and pike, safe from the angler, are frequently being fed by visitors.

A stroll around the meadow, only a few hundred yards from the traffic-clogged High, will transport you into a completely rural atmosphere. This walk, under chestnut trees with may and hawthorn blooming pink and white in spring, is perhaps the most charming in Oxford. Part of it runs along the meandering **Cherwell,** a stream overhung with willows and only about ten yards wide. At the far end you will find a little footbridge amid luxurious foliage. Pause on the bridge for a few moments and watch the punts go by.

After returning from this twenty-minute excursion, you should visit Magdalen's **deer park** just beyond the **New Build-ings,** which, despite their name, were constructed in the eighteenth century. There, under a grove of tall and luxuriant oaks, chestnuts, and elms, the sight of the college herd adds a special old-world touch to these academic surroundings. There are about fifty deer, one for each Fellow of the college. Nearby on the left you will spy a lawn on raised ground next to

ELD

ST. CATH.'S
COL.

N

HOLYWELL ST.

NEW
COL.

GARDEN

DEER
PARK

ADDISON'S WALK

NEW COLLEGE LA.

QUEEN'S
COL.

SOULS
COL.

FINISH 2

ST. CROSS RD.

LONG WALL ST.

MAGDALEN
COL.

VERSITY
COL.

EXAM
SCHOOLS

ST.

RTON

MERTON
COL.

MAGDALEN
BRIDGE

START 1

BROAD WALK

CHERWELL R.

COWLEY PL.

ST. HILDA'S
COL.

IFFLEY RD.

CHERWELL

OXFORD

ROUTE 1 →－－→

ROUTE 2 •▷•••▷•

100   50   0   100   200   YARDS 300

a delightful garden. From this vantage point on the lawn, you have an unusual view of **Magdalen Tower** rising above the college buildings.

You leave Magdalen through the main gate and proceed up The High, universally recognized as one of the finest streets in Europe. In a few moments the famous and graceful sweep of **Queen's** and **All Souls** colleges and the spire of **St. Mary's Church** in the distance comes into view. A bit further on, you should stop at the corner of Queen's Lane and study the college buildings on both sides of the street.

The entrance to **The Queen's College,** founded in 1340, is just ahead on the right. (Open in term, 2:00–5:00; in summer, 10:00–7:00.) Pausing under the cupola at the gate, you will be struck by the stately proportions of the eighteenth-century **front quadrangle,** cloistered on three sides. It was designed by Nicholas Hawksmoor, an associate of Wren. Directly ahead, beyond the velvetlike lawn, stands the classic chapel and the hall surmounted by a clock tower. The view of this cupola, outlined by the entrance archway, as seen from the outside steps, is particularly effective against the background of open sky.

The finest façade of Queen's—and one of the most magnificent in Oxford—is the west front of the **library,** overlooking the **Fellows' Garden** and surmounted by a stone eagle, the insignia of the founder. But the upper library's interior, with its superb proportions, exquisitely carved dark woodwork, and highly decorated white plaster ceiling, has few rivals in England in classic nobility and dignity. (If the library is closed, request the porter at the gate for permission to see both it and the Fellows' Garden.)

You should now wander along a narrow passageway next to the library into the old **Nuns' Garden,** a restful spot beside **Drawda Hall,** whose gables rise over apple trees and rosebushes. After viewing the college dining hall, ask the porter to let you see the college's collection of silver, including the founder's ancient drinking horn. During term, a trumpet is blown each evening to announce dinner in accord with the founder's instructions.

Turning left outside Queen's, walk along the winding lane which runs below high stone walls to **New College** on the right. You will notice that the top of the wall is spiked to discourage students from climbing in or out after the college gate is closed.

After passing through the entrance to New College (open Monday–Friday, 2:00–5:00; Saturday and Sunday, 12:00–6:00), turn sharply to the left to reach what is probably the most peaceful spot in Oxford—the **college cloisters.** Rising above the wood-vaulted cloisters stands the crenelated bell tower, once part of the city wall. While you pause at the far edge of the perfect lawn, dominated only by a venerable ilex tree, you will sense the calm and meditative air of the Middle Ages that has survived the centuries in this place.

New College, founded in 1379 by William of Wykeham, Bishop of Winchester, is the first college whose buildings, most of which still stand, were planned as a college by its founder.

On leaving the cloisters, you should visit the chapel to see the fourteenth-century stained-glass windows, the founder's pastoral staff, and Sir Jacob Epstein's dramatic statue depicting the rising of Lazarus. From the chapel, walk to the left through two quads to a superb wrought-iron gate, the entrance to the college's spacious **garden** (open 2:00–5:00 P.M.). In the center of the garden is a high mound covered with trees and shrubs, and around the lawn the battlements of the original medieval city wall look down on an exquisitely planned herbaceous border. Here is a perfect spot to sit for a while on a summer day.

Having seen several of the leading colleges, you should now have a look at the finest buildings of the university. Most buildings in academic Oxford belong to the individual colleges, while the university provides the special facilities like the building called **The Examination Schools** or scientific laboratories used by all the colleges in common.

After leaving New College, you pass under **Hertford College Bridge.** Just ahead you will see the refaced **Sheldonian Theatre** a smaller copy of the Roman **theater of Marcellus.** It was designed by Sir Christopher Wren, and university ceremonies, such as the granting of degrees, take place in it. The flat, highly decorated ceiling, apparently unsupported, is one of Wren's mathematical achievements. The interior has been repainted as it was in Wren's time. Outside the theatre (open 10:00–11:00, 2:00–6:00) the weather-beaten stone heads of Roman emperors face "The Broad," Oxford's term for spacious **Broad Street.**

The world-renowned **Bodleian Library** stands next to the Sheldonian. The main gateway, which passes through the **Tower of the Five Orders of Architecture** (Tuscan, Doric, Ionic, Corinthian, and composite) to the Bodleian quadrangle, is only opened on ceremonial occasions. The quadrangle within, dating from the early seventeenth century, was built to house the books Sir Thomas Bodley began to collect in 1602 when he refounded the former university library, which had become dispersed. You should visit the fifteenth-century **Duke Humphrey's Library** and exhibition room (open weekdays, 9:30–5:00). Note the painted ceiling and oak beams, and the shelves, which contain old books still arranged in their seventeenth-century classification by size and subject (Theology, Medicine, Law, and Arts). In keeping with Bodley's instructions a bell is still rung when the library opens and closes. Upstairs are reading rooms with decorative friezes and ceilings. Nearby is the **Divinity School** with its fine stone-vaulted ceilings. The House of Commons met there in 1655 after having been driven from London by the plague. To the south stands the **Radcliffe Camera,** a circular building, mainly a reading room of the Bodleian.

Just a few steps back to The High will bring you to **All Souls College** (open 2:00–5:00), the only college without undergraduates, only Fellows. The resident members here are called Research Fellows. Hawksmoor's **twin towers** in the north quadrangle are a familiar feature of the Oxford scene. You should ask the porter at the gate for permission to see the lofty **Codrington Law Library,** an extremely well-designed room where the annual Encaenia luncheon for recipients of honorary degree takes place in June. Note Wren's great sundial over the library door.

Retrace your steps along **Catte Street;** turn left into The Broad, passing the new Bodleian Library (erected largely through a Rockefeller Foundation grant); and so a few steps beyond **Blackwell's,** Oxford's famous bookstore, to reach the fine entrance gates and extensive grounds of **Trinity College** (open from 2:00 P.M. until dusk). During the summer term it is interesting to watch members of Oxford's dramatic society rehearsing Shakespeare under the blossoming fruit trees. Trinity's seventeenth-century ornamental chapel, with its elaborate woodcarving, is well worth seeing.

Continuing along The Broad, you pass **Balliol College,** noted more for its academic excellence than for its monstrous architecture. After turning right along **St. Giles Street** (known in Oxford as "The Giler"), notice on your left the **Martyrs' Memorial,** commemorating the burning here of both the Protestant reformers Latimer and Ridley (condemned during the reign of Catholic Queen Mary) and Archbishop Thomas Cranmer.

St. John's College should not be missed on any tour of Oxford, mainly because of its unusually attractive **garden** (open weekdays, 9:00–5:00; Sunday, 10:00–1:00). It is the largest in Oxford and was laid out in 1777–1778 in the style of Capability Brown. Its extensive lawn, rockery (one of the oldest in England), and groups of trees, as well as its attractively arranged herbaceous border, make this garden one of Oxford's most delightful havens of repose. **Canterbury Quad,** named after William Laud, Archbishop of Canterbury, who built it, is perhaps the outstanding example of early seventeenth-century architecture in Oxford. Its graceful Italian colonnades are unusually lovely. You should also see the **Hexagon Building,** a modern college dormitory (built in 1960). It has an unusual design in stone and glass and is considered one of the best pieces of contemporary architecture in Oxford.

You will find the gardens of St. John's just the place to end this first stroll through the colleges of Oxford.

Toward the Isis

As a change from touring colleges, you ought to start your second walk in Oxford by spending some time in the **Ashmolean Museum,** the university's important art and archaeological collection on Beaumont Street, just around the corner from St. Giles (open weekdays, 10:00–4:00; Sunday, 2:00–4:00).

The Ashmolean is particularly distinguished for its rare Egyptian and Cretan treasures, but it also has on exhibition a representative selection of paintings and sculpture ranging from the early Italian masters to contemporary artists.

Straight ahead down Beaumont Street you will see **Worcester College.** Inside the gate on the left is a row of relatively untouched medieval cottages. These were originally separate monastic houses, and the ancient shields over the doorways show the different abbeys with which they were connected. Passing through an archway, you enter a large and delightful garden with noble trees. Its unique feature is Oxford's only lake.

On leaving Worcester, you should turn right into Worcester Street and left into George Street. When you reach the Cornmarket (Oxford's main shopping thoroughfare) you will realize what a busy, industrial city Oxford has become. **Carfax,** the center of the city, is the main crossroad at the end of the Cornmarket. Continuing straight ahead down St. Aldate's, you will see on the left the familiar **Tom Tower** of **Christ Church,** known in Oxford as "The House." (Open 9:00–6:00.)

Before entering the grounds of Christ Church, the most extensive of any in Oxford, you should step back from St. Aldate's a few yards along the lane leading to **Pembroke College** and study the details of imposing Tom Tower. It was completed by Sir Christopher Wren in 1682, after the lower part had been begun by Cardinal Wolsey, Christ Church's founder. Every evening, at five minutes past nine, the great bell tolls 101 times, once for each of the original 101 scholars. After passing through the huge gateway of Christ Church, you will be spellbound by the grandeur and size of **Tom Quad.** Walking around the stone terrace to the far side, notice the arches built in the walls; these indicate that Wolsey intended to construct a cloister around the quad. In the center of the perfect lawn is a statue of Mercury surrounded by a small pool. Pause for a moment at the archway in the southeast corner of the terrace for an unusual view of Tom Quad, perhaps the most impressive and yet tranquil quad in Oxford.

Just beyond the archway you should study the magnificent wide stone staircase with its beautiful fan-tracery roof. The **Great Hall** (open 11:00–12:00; 2:00–4:00) at the top of the stairs, with its elaborately carved oaken roof and superb paneling, is the largest and finest in Oxford. Many interesting portraits adorn the walls, including paintings of Wolsey, who built the hall; Henry VIII, the royal founder; Queen Elizabeth I; Charles Lutwidge Dodgson ("Lewis Carroll"), a former canon of Christ Church; and William Penn, an old member of the college. In this hall, stage scenery was used for the first time in England, to produce a play before Charles I in 1636.

Outside the hall is **Wolsey's huge kitchen,** the oldest part of the building, still in use, and most interesting. The original oak roof is over fifty feet high. You can see the original spit, which is still operated on special occasions, and a serving table, six to eight inches thick, made in 1734, and used for 210 years. Colorful copper skillets hanging on the walls are used regularly.

Only a few steps away you will find the Norman and early English **cathedral,** which, though small, is the most beautiful in Oxford. Also take a look at the adjoining fifteenth-century **cloisters.**

Before leaving Christ Church, walk along the quad to the towered gateway that leads to **Peckwater Quad** and the **college library.**

Returning through Tom Quad, you should make your way through several passageways of the newer buildings into **Christ Church Meadow.** It is a few minutes' stroll down the New Walk to the river **Isis,** where the gaily colored college barges are tied up. You can make a delightful circular walk along the tree-covered banks of the **Cherwell** (which joins the Isis nearby) back to the **Broad Walk.** As you stroll along this avenue of fine trees, you will see on your right a striking view of the towers of Merton and Magdalen.

Proceeding up the path to Merton Street, past its massive tower, you will reach the entrance to **Merton College** on the right. The College's fourteenth-century **Mob Quad** is the oldest surviving quadrangle in Oxford. The **medieval library** on one side of this simple quad is one of the most fascinating in England (open 2:00–5:00). It has an intimate air, with its old fittings and paneled ceiling. Built in 1371–1379, this relic of early Oxford still retains an original bookcase with chained volumes.

On leaving Merton, turn left and saunter along **Magpie Lane** with its odd little houses. Up ahead, the spire of **St. Mary's** looms at the end of the narrow street. If you want a fine view over Oxford, you can climb St. Mary's 95-foot **tower** (open weekdays, 10:00–5:00; Sunday, 1:00–5:00). Once again in "The High," you turn right to visit **University College,** founded in the thirteenth century. Although Shelley was "sent down" as an undergraduate for publishing a pamphlet on *The Necessity of Atheism* in 1810, the college later repented by erecting a memorial to him. University College is the first Oxford college ever to elect an American as its Master, Professor A. L. Goodhart, who donated the new Goodhart Quadrangle, one of the best examples of modern architecture in Oxford.

As you approach **Magdalen Tower** pondering the beauties

of the quads, halls, chapels, and gardens, you will realize that such a stroll as this has only served to whet your appetite to spend many more days in the inimitable atmosphere of Oxford.

III CAMBRIDGE

WHERE THE BACKS ARE FRONTS

From King's to Queens'

"The other place," as Oxonians disparagingly describe **Cambridge,** the junior university, is historically as fascinating as Oxford and in many ways more beautiful. Cambridge's locale in a rural community contrasts with Oxford's in an industrialized area and, with its interesting and lovely surroundings, lends itself particularly to walking.

The famous **"Backs"** of the colleges—those sweeping, carpetlike lawns along the languid little **river Cam**—and the luxuriously colorful college gardens provide a spaciousness unmatched in Oxford. The several colleges along the stream seem to merge into one another; you are not conscious of the walls that separate them. Standing on one of the many picturesque bridges you sense a calm, restful unhurried air as the branches of the overhanging lime trees sway in the breeze. Altogether, the view of elegant buildings and carefully tended gardens creates the contemplative atmosphere that marks the ideal university community.

Upon arrival, as a stroller in Cambridge, you should absorb its unique mood before exploring the byways of the varied college quads. (The colleges are usually open during the daytime, but in term time some may be closed before noon.) To absorb this mood you should get your first impression by entering the main gate of **King's College** and walking to the left down the path that leads to **King's Bridge** over the Cam. Pause on the bridge for a few minutes and face the town. There looms to the left over the close-cropped greensward the pointed Gothic pinnacles of the world-renowned **King's**

Chapel. Close at hand, are the seventeenth-century stone arches and balustrade of **Clare Bridge,** without doubt one of the most graceful anywhere, which leads to the **Fellows' Gardens.** Behind this bridge, on both banks, rise stately and luxuriant trees with a green richness that only English dampness can create.

In the opposite direction, the half-timbered and deep red brick of **Queens' College** strikes a remarkable contrast in color against the sloping turfed banks of the river.

On the river below, you will see undergraduates, and often undergraduettes, maneuvering their punts by manipulating a huge pole from the rear platform.

After a few minutes spent in absorbing the spirit of Cambridge, you wander back into the main court of King's and approach the glorious **chapel** founded by Henry VI and considered by many the finest example of Perpendicular style in England. Inside the chapel, you will be struck at once by the lofty lacelike fan vaulting in the stone roof of "the loveliest chapel in England," which Henry VIII completed in 1515. The Tudor heraldic carving is highly decorative. The early sixteenth-century stained glass in the great windows was made by both Flemings in England and Englishmen working under Flemish inspiration from Flemish designs. The organ screen, one of Europe's finest pieces of woodwork, carries the arms of Anne Boleyn. You should inquire when the next service will be held and return, if possible, to hear the celebrated voices of the King's College Choir in this incomparable setting.

Leaving King's by the gate on the north side of the chapel, you turn left into **Clare College.** Proceed through the old court to **Clare Bridge**—the oldest in Cambridge (1640)—with its famous row of stone balls. Crossing the stream—but stopping for at least a moment to enjoy a still different view of the "Backs"—you pass through handsome eighteenth-century wrought-iron gates. It's worth while to inquire whether, by chance, **Clare's Fellows' Garden** may be open, before leaving the park by the back gate on **Queens' Road.**

A few hundred yards either way on Queens' Road, are

CAMBRIDGE

ROUTE ->- - ->

100 50 0 100 YARDS 200

extensive and delightful gardens—**King's Fellows' Garden**
(to the left) and **Trinity Fellows' Garden** (to the right), both
of which are usually open. The variety of the flowers, shrubs,
and trees in these well-planned and carefully maintained gardens is quite unusual. You owe it to yourself to wander
around them leisurely or find a secluded spot and sit for a
while.

After leaving Trinity Fellows' Garden, cross Queens' Road
and take the path leading to **Trinity Bridge,** from which
you will get an excellent view of **St. John's College.** Directly
ahead, in the grounds of **Trinity College,** is the **Avenue**—one
of the finest walks in Cambridge—which leads to **New Court.**
On the left lies the magnificent classic façade of **Sir Christopher Wren's library,** built with cream and pink stone over a
covered piazza. The visitor should proceed into the cloisters
of **Nevile's Court** and enter the library at the far end of the
classic arches (usually open weekdays, 1:00–4:00). Wren's
interior design of the beautifully proportioned library "touches
the very soul of any one who first sees it," as Roger North
wrote in 1695. The walls and bookcases exhibit the best examples of Grinling Gibbons' woodcarving. The library also
contains the private book collection of Sir Isaac Newton, one
of Trinity's most distinguished sons. You may even find the
manuscript of Milton's shorter poems, in his own handwrit-
ing, on display among the library's many treasures.

The **dining hall** of the college, one of the most magnificent
Elizabethan halls in England, with its carved oaken beams, is
just off a passage above Nevile's Court and is generally open
between 1:30 and 3:00. Opposite the entrance to the hall
you will notice the colorful portrait of Henry VIII hung on
the fine paneling immediately above the high table. Among
other interesting pictures is a contemporary portrait of Francis Bacon, painted on wood. Overhead is the Minstrels'
Gallery.

On your way out of the hall you should stand for a moment
at the top of the stone steps to admire the **Great Court,** the
largest of any college in Oxford or Cambridge. All the build-

ings are in the Tudor-Gothic style except for one section. On the left is Trinity's medieval clock tower, decorated with armorial crests, and in front is Nevile's lovely stone fountain. Near the chapel at the far end are the rooms in which Sir Isaac Newton worked out the proofs of his great scientific discoveries. After wandering around the court, you should stop by the sundial near the fountain and study the noble great tower; then leave the college through the massive Tudor archway.

Just a few yards to the left along **Trinity Street** stands the imposing stone and brick gateway to **St. John's College,** bearing the elaborately painted and gilded arms of Lady Margaret Beaufort, the foundress. You should ask for permission to see the **Combination Room** in the Elizabethan brick second court. This paneled gallery, one of the most stately in England, is nearly a hundred feet long, with a decorated plaster ceiling worked in 1600.

Beyond the third court, the **"Bridge of Sighs"** (somewhat like the one in Venice) over the Cam leads to the delightful cloister in the **New Court.** From here you should wander into the college grounds and back across the old bridge, through the courtyards, to the main gate.

A few minutes' walk along **Bridge Street** will bring you to **Magdalene College** (pronounced Maudlen) to see the fascinating library of Samuel Pepys exhibited in the original bookcases he had made for it. The manuscript volumes of his diary are also in this collection. (Ask the porter at the gate when the seventeenth-century library building is open.)

Returning along Bridge Street, you should look in at the **Round Church.** Built during the twelfth century, it is the oldest of the four round churches in England. A little farther along on the left, across Jesus Lane, **Sidney Street** brings you to **Sidney Sussex College.** After glancing around its ivy-covered walls, continue to the delightful gardens of **Christ's College** on the left—perhaps the loveliest in Cambridge. (The gardens are usually open from 2:00 to 4:00.) The mulberry tree on the lawn is supposedly associated with the poet John

Milton, Christ's College's most distinguished old member.

If you are interested in the fact that Harvard was founded by an Emmanuel man, walk along **St. Andrew's Street** a couple of hundred yards to **Emmanuel College.** The college chapel contains a tablet and stained-glass window in memory of John Harvard.

Returning to Sidney Street, you will see opposite you a narrow street called **Petty Cury.** Walk past its old buildings and you will shortly come to **Market Hill,** a shopping center since medieval days. Open stalls display colorful flowers, fruit, and vegetables. A few steps through **St. Mary's Street** will bring you to **King's Parade.** Across the street stands the classic **Senate House,** where the chief university functions, like the awarding of degrees, take place. Just to the right rises the lovely old **Gate of Honor** of **Gonville and Caius** (pronounced "Keys") **College.**

From the Senate House, walk past King's and on the left you will shortly come to **Corpus Christi College,** where you can visit one of Cambridge's treasures—the **old court,** built in 1377 and considered the earliest example of a complete medieval academic quadrangle still standing. Look for the tablet to Christopher Marlowe, who lived in a ground-floor room on the right.

Cross **Trumpington Street** and turn right into **Silver Street** to **Queens' Lane.** Here is the entrance to **Queens' College,** whose fifteenth-century mellow, dark red brick construction lends a distinct and picturesque quality to its several small courtyards. Queens' has the most complete set of medieval college buildings in Cambridge. The embattled turrets of the fifteenth-century gateway are particularly impressive. Wander into the cloister court to look at the old half-timbered **President's Lodging,** with its bay windows supported by wooden columns, surely one of the most charming corners of Cambridge. The large sundial in a nearby court below a sloping red roof adds an attractive touch. Returning through these courts, in one of which lived Erasmus, you cross the famous wooden **"Mathematical Bridge"** (so-called because of the care-

ful calculation of strains which went into its construction)
to the college gardens.

Returning to Trumpington Street you should end your tour
of Cambridge colleges by visiting the oldest of all, **Peterhouse,** founded by Edward I. Be sure to see the church of **St.
Mary the Less** for the tablet to Reverend Godfrey Washington, a Fellow of Peterhouse. The Washington coat of arms
displayed here later became the Stars and Stripes. The college **hall** and **buttery** are original late-thirteenth-century buildings.

Just beyond Peterhouse on Trumpington Street you will
find the **Fitzwilliam Museum,** containing one of England's most
extensive and outstanding collections of all forms of art. The
museum is open weekdays from 10:00 to 5:00; Sunday from
2:00 to 5:00 (closed the first Wednesday of each month).
The paintings, including excellent examples of English as well
as most Continental schools, are well exhibited in light and
spacious galleries.

As a suitable end of the day's tour you will enjoy having
tea or dinner at the delightful **Garden House** hotel, which you
reach by walking down little **St. Mary's Lane,** just north of
Peterhouse. The hotel gardens run right along the river. There
you might decide, if you can, which spot in Cambridge is the
most fascinating of all.

IV EDINBURGH

"AULD REEKIE"

The Royal Mile

You will find **Edinburgh** a delightful city for walking. It is not only scenically beautiful but full of historical interest. The **old town,** perched on a long, high rocky ridge, sits in a most dramatic position overlooking the **new city,** which spreads northward toward the **Firth of Forth.** The old and the new (most of it was built during the late eighteenth and early nineteenth century) are divided by Princes Street. Considered one of the finest avenues in Europe, it owes its reputation largely to the striking view of the old town directly opposite.

Begin this walk in Edinburgh at the west end of spacious **Princes Street,** in full view of the old section, which you should visit first. Rising sharply to the right is **Edinburgh Castle** high on the cliff—in earliest times the stronghold of a Pictish king. Proceeding east, you should enter the beautifully landscaped **Princes Street gardens** on the right just opposite **Charlotte Street.** As you stroll along, you will enjoy the lawns and flower beds that provide an attractive foreground and brighten the scene of the turreted castle, the stone houses, and the church steeples rising above the rock. At any moment a Scotsman in kilts may saunter by. Take a few minutes to wander through the charming gardens, built on filled ground, the site of a former loch. Midway down the main walk below Princes Street is the impressive **memorial**—a soldier in kilts—erected by Americans of Scottish blood and sympathy to Scotsmen who were killed in World War I. Ater passing an attractive display of heather—white, purple, and mauve—you will reach the lovely **Floral Clock,** the oldest of its kind in the

74

world. Each quarter hour a cuckoo appears to sound the time. During the festival season (late August to early September) band concerts take place in an open amphitheatre nearby, and at night the gardens are beautifully floodlit.

At the top of the steps beyond the clock, pause for a moment and look at the skyline silhouette of the houses and churches of the old town. On leaving the gardens, start up **The Mound,** the street that crosses the park into old Edinburgh. On the left are two large buildings designed in the classic style—the **Royal Scottish Academy,** a building of pink stone, and the **National Gallery.** The Academy features contemporary works of art from April to mid-September (open 10:00–9:00) while the National Gallery houses a fine selection of Italian and Dutch masters, as well as the most complete collection anywhere of Scottish artists, including Sir Henry Raeburn (open weekdays, 10:00–5:00; Sunday, in summer, 2:00–8:00).

Continue to the right up the hill into **Mound Place.** As Mound Place turns left into **Ramsay Lane** a bit of the Firth of Forth is visible in the distance. Keep right past turreted houses to the large **Esplanade,** the castle's parade ground. In former days the burning of supposed witches took place here, but in summer, during the **Edinburgh Festival** season, it is the scene of the stirring military tattoo, a thrilling performance held at night under floodlighting, featuring massed bands. (The castle is open from June to September: daily, 9:30–6:00; Sunday, 11:00–6:00; but state apartments are closed Sunday.) **Castle Rock** is so steep on three of its sides that it was an almost impregnable fortress.

Statues of the Scottish heroes Robert Bruce and William Wallace on either side of the gateway are reminders that you are on historic ground. Kilted soldiers stand on guard outside the entrance. A steep road winds to the right past the drawbridge and under an ancient prison. In a few moments you will reach a terrace where a battery of old cannon are still in their emplacements. Here you will be rewarded by a magnificent panorama over the city, the wide Firth of Forth, and the hills

EDINBURGH

ROUTE 1 -›--›--›-
ROUTE 2 ·—··—··—·

100 50 0   100   200   300 YARDS

of **Fife** on the horizon. At the summit, a little farther along, stands the tiny, low stone non-sectarian Norman **Chapel of St. Margaret,** the most ancient building in Edinburgh. It was built in 1073 and restored about a century ago. Some of the original gray stone is still visible in the walls. Fresh flowers in the chapel are changed every week by a group of Edinburgh ladies named Margaret under the patronage of Princess Margaret. In front of the chapel on the ramparts is **Mons Meg,** a huge fifteenth-century cannon. One of Europe's oldest artillery pieces, it fired a stone ball weighing 400 pounds a mile and a half.

The **Scottish National War Memorial** is located inside **Palace Yard.** In the **Hall of Honor** you will be deeply impressed by the central shrine, consisting of banners, campaign flags, and regimented panels in memory of Scots who fell in two world wars. To see a display of Scottish military uniforms and an exhibit of memorabilia pertaining to the Scottish sailor John Paul Jones, "the Father of the American Navy," you should also stop in at the **United Services Museum.** Be sure to see the great **banqueting hall,** decorated with crests of governors of the castle, with its fine hammer-beamed roof on the south side of the quadrangle. It was in the banqueting hall that the early Scottish Parliaments met. Now it houses a collection of armor and ancient weapons. In addition, you should visit the **Royal Apartments,** also in the courtyard, to see the tiny bedroom where Mary, Queen of Scots, gave birth to James VI of Scotland (James I of England). A fascinating display of Scottish regalia—crown, scepter, and sword of state (last carried in state on Queen Elizabeth's coronation visit in 1953)— is on exhibition in the **Crown Chamber.**

After wandering around the castle long enough to absorb its memorable history, return by the **Argyll Tower** with its portcullis leading to the Esplanade. You are now starting on the famous **Royal Mile,** so named because it descends from the Royal Palace in the castle to the Royal Palace of **Holyroodhouse.** It is one of the most renowned walks in Europe, and it promises to become even more so, for an extensive and gradual program of restoring the dilapidated old buildings along the Royal Mile is now in process.

On leaving the Esplanade you may notice a cannon ball (dating from 1745) embedded in the wall of the first house (1630) on the right just above the central window. A few yards farther along on the left, the **Outlook Tower** is worth visiting and is particularly fascinating for children. In the roof there is a **camera obscura.** The reflection of light through this device enables you to see on a clear day the details of the new town and surrounding country projected on the floor (open weekdays, 10:00–6:00; Sunday, 12:30–6:00).

You now enter the wide **Lawnmarket,** so named because the booths of lawn, or cloth, sellers were located here. On either side of the Lawnmarket there are narrow alleyways, or closes, where many distinguished figures lived. In **Milnes Court** on the left you will note a balustrade with curved bars which permitted eighteenth-century ladies in their wide crinoline dresses to pass. The old houses in the closes deteriorated into slums during the nineteenth century, when the new town became fashionable. However, in recent years, these multistoried dwellings have been restored, so now it is interesting to wander around the closes. Turn right down the steps in front of the church to ancient **West Bow,** a short, steep street lined in canyonlike style with high houses through which royal processions and victims on their way to the execution block passed to and from the castle. At the foot, beyond the old shops, you will come into a large square called the **Grassmarket,** where for several hundred years cattle and grain were sold. Then return by West Bow to the Lawnmarket.

In **James' Court** on the left lived the Scottish philosopher David Hume. Dr. Johnson stayed with his host and biographer James Boswell in the eastern corner. In another close, where the poet Robert Burns lived in 1786, on the left of the Lawnmarket, is **Lady Stair's house,** now restored and a museum. Under the archway through which you pass from the Lawnmarket, note the tablet, which records that "in a Tavern of 1717 Sir Richard Steele gave supper to a company of eccentric beggars." Opposite is the close where Deacon Brodie lived. He is believed to have been the character whom Robert Louis Stevenson had in mind when writing *Dr. Jekyll and Mr. Hyde.*

As you wander around the closes or closed courts and down the Royal Mile, try to spot the **"marriage lintels"** (stones over the doorways), giving the date and initials of the original owner.

The Lawnmarket opens into **High Street.** On the right is **Parliament Square** and the **High Kirk of St. Giles,** whose tower is shaped like the Crown of Scotland. If you look carefully in the square outside the west end of the church, you will see the design of a heart in the cobblestones, which marks the site of the old **Tolbooth,** or prison, popularized in the opening scene of Sir Walter Scott's novel *The Heart of Midlothian.* Although founded in the eleventh century, the High Kirk is known primarily as the mother church of Presbyterianism because John Knox, the reformer, was its first minister.

The small **Chapel of the Thistle** (the thistle is the emblem of Scotland's highest order of chivalry), with its exquisitely carved stalls bearing the coats of arms of the knights, is an elegant though recent addition to the church's interior. The fine nave is hung with old battle flags and regimental standards.

At the east end of the square you will see the **Cross of Edinburgh,** which in days gone by marked the center of the city's life as well as the scene of burnings and beheadings, and today is used as a forum for official proclamations. On the opposite side of High Street stands the **City Chamber,** or town hall.

The adjoining group of buildings includes **Parliament Hall** (open weekdays,10:00–5:00; Saturday, 10:00–1:00) with a lovely hammer-beamed roof, where the Scottish Parliament met from 1639 to 1707, and the **Signet Library** (open weekdays, 10:00–4:00; Saturday, 10:00–1:00), whose upper room is nobly proportioned. The burial place of John Knox in the courtyard near the cathedral is indicated by a circular spot in the tarmac of the present parking lot.

After passing several closes and crossing the busy junction of **North** and **South Bridge** (the **University of Edinburgh** is off to the right), you will come to the picturesque sixteenth-century house on the left where John Knox died in 1572. Inside are many interesting exhibits relating to the "great reformer" (open weekdays, 10:00–5:00). Moubray House next door is considered the oldest private dwelling in the city. An interesting historical collection of toys can be seen in the **Museum of Childhood,** in **Hyndford's Close** (open weekdays, 10:00–5:00). Look down some of the narrow alleys or closes on the right to get glimpses of industrial Edinburgh, almost obscured in smoky fog. In fact, Edinburgh is called "Auld Reekie" because of the pall of smoke that used to hang over the city in the morning.

After passing what was once **Nether Bow,** the east gate to the old city, you enter **Canongate.** A marriage lintel dated 1677 is over the doorway at No. 185. A few hundred yards farther, on your left, you will see the turrets and projecting clock of **Canongate Tolbooth,** a former courthouse and prison, built in the sixteenth century, that reflects the French influence in Scottish architecture. Today, it is a city museum containing an interesting tartan collection. Adam Smith, the author of *The Wealth of Nations,* which so greatly influenced eighteenth-century economic thinking, is buried in the adjacent churchyard.

On the opposite side of the street is **Moray House,** once used by Oliver Cromwell as a temporary residence. You should visit sixteenth-century **Huntly House** (open weekdays, 10:00–5:00), a city museum where the local history of Edinburgh is shown in several seventeenth-century oak-paneled rooms. A copy of the National Covenant and John Knox's Psalter are on display. Go through the pleasant tearoom (Scottish scones are served) to a charming courtyard. On one side clay pipes are being made in a small workshop. Also see the typical Scottish kitchen of a hundred years ago. Now turn right just beyond Huntly House and stroll into **Bakehouse Close,** the best-restored of the many closes in the Royal Mile.

Acheson House (1633), now a craft center, on the east side, is also particularly attractive. **Arthur's Seat,** the rocky mountain that rises above Edinburgh, can be seen in the distance. At the bottom of the hill on the left, the famous **White Horse Inn,** an artistic corner of old Edinburgh, is being reconstructed.

Just beyond the square is Holyroodhouse, the Queen's official residence, built about 1500 by James IV and for years the Scottish Royal Palace. But before entering its historic grounds, take a turn down Abbeyhill to the left to see **Queen Mary's Bath House,** which dates from the late sixteenth century and was originally a postern gate in the palace's wall.

Holyroodhouse is best known for the period when Mary, Queen of Scots, resided there (1561–1567), but the palace as it stands today dates mainly from the reign of Charles II, who rebuilt it in 1671 (open June–September: daily, 9:30–6:00; Sunday, 11:00–6:00). The long **Picture Gallery** and **State Apartments,** including the **throne and dining rooms,** are interesting because of their paneling, ceilings, paintings, and tapestries. The smaller rooms have a lived-in quality unlike many palaces. Queen Elizabeth II and Prince Philip take up residence in Holyroodhouse every summer. But the most fascinating apartments in the palace are those connected with the tempestuous days of Mary, Queen of Scots. Here, in the main tower—the oldest part of the palace—is located the **secret staircase** and tiny apartment where the bloody murder of the Queen's secretary, David Rizzio, took place before Mary's eyes. In fact, a brass marker in the floor of the audience chamber, outside of the apartment, marks the spot where on March 9, 1566, the corpse lay with its fifty-six dagger wounds.

After touring the palace, you should visit the ruins of the twelfth-century **Abbey Kirk** on the left of the central courtyard. Then stroll around the beautifully landscaped grounds, where each summer the Queen holds a garden party. The artistically planted flower borders, charming rockery, shrubs, carpetlike lawns, and towering trees lend a country atmosphere to the palace park, which seems to nestle so fittingly beneath the high green slopes of Arthur's Seat, Edinburgh's mountainous landmark.

The New Town

Start your stroll through the **new town of Edinburgh** on Princes Street at the corner of **St. David Street,** opposite the Gothic monument to Sir Walter Scott, Scotland's great historical novelist and poet. As you wander along stately **Princes Street,** you will enjoy indulging in some window-shopping, for Edinburgh's leading stores are located here.

When you reach Charlotte Street, at the west end of Princes Street, turn right and in a minute or two you will be in **Charlotte Square,** one of the most delightful in Edinburgh. The lawns, trees, and gardens of the squares in the new town lighten up the rather forbidding stone of the houses around them. If you walk to the left around the square you will pass the imposing **St. George's Church.** The delicate detail of the classic façades on the north side is one of the outstanding works of the great eighteenth-century architect Robert Adam.

There is one other spot nearby which is architecturally appealing—the circular **Moray Place,** just two blocks north from the west side of Charlotte Square, beyond **Ainslie Place.** At Moray Place turn right on Darnaway Street and walk along **Heriot Row,** with the residents' private gardens on your right and attractive homes on your left, to the next corner. A right turn into Frederick Street and another right at the next corner will bring you into Queen Street. At the next corner take a left turn into **Castle Street** and in the second block on your left you will come to **No. 39,** an Adam house with a circular window on the ground floor. Sir Walter Scott lived here from 1802 to 1826.

A few yards farther on, is **George Street,** which is half a mile long and was originally planned as the main avenue of new Edinburgh. An impressive thoroughfare, wide enough so that parking space is provided in the center, George Street, with its fine buildings and monuments, may strike you as even more distinguished than Princes Street. You can see at the west end of George Street the dome of St. George's Church in Charlotte Square and at the east end the high column in St. Andrew Square.

A few minutes' stroll to the left along George Street will bring you to **St. Andrew Square,** one of Edinburgh's finest. The massive stone buildings around the square—some of them eighteenth-century—house many of Scotland's leading banks and insurance companies. If you look right, toward Princes Street, you will get an unusual view of the **Scott Memorial.** Its tower rises above the crest of **St. David Street,** making it seem as though it were located there instead of on Princes Street, its actual site. At the far end of the square turn left one block down St. Andrew Street to visit the Scottish Museum of Antiquities and the National Portrait Gallery (open weekdays, 10:00–5:00; Sunday, 2:00–5:00) just around the corner to the left on Queen Street. The **Museum of Antiquities** contains a varied assortment of Scottish historical objects from the days of the Picts and Romans. John Knox's pulpit from St. Giles' Cathedral and the "creepie," or stool, which Jenny Geddes is believed to have thrown at the Dean's head when he was reading Archbishop Laud's liturgy in 1637, are also on exhibition. In the **National portrait gallery** you will find paintings by Sir Joshua Reynolds and bronzes by Sir Jacob Epstein.

Return along St. Andrew Street to Princes Street and then turn left to **Register House,** the repository of Scottish national and historical records. This building is regarded as an excellent example of Robert Adam's design.

Just a few yards ahead, along **Waterloo Place,** you can locate on the right the **Old Calton burial ground,** where you will be interested in a monument to the memory of Abraham Lincoln and the Scottish-American soldiers killed during the American Civil War.

Continuing along Waterloo Place, take a turn to the left and climb a flight of steps to the top of **Calton Hill.** From here you can see a magnificent panorama spread below—the new town at the foot; to the right, the **Firth of Forth,** the port of **Leith,** and the **North Sea;** and in the other direction, the ridge of the **Royal Mile** and **Arthur's Seat.** The **two monuments** on the crest of Calton Hill are quite unusual: one a row of classic pillars, intended as a memorial of the Napoleonic Wars, which, if completed, would have been a reproduction of the Parthenon; and the other a telescope-shaped tower, in memory of Lord Nelson.

As you stand at the top of Calton Hill looking out over Edinburgh, with its striking contrast of ancient and modern, you are at the right spot to end your walk in this picturesque and lovely capital of Scotland.

The Continent

V COPENHAGEN

THE CITY OF COPPER ROOFS
Skirting the Canals

Copenhagen's gay, intimate atmosphere, the charm of its delightful old houses and squares, and its stately palaces with their copper roofs and beautiful parks has made this Scandinavian capital increasingly popular, particularly with Americans. Also, you will discover, like most visitors, that the Danes are a friendly, hospitable people with whom you will feel at home. Incidentally, English is really a second language in Copenhagen, which makes it easier for many to find their way.

The center of the **old city** through which you will walk has not only considerable historic interest but also the seafaring spirit of a throbbing harbor and free port. One of the attractions in walking around Copenhagen is the considerable variety that you encounter—medieval streets, fascinating palaces and churches, canals and quays, and the latest shops, all comparatively close together and in one general area.

As a convenience to the stroller, this walk through Copenhagen has been divided into two parts, each of which should require about half a day. The first part includes the oldest section as well as the palaces of Christiansborg and Amalienborg. The second stroll covers the park, Rosenborg Palace, and the university and shopping sections.

You should begin your walk (in the morning, if possible) in the center of Copenhagen at the **City Hall Square,** or **Raadhus Pladsen.** When you stand in front of the Palace Hotel, by the column depicting two Vikings blowing their horns, you are at the spot where some of the oldest habita-

89

COPENHAGEN

ROUTE 1 ——————→
ROUTE 2 ——•••••→

100 50 0   100   200 YARDS 300

tions were located in earliest times, for Copenhagen's history goes back to the Stone Age.

Opposite the City Hall tower, you enter the old part of town by turning left into **Lavendelstraede.** Mozart's widow, who later married a Danish diplomat, lived at **No. 1** from 1813 to 1819. Now cross Hestemollestraede, named for a mill that was driven by horsepower, and wander under the arch along a little winding street, Slutterigade. After passing through another arch you will be in **Nytorv,** the new market place. The classic building on the left with the large Ionic columns is the **City Courthouse;** formerly, it was the Town Hall until the new one was erected in 1906. Søren Kierkegaard, the famous Danish philosopher, was born next door in 1813.

From Nytorv turn right into **Raadhusstraede,** crammed with old brass and copper shops. You may be attracted by the many ground-level display windows and wish to browse around them for a bit. These houses were built in 1795, after the second great fire.

At the second corner turn left into the narrow street **Magstraede,** once the shoreline of the old town. It still preserves the atmosphere of early days. The two red brick gabled houses on the right, are about the only bourgeois homes dating from 1650 that survived the first conflagration, which devastated Copenhagen in 1728. Many of the Dutch-style houses on this curving street have antique shops in the basement. On the other side of Knabrostraede, Magstraede changes its name to **Snaregade,** although it continues to be just as narrow. The ancient house at **No. 5** is unusual for its fine timber beams and original early eighteenth-century hand-fashioned blown glass windowpanes. Cross over to the opposite side to **No. 10** and look at a semicircular courtyard below ocher-colored buildings (1792). Note the chimney that leans at a rakish angle and the fine carved-oak door just inside the entrance. For a bit of variety, stop in at **No. 4** to see the series of amusing modern frescoes depicting the different owners who have lived there since 1397.

Straight ahead is **Gammel Strand,** which faces the **Frederiks-holms Canal.** At the far end of the street you will come to one of Copenhagen's most picturesque scenes, the old red-faced women cleaning and selling fish. In the midst of the stalls, there stands a granite monument of a typical fishwife to perpetuate the spirit of this colorful market.

Bishop Absalon's statue is in the square in front of you, **Højbro Plads.** This medieval warrior founded the town in 1167 by building his fortress on the island across the canal where Christiansborg Palace stands. You can see the foundations of this and later castles when you visit Christiansborg. Beyond the statue, the corner house with pilasters was the home of the Melchior family; in the second-floor drawing room Hans Christian Andersen used to read aloud his popular fairy tales.

Return now along Gammel Strand, where there is a very good fish restaurant, **Fiskehusets.** Across the canal you will notice two buildings; the one with a green cupola is **Slots-kirchen,** the castle chapel, and next to it is a museum featuring the works of the Danish sculptor Thorvaldsen. Excellent free concerts by the **Copenhagen Boys' Choir** are held in the chapel during the winter. But you should pay particular attention to the very fine old houses on your right. Notice how some have pulleys on top to haul up furniture. **No. 48,** a wonderful baroque red brick house dating from 1750, is perhaps the most outstanding. It now belongs to the Art Association, which exhibits Danish and foreign paintings and sculpture.

Continuing along the canal, you follow **Nybrogade** to the end. Looking back along the canal, there is a superb view from here of the copper steeple of the **Nikolaj Church** reflected in the water. Now turn left just before the **National Museum.** This museum contains, among other things, important and interesting ethnographic and prehistoric collections related to Danish culture (open 10:00–4:00, except Tuesday).

Pause for a few moments on the marble bridge opposite, with its exquisite rococo pavilions on either side. To your left is another view of the row of attractive houses, which have survived the centuries. Also, you will see the high sloping roof of **King Christian IV's huge brewery.** The canal itself is full of interest and activity, because in summer big wooden-hulled sailing ships and small steamers tie up at the wharf.

You now enter **Christiansborg Palace** and make your way over the cobblestones to the royal riding ring straight ahead, attractively landscaped with rows of pollarded trees. The curved archways and the symmetrical buildings on either side are the only remains of the original eighteenth-century palace. The building on the left is the indoor **riding hall,** and on the right is the **King's stables,** which you may be able to enter for a peep at its beautiful interior. If you happen to be here on Wednesday or Sunday between 2:00 and 4:00, stop in to see the old **court theatre** also on the right, which now houses a **museum of Danish dramatic art.**

At the end of the open space, you walk under a colonnade to the right of the large palace and go into the courtyard of the **Folketing,** the Danish Parliament. In the building opposite, you will see five low arches. Through the arches and down a couple of steps you will come to the most delightful part of Christiansborg, the marvelously landscaped gardens of the red brick **Royal Library** directly facing you. Here is a most inviting and quiet place to sit for a while, under chestnut and lime trees, near the lovely large rose garden around the square pond. This enclosure used to be a naval harbor long ago. On your way out, you will see two of the iron rings to which the ships were tied.

Now turn right and go through a low archway into a large square in front of the palace. To your right is the old corn exchange, built in 1619, one of the most interesting and unusual Dutch Renaissance buildings in Copenhagen. It now houses the stock exchange. (Open Monday–Friday, 12:45–3:15; Saturday, 11:45–2:15.) Saunter along **Slotsholmsgade** on your right to get a better view of the exchange and, especially, its corkscrew spire of four entwined dragon-tails rising above its shining green copper roof. You will see lots of bicycles parked on the right—a characteristic sight in this flat country where bicycle-riding is so extremely popular. From the end of Slotsholmsgade you can see another twisted spire. This one has an external staircase and is across the busy harbor in the old part of **Christianshaven.**

Walk around the **Royal Exchange,** or **Borsen,** to the canal on the far side. Here you will sense the busy life of the port. Ships for other parts of Denmark and Sweden dock along the wharves to your right. As you stroll along the quay you will pass barges from the Danish islands, selling fruit, flowers, and vegetables—a gay and colorful sight. Every twenty minutes after 10:00, boats leave from here for **Langelinie,** a favorite promenade for Copenhageners, which runs along the harbor. From Langelinie the famous **bronze statue** of *The Little Mermaid* looks out to sea. If you have an hour or more to spare, this trip will give you a good idea of the nautical side of Copenhagen.

Cross the bridge where you see the sign reading "Ring II" to reach the **Holmenskirke,** which originally was a sixteenth-century anchor foundry for the Danish Fleet. You follow the broad avenue, **Holmenskanal,** as it curves to the left to the large square, **Kongens Nytorv,** which is pleasantly landscaped with attractive flower beds inside a ring of pollarded trees. **The Royal Theatre** for opera, drama, and ballet is on the right. **Grumstrup,** a leading antique dealer, is nearby. Just beyond you will notice a beautifully proportioned building of dull red brick, built in the late seventeenth century. This is **Charlottenborg,** now the home of the **Royal Academy of Art.**

If you keep to the right around the square, you will reach **Nyhaven,** where sailing ships often are tied to the pier. This street along the canal, a popular resort for sailors, is filled with picturesque old houses, now cheap restaurants and seamen's dives. A short distance along Nyhaven will bring you to Lille Strandstraede, an interesting street, where you turn left. Wander under the archway of **No. 6** to a small courtyard where you will find an old timbered house. When you reach **Sankt Annae Plads** just a little farther along, turn right a few yards for the memorial bust of President Franklin D. Roosevelt, which the Danes erected after World War II.

You now walk along **Amaliegade** to the left for a few minutes to visit the **Amalienborg Palace,** the residence of the Danish King. Enter the royal square through a colonnaded arch. The spacious courtyard with a fine equestrian statue in the center is most impressive. Four distinguished rococo mansions of lovely proportions occupy the four corners. The residence of the King is at the far right; other members of the royal family occupy the other buildings. At noon, when the King is in residence, the ceremony of changing the guard takes place. You leave the square on the left opposite **Frederick's Church,** and then return to Kongens Nytorv by **Bredgade.**

If you started this stroll in the morning, you probably are ready for a good lunch. Around the square are several attractive restaurants—one is **A Porta**—where you can relax and enjoy the tasty open sandwiches which the Danes prepare so well.

Rosenborg to Tivoli

If you take your second stroll through Copenhagen in the afternoon, start before 2:00. You should begin at the entrance to **King's Garden (Kongens Have).**To reach it from Kongens Nytorv, you walk a few blocks along Gothersgade through a dull business section to the corner of Kronprinsessegade.

The King's Garden, Copenhagen's first public park, was originally planted in the French style. Its extensive lawns (as green as those in England), luxurious trees and shrubbery, herbaceous borders, and flower beds make this park exceptionally charming. A few steps inside the entrance you will reach an avenue of trees, then straight ahead you will see **Rosenborg Palace,** which used to be the King's summer home. To the left, beyond a narrow avenue of lime trees, you will have a glimpse of the Round Tower and **Our Lady's Church (Vor Frue Kirke).**

Take the path branching to the right and at the end you will come to a good **statue of Hans Christian Andersen,** surrounded by a bed of flowers. From here keep to the left past the herbaceous border to the parterre rose garden by the moat which flows around the palace. This is a delightful spot to pause for a moment while you study Rosenborg's rather fancy seventeenth-century exterior.

You leave the park by the **Queen's Gate** in the far corner and then turn left down Ostervoldgade, and go a few hundred yards to the entrance of **Rosenborg Palace** (open 11:00–3:00). Inside there is a museum with exhibits pertaining to the Danish royal family, including the crown regalia and an unusual collection of china, glass, and paintings.

On leaving the palace, continue along Ostervoldgade a few blocks into Norre Voldgade. At the **Norreport underground station** turn left into Fiolstraede, the beginning of **Copenhagen's Latin Quarter.** You are now approaching the university section. As you wander along **Fiolstraede** you will be enticed by the mass of old copper and brass bowls, plates, etc., hanging outside its many antique shops. Several second-hand book shops display their wares on outside racks. At the corner of **Krystalgade** you will find a lovely yellow half-timbered house that dates from 1734.

A block farther along you will reach Frue Plads, the square dominated by Our Lady's Cathedral (open 11:00–3:00) and the old buildings of **the University of Copenhagen** founded in 1479. Have a look at the hall and staircase through a large door marked "Gate A" opposite the cathedral. At one side of the courtyard, under a large tree, you will see the **Konsistorium,** a building of red brick and the oldest in the city. Opposite the front of the cathedral you should walk through an arch into the delightful courtyard of the **Bishop's Palace,** shaded by trees and vines. Practically next door is **St. Peders Church** with a beautiful herb garden.

Return to the cathedral square and beyond the university on the far side saunter along Store Kannikestraede to **No. 10** where, in a quiet courtyard, you will discover a charming old house. This timbered building of varying height has a warm ocher coloring. The large trees, vine-covered walk, and small fountain lend great charm to this out-of-the-way corner of Copenhagen. Just a little farther along the street you will come to the seventeenth-century **Regensen,** the university's oldest dormitory. Here you will see another charming courtyard, ivy-covered buildings with slate roof, a clock tower and belfry, and, just above, the upper part of the **Round Tower.**

You should climb the wide spiral ramp of the tower—Czar Peter the Great once did it on horseback. The tower, built in 1637, was an observatory until a century ago. From the top you get an excellent and close impression of Copenhagen's old houses, with their gabled sloping roofs and tree-shaded courts.

After climbing the Round Tower, you should wander around the nearby streets and visit two attractive squares. From the Round Tower go left a few yards on Kobmagergade, then right on Skindergade, and in a moment left on Niels Hemmingsensgade to **Graabrodretorv,** a square of great charm and quaintness. Eighteenth-century gabled houses painted in pastel colors surround a green lilac-covered mound in the center.

Return to Niels Hemmingsgade and on the other side of Valkendorfsgade you will come to **Helligandskirken** (Church of the Holy Ghost). You are now on **Strøget,** Copenhagen's famous and crowded main shopping street, which is really five streets continuing one another. Just across Strøget is a pleasant square with a flower market, from which you get a good view of Christiansborg Palace. **Illums Bolighus,** perhaps the city's leading department store and a center of modern design, is nearby and well worth looking around.

Now walk past the many shops along Strøget toward Gammel Torv, and then on Frederiksbergade back to City Hall Square. Cross the busy square and shortly, on the left side of wide **Vesterbrogade,** you will reach the entrance to **Tivoli,** the world-famous amusement park. Even though you will want to return one evening for dinner and a taste of the great variety of entertainment—concerts, outdoor vaudeville, and pantomime shows, as well as the traditional "Fun Fair,"—it's pleasant to sit, perhaps by the lake, in these beautifully land-scaped gardens—a fitting finish to these strolls through attractive Copenhagen.

VI AMSTERDAM

HOLLAND'S CITY OF CANALS
The Old Town

Amsterdam combines business with art—the modern with the old—an active commercial port with the charm of the days of Rembrandt. It's a colorful city, with flower markets along the quays and music in the streets. It's a city of some fifty canals. But unlike Venice, most of Amsterdam's waterways are lined with cobblestoned streets.

In fact, there are two Amsterdams: the old town dating from the thirteenth century and the new, which developed some three-hundred years later. Both are intensely interesting, quite different from other important European cities, and steeped in the history of the seventeenth century, when Holland with her Hanseatic merchants was a world power.

The art lover will be attracted to Amsterdam because it was the home of Rembrandt and because its world-famous Rijks Museum houses probably the greatest collection of Dutch art to be seen anywhere. Those who admire fine old houses will derive much pleasure from the fascinating gabled residences of the great Dutch merchants that line the broad canals in the newer section. And if you like to stroll about a city where you continually encounter enchanting views, Amsterdam will delight you with its long vistas of tree-lined canals spanned by graceful bridges. Combine all this with the throb of a vigorous commercial community, its busy harbor teeming with activity, and you have an unusually attractive tourist center.

Here is a modern metropolis—one of the greatest ports in Western Europe—built on piles driven into the sand and composed of seventy islands. Although you will always sense the bustle and activity in Holland's financial and trading capital, you will find that the quiet and picturesque canals best express the spirit of this ancient city.

As you walk around Amsterdam, you will understand that its charm does not depend on the artistic views from its bridges or the stillness of its broad canals. It springs from a combination of sights and sounds, and the vivacity of the residents, reflected in its street life. Thousands of cyclists seem to overwhelm motor traffic. Concertina players can be heard, helping to satisfy the city's centuries-old craving for music, although Carillons every quarter-hour from church towers in the old section of the city are a more traditional feature of the city's musical life. Not only do the people of Amsterdam love music, but they adore flowers, which, during the growing season, seem to be everywhere—in markets, window boxes, barges, gardens, and parks.

Amsterdam, now a city of almost 900,000 people, looks back on the sixteenth and seventeenth centuries as the period when it became a great commercial and cultural center. It won its freedom in 1578 during the Netherlands War of Independence. Shortly afterward, merchants and artists began to move to Amsterdam from Antwerp and Ghent; the size of the city doubled in the closing years of the sixteenth century. A few years later Amsterdam became the foremost trading port of Europe, and not long thereafter, Rembrandt, Bol, Van Ruysdael, and others established its artistic reputation.

For your convenience, two walking routes are recommended, the first concentrating on the **old town** and the second mainly centering on the **newer city** (built up during the seventeenth and eighteenth centuries) with its stately homes, its broad, peaceful canals, and its great museums.

Begin your first walk (women should wear flat shoes because of the brick sidewalks) at the **Dam**—the center of Amsterdam life—the huge open square in front of the Royal Palace (open weekdays, 10:00–4:00). The Dam is the central

point around which the **five canals** that mark off the old section of the city fan out in concentric semicircles.

The Royal Palace, an imposing brick building which was originally the **Town Hall,** is a remarkable structure because its foundations rest on thousands of piles driven into the ground. The Queen resides here when she is in Amsterdam. The palace's **Great Hall** has an impressive air, particularly on state occasions, when thousands of candles sparkle from the large glass chandeliers.

The **Nieuwe Kerk,** Holland's coronation church and one of Amsterdam's oldest, stands opposite the palace at one end of the square. If you go inside to visit the burial place of Dutch heroes, you will notice the church's unusually fine vaulted wooden ceiling.

In Amsterdam there are many narrow streets down which cars tear at a terrific pace—so watch your step.

Stroll along the wide Dam a couple of blocks to a small square, **Beurs Plein.** At the far right-hand corner, go left in front of a red brick building, then right down an alley, Paternoster Steeg, and across busy Warmoes Straat, the oldest street in the city. Straight ahead you will see the **Oude Kerk,** founded in 1306. This typical Dutch town church is worth examining for its spacious interior, stained-glass windows, and 223-foot sixteenth-century spire. Note the tiny houses built into the church tower on either side of its base.

Now stroll to the far side of the church and walk to the left along the picturesque **Voorburgwal.** Looking across the canal, you will be enchanted by the ancient houses that actually lean forward. Look up and you will see the hoisting beam, a particular Amsterdam phenomenon, that has been used for hundreds of years to raise furniture and merchandise from barges to the upper floors.

Proceed along the canal a few yards, and shortly you will come to the **Amstelkring Museum** (open weekdays, 10:00–5:00; Sunday, 1:00–5:00), which contains a collection of Roman Catholic objects. Opposite, there are some fine rococo houses with stone pediments.

Before turning to the left on Zee Dijk to **Prins Hendrik Kade** in the inner harbor, turn around and look back along the colorful canal. Near the wide bridge you will find the wharves, where glass-covered excursion boats leave frequently, both during the day and in the evening, for an hour's delightful cruise through the network of canals—a trip you will enjoy even more after touring the city on foot, for then you will recognize many of the interesting places you have already visited.

Just to the right along the waterfront, past the bridge that leads to the **railroad station,** you will find around the corner an ancient stone tower, the **Schreierstoren,** which now houses the Master of the Port of Amsterdam. A tablet on the tower commemorates Henry Hudson, the discoverer of the Hudson River in New York, who sailed past here in the *Half Moon* in 1609. Another and more sentimental stone plaque on the opposite side shows a woman weeping as the ships sail away. As you stand facing the **Gelderse Kade**—the wide canal that runs into the harbor—you will be interested in the varying ornamentation of the houses, especially that of the shipchandler's warehouse on the right.

If you want to stroll along what was one of Amsterdam's famous old dikes and is now a street, turn right for a moment on Stormsteeg to **Zee Dijk.** But if you do, be prepared to confront a rather disreputable section of Amsterdam, for this is the sailor's **"red-light" district.**

Turn back, and at the end of the Gelderse Kade you will find yourself in the **Nieuwe Markt**—still an active street market—where the seventeenth-century gatehouse, called the **Waag,** houses the **Amsterdam Historical Museum** (open weekdays, 10:00–5:00; Sunday, 1:00–5:00). Rembrandt painted his famous *Anatomical Lesson* in one of the upper rooms that formerly were guild chambers. The museum's **Jewish collection** is a most interesting chronicle of Amsterdam's Jewish community, which for several hundred years played such a vital role in the growth of the city and whose destruction by the Nazis is also recorded in a special exhibition.

A few minutes' detour from Nieuwe Markt along **Kloveniersburgwal** to **No. 12** will bring you to a two-hundred-year-old herb shop. You might like to putter about here and watch the shopkeeper weigh the herbs in his brass scale.

At the far corner of the Nieuwe Markt you will find **Sint Antonies Bree Straat,** rather a dull street which leads to **Rembrandt's house,** with its red wooden shutters (open weekdays, 10:00–5:00; Sunday, 1:00–4:00). This is just beyond the bridge, from which you have a good view along the canal to the left. The house is now one of the most interesting museums in Amsterdam. The interior has been restored and is very much as it was when Rembrandt lived here from 1639 to 1658. The art collection contains a fine group of his etchings, water colors, and drawings.

From Rembrandt's house, turn left along Zwanenburgwal beside the canal, and continue over the bridge. The spire of the **Zuider Kerk** rises in the distance. Just beyond the bridge, you will come to the juncture of the canal and the **Amstel River.** Here is a good spot to rest for a bit on a bench and look out over Amsterdam's network of waterways.

On the other side of the bridge you will be in **Staal Straat;** in a moment you will come to an old wooden drawbridge. To your right, the tree-lined **Groenburgwal** with the towering steeple of the **Zuider Kerk** at its end makes a picturesque scene. Now turn left and walk around the quay by the Amstel. At the center of the bridge, look across the river, and you will see a good view of the **Mint Tower.**

Go back to the long canal on your right—**Kloveniersburgwal**—which flows into the Amstel, then cross the steel drawbridge and turn right for perhaps a hundred yards along the canal to an archway. Colorful barges will very likely be moored to the quays.

You make your way down the dark narrow cloistered passageway, lined with second-hand bookstalls and called **"Oudemanhuisport."** On your right the delightful courtyard shaded by a majestic copper beech is enclosed by the ivy-covered buildings of **Amsterdam University,** a seventeenth-century municipal institution with six thousand students. After wandering about the courtyard and browsing among the prints and maps farther along the passageway, you come out, after crossing a little bridge, at the juncture of three canals. The scene you will see along the tree-lined **Oude Zijds Canal** is one of the most paintable in old Amsterdam. At this corner you will discover a tablet on an old brick house identifying it as the **Fluwelenburgwal** or "Velvet Town Hall," a residence of the wealthy or velvet-clothed citizens.

Stroll across the bridge into Grimburgwal, and on to the wide **Rokin,** where there is a gay **flower market.** Just ahead you will be in the **Spui.** Cross Kalver Straat, one of the city's most crowded shopping streets, usually jammed with pedestrians, and on your right, through a little gateway off the Spui, you will discover a charming and quiet oasis, the **Begijnhof.** This is a somewhat circular group of old narrow brick houses where, following a characteristic Flemish custom, widows and elderly women live. Each gabled house with its white window frames has a little garden in front facing the common lawn and overhanging trees. Notice the leaning tower of the brick church in the courtyard. The whole effect of the ivy-covered houses with sloping tile roofs, the old church, and the brick walk around the central lawn will captivate you. It's as if an old Dutch painting had come to life.

After this delightful interlude, continue along the Spui to the **Singel,** where you will be fascinated by a **floating flower market.** If you don't find what you want on the street, you can climb aboard the barges moored to the cobbled quay and join Dutch housewives as they shop for flowers and shrubs. It's one of the most unusual and attractive flower markets you will encounter in Europe. As an extra touch, you can hear the bells of the Mint Tower chime the hour. Enthusiasts for flower decorations should be sure to visit the shop almost opposite along the quay, where flowers and plants are artistically arranged in special containers. It is called the **Aziatische Bloemsierkunst No. 506 Singel.**

Now that you have started your shopping, return to the

Spui and turn either left or right on **Kalver Straat,** where many of Amsterdam's most popular stores are located. This is just the place to interrupt this walk through old Amsterdam, either for shopping or for luncheon. There are several good restaurants nearby, including the **'T Binnenhofje** in the Singel or **Five Flies** at 294 Spuistraat. Both have an old-world atmosphere but are fairly expensive.

By the Canals to the Rijks Museum

The Mint Tower, an Amsterdam landmark and favorite meeting place, is the best starting point for your second walk, through the **newer section** of the city. Years ago the city's coinage was minted in this old rounded brick tower surmounted by a belfry. Flower stalls now decorate its base.

Walk along the **Amstel River** straight ahead and turn right at the bridge along Halvemaansteeg. After a short block you will be in the **Rembrandts Plein,** a small green square bordered with flowers and enlivened by sidewalk cafés and places of entertainment. Continue along **Amstel Straat** to the bridge over the river. From here you will see one of Amsterdam's most famous and most picturesque bridges, the **Magere Brug.** Its characteristically Dutch balance levers are well known to devotees of Van Gogh and other Dutch painters.

Now you are about to walk along the first of the **three wide parallel canals** that give such a feeling of nobility to the newer part of the city. (You should also walk through this section at night when the houses are floodlit.) The most beautiful and distinguished of these tree-lined promenades is the **Heren Gracht.**

After returning to the Amstel Straat approach to the bridge, you will find the Heren Gracht the first turn to your right. Stand for a moment on the bridge and look down this lovely canal. The house on the far corner has particularly beautiful brickwork.

If possible, try to visit the **Six Museum** at 216-218 Amstel, just across the Herengracht. You must obtain a card of introduction by applying either to your government's consul-general or the director of the Rijks Museum. One of the finest private art galleries in Holland, its collection was started by Rembrandt's patron Jan Six. Its masterpiece is Rembrandt's painting of his friend Six, certainly one of the artist's greatest portraits.

Now return to Heren Gracht and saunter along the tree-covered quay. As you wander past the four- and five-story narrow brick mansions with their decorative stone garlands, you will get an idea of the kind of life Dutch aristocrats lived in the seventeenth and eighteenth centuries. Now, many of the houses are occupied by banks, law offices, and business firms. It's also a fashionable neighborhood for wealthy young married couples. If by chance you should notice a door that is open, perhaps a discreet inquiry will result in an invitation to see the rich ornamentation of the interior decoration done in the French style of that period. You might stop in at the **Willet-Holthuijsen Museum,** the building with fine metal and stone works at No. 605, where furniture, glass, porcelain, and *objets d'art* from the sixteenth to the eighteenth centuries are on exhibit. (Open weekdays, 10:00–5:00; Sunday, 1:00–5:00.)

No. 284, once the **Van Brienenhuis,** an early eighteenth-century mansion now occupied by the **Hendrick de Keyser Society,** is open to visitors.

At the second bridge, **Reguliers Gracht,** you have a fine view of the canal in each direction. Often private sailboats are moored along the quay.

Continue your stroll along the curving canal, past another bridge, until you reach **Leidse Straat,** where you turn left. Most of Amsterdam's quality stores, as well as the city's finest restaurant, **Dikker and Thijs,** are located here. As you walk along, you will cross two other broad canals, the **Keizers Gracht** and the **Prinsen Gracht.** Notice that the trams make their stops on the bridges. The large square you are approaching is the **Leidse Plein,** where the **Municipal Theatre** is located. Just beyond the square you cross **Singel Gracht,** a wide and curving canal.

Turn to the left through the beautifully landscaped little park. Across the canal, rose gardens decorate the banks. In a couple of blocks you will come to the world-renowned **Rijks Museum** on your right (open weekdays, 10:00–5:00; Sunday, 1:00–5:00). Its collection of Dutch paintings is unrivaled; Flemish and Italian artists are also well represented. In addition, the gallery has fine exhibits of Dutch arts, crafts, and sculpture. But if you have only a limited amount of time, you will want to concentrate on Rembrandt's *The Night Watch, Anatomy Lesson, The Staalmeesters,* and the other fine examples of his work. Also, you will be thrilled by the superb, though few, Vermeers on exhibit.

If you prefer modern art, you may wish to limit your time in the Rijks Museum and save yourself for the **Stedelijk Museum,** just two blocks behind it. Here you will find a magnificent and large group of paintings and drawings by Van Gogh. In addition there are works by twentieth-century Dutch painters and many French impressionists.

After reveling in this artistic feast you will feel like sitting quietly and enjoying tea or a drink, so cross the Singel Gracht and find a table on the attractive outdoor terrace of the **Lido** overlooking the canal. This is just the spot to contemplate the fascinating places you have visited while strolling through Amsterdam.

VII   BRUGES

THE WORLD OF THE MIDDLE AGES

To the Lake of Love

Bruges is unique. The medieval and Renaissance world has miraculously survived in this Flemish city. Here, encircled and intersected by quiet waterways, the past has been preserved for the enjoyment of the present. Though there are a few other relatively untouched medieval towns in Europe, none is quite so accessible to the mainstream of tourist travel, for Bruges is only fifteen miles from **Ostend,** on the **English Channel,** and sixty from **Brussels.**

When you cross the outer ring of canals and enter the **old city,** you feel at once transported into the days of Bruges' greatest glory, the fourteenth century. Then, through its trade both in wool and cloth with England, its status as a Hanseatic town, and its commercial ties with Italy, Bruges was one of the great trading and artistic centers of northern Europe. In those days the medieval guilds flourished and the wealthy Flemish merchants made possible the northern Renaissance.

Today as you wander down the narrow streets past the ancient houses and along the tree-lined quays, the spirit of old Bruges lingers on. The reflections of the ivy-colored buildings and tall Gothic towers in the waters of the canals remind you of the time when Bruges, at the junction of the trade routes between the Baltic and the Mediterranean, was the home of humanism, when Italian bankers sat for Van Eyck, and Memling painted his marvelous triptychs.

Being so concentrated—it's hardly half a mile from one

111

side to the other—and packed with such fascinating detail, Bruges is perfect for the tourist who wants to do his sightseeing on foot. In fact, you couldn't properly see the city any other way. By walking you have time to stop and admire the picturesque corners, medieval towers, and lovely façades with which Bruges abounds.

Before starting on your walk, you should buy a museum card, which entitles you to a reduced rate, is transferable, and can be purchased at any museum or at the **Bruges tourist office** located in the **Government Palace** in the **Markt,** or Market Place. Unless otherwise mentioned, the public buildings and museums are open weekdays from April 1 to September 30, 9:30–12:00 and 2:00–6:00, and during the rest of the year, 10:00–12:00 and 2:00–4:00; all Sundays, 10:00–12:00.

Let us start our walk here in the **Market Place**—the main square of Bruges. There before you rises the impressive, lofty tower—one of the most significant Gothic structures anywhere —soaring above the fourteenth-century market house. Stand well back in the square so you can see the graceful turrets of the 280-foot belfry. The world-renowned **carillon,** which is composed of forty-seven bells, is played on Monday, Wednesday, and Saturday evenings from 9:00 to 10:00 and on Sunday mornings from 11:45 to 12:30, June 15 to September 30; from October 1 to June 14 it can be heard Sunday, Wednesday, and Saturday mornings from 11:45 to 12:30. Listening to its majestic tones is a thrilling experience.

As you start toward the **tower,** you may be surprised to note that it leans slightly to the southeast. If it is a clear day and you want to enjoy a wonderful view of the city and the sea, you may climb some 360 steps to the top.

Wander around the square to look at the old **guild houses** opposite the bell tower. The **Fishmongers' Guild** can be easily spotted by the fish-shaped sign on its building.

Now follow Wollestraat along the side of the bell tower to the bridge over the canal. Then turn right along the **Dyver,** an embankment shaded by chestnut, linden, and weeping beech trees, and lined with cream- and gray-colored houses. Just to the left, enter a gateway to a rose garden. This will bring you to the **Groeninge Museum,** the city art gallery. You should go in to see the important paintings by such great Flemish artists as Rogier van der Weyden, Jan van Eyck, Hans Memling, and Gheerardt David, as well as modern works. A fifteenth-century Van Eyck, painted on wood, is remarkable for the extraordinary quality of its blues and reds.

At the end of the quay the **Gruuthuse Museum** is well worth a visit for its fine collection of *objets d'art,* silver, china, and musical instruments, as well as lace and pottery, for which Bruges is still famous. The building itself is a splendid medieval mansion decorated with great fireplaces, beautifully tiled floors, and rich woodcarving. The exhibits and furniture are arranged to show how people lived during the fifteenth and sixteenth centuries. You will find the kitchen fascinating, with its huge brick fireplace. Giant hooks hold kettles and pots. There is a huge iron caldron which was used for washing utensils. The motto above the fireplace, "Plus est en vous" ("You can always do better"), will amuse you. A less attractive relic is an eighteenth-century guillotine, formerly used in Bruges.

A little farther along is the **Church of Our Lady**. Its tower is 375 feet high. Inside, you will be excited by Michelangelo's exquisite marble statue of the Virgin and Child in the south transept. The great sixteenth-century artist Albrecht Dürer expressed his admiration of the statue on a visit to Bruges.

Although these two museums are interesting, you should save your most intensive sightseeing for what is probably the finest art collection in Bruges, the **Hans Memling Museum** in **St. John's Hospital,** just across the street through an archway from the Church of Our Lady. The Memling masterpieces are hung in a corner of the fifteenth-century, early Gothic hall. Its high roof, original oak beams, and huge windows give it an atmosphere of great spaciousness. The six outstanding works in the former **Chapter Room** include *The Shrine of St. Ursula* (perhaps the most notable), *The Mystic*

Marriage of St. Catherine, and *The Adoration of the Magi.*
(Open 9:30–12:00, 2:00–6:00.)

As you leave the hospital, glance up at the sloping tile roofs
against the background of the lofty church tower. This is one
of Bruges' many picturesque touches.

Turn right along **Maria Straat** to the nearby bridge. Pause
for a moment and study the odd angles of the old houses on
either side. Now continue on Sinte Katelijnestraat to the
third turning on the right, Wijngaardstraat, which you follow
to the canal.

As you cross the bridge to enter the beautiful grounds of
the thirteenth-century **Beguinage** (a modified nunnery
founded by the Beguines, a charitable community of lay
women) stop for a moment and look at the delightful vista in
both directions. Below you there probably will be many swans
adding a decorative note to the placid canal waters. In Bruges,
they say the swans are kept in the canals because of an ancient
legend. While you are enjoying this peaceful scene, black-
frocked Benedictine nuns may pass to and from the Beguinage
(open weekdays, 9:30–12:15, 2:00–7:00; Sunday, 10:00–
12:15, 2:00–7:00).

Walk into the quiet courtyard enclosed by trim whitewashed houses and shaded by lime trees. You will find the
Beguines' house most charming and it will give you an idea of
the meditative life led by the Benedictine Sisters who live
there now. You leave the delightful grounds on the far side
through the south gate, cross a bridge, and, after passing
through a brick gate, you face the **Minnewater,** or the **Lake
of Love**—a harbor during the Middle Ages. From the stone
bridge at the far end, near the fourteenth-century tower, you
have a fine perspective of the diverse foliage, reflected in the
water in the foreground, and the spire of Our Lady's Church
in the distance.

There is a small turreted brick castle on your right, partly
hidden by copper beeches. Return along the tree-sheltered
path to the old lockhouse. From here turn slightly right past
the little green where the swans are preening themselves into

Wijngaardstraat. To the left on **Wal Plaats** you will probably see elderly women making lace in the doorways of their homes. Just to the right you will once again be in Sinte Katelijnstraat. After you pass Our Lady's Church, take the left fork, Heilige Geeststraat, to the **cathedral, St. Savior's Church,** the oldest in Bruges. Its interior is well proportioned and includes a **museum** with several fine Flemish paintings. But if you feel you have done enough sightseeing, just walk around the cathedral and follow Steenstraat for about three-hundred yards back to the Market Place.

If you started the first walk in the morning, you may have returned to the Market Place in time to lunch at one of the two good restaurants in the square, the **Panier d'Or** or the **Civière d'Or,** decorated with original paintings by Toulouse-Lautrec and Renoir. Bruges also has several excellent pastry shops, so keep that in mind for now or later.

Reis and Waterways

Begin the second stroll by following Vlamingstraat for two blocks to **Theater Plaats,** where you will find a fourteenth-century residence at **No. 33,** occupied centuries ago by merchants from Genoa. Turn left down Grauwwerkensstraat to No. 35. On this site was a building, which belonged to the Van der Beurze family, where merchants gathered in the fifteenth and sixteenth centuries to transact business. Hence the word "bourse" or "beurze" came into use for commercial centers all over the world. Now return to Vlamingstraat and cross into Akademiestraat; a few yards farther on, you come to **Van Eyck Square,** one of Bruges' most historic sections. There are several interesting narrow streets here, where you can wander. On one side of the square stands the fifteenth-century **Customs House,** which contains the **Public Library.** Inside you may see the exhibit of paintings by William Caxton, who printed the first book in English and who lived in Bruges during the fifteenth century.

The square overlooks a **wide canal**—one of the loveliest scenes in Bruges. Gray and white brick and stucco houses with tiled roofs face one another across the canal. At the far end you will see a lovely white house that looks like a French hunting lodge. It was once the Spanish Embassy. Walk along the quay on the right, **Spinolarei,** to the first bridge. Look back at the Van Eyck statue and the Gothic tower above. Continue along the quay to the end, study the lovely houses, and turn right on Verwersdijk. Pause on the first bridge for the fine vistas on both sides. Just ahead is the mellowed brick **Church of St. Ann.** Its simple exterior contrasts with its impressive Renaissance interior, which has the carved woodwork and brass candelabra so often seen in Flemish paintings. Just behind the church, by taking a right turn, you will come to the **Jerusalem Church,** noted for its stone altarpiece and stained-glass windows, the oldest in Bruges (1483). For admission, you must ring the bell at the gate on the right.

Take Molenmeerstraat opposite the Jerusalem Church, make a left at the end, and in a few yards cross the bridge. Then turn right along the **Groenerei,** one of the most delightful canals in Bruges. The **first bridge** you come to dates from the late fourteenth century and is the oldest of all.

As you saunter along here, you will be entranced by the effect of the ivy-covered buildings on the opposite side, the huge overhanging trees, and the greenish water of the canal.

In a few moments you will reach the **Fish Market,** which is located under a colonnade. Turn left and in a few yards you will be on the Rosenhoedkaai. Here, by the **Brick Tanners' Guild building,** is one of the most romantic and beautiful sights in Bruges—the old brick houses on either side of the canal and, soaring above them, the magnificent belfry tower and spire of Our Lady's Church. Many artists, including Sir Winston Churchill, have found this an irresistible setting, beautifully modulated by the reflections in the water at different hours of the day.

When you can drag yourself away from this incomparable scene, walk back toward the Fish Market past the Tanners'

Guild (now an exhibit of modern handicrafts) and the ancient Duke of Burgundy hotel (its dining room, hung with an unusual collection of modern paintings, has a wonderful location overlooking the canal).

Linger for a few minutes on the bridge by the Fish Market. You will be fascinated by this charming corner of Bruges— with the old buildings along the quay, the hanging gardens and luxuriant trees shading the water, the donkeyback bridges, and the Gothic towers and spires. Motor launches leave from the dock just below the bridge for a **tour of the canals**—a delightful half-hour trip which you might make as a finale to your visit. It's particularly attractive after dark, when many of the buildings and towers are floodlit.

From the bridge walk along the Blinde Ezelstraat to the **Burg,** or **Castle, Square,** named after the fortress formerly located here that belonged to the Dukes of Burgundy and which was then protected by moats.

Several interesting ancient buildings of varied architectural styles surround this small square. The first one you should visit is in the left-hand corner, the **Basilica of the Holy Blood** (open in summer, 9:00–12:00, 2:30–6:00; in winter, 9:00–12:00, 2:30–5:00). This Romanesque chapel is really divided into two chapels, an upper one and a lower one. The **upper chapel,** Gothic in design and ornate in decoration, contains the relic in which, it is said, there are drops of Holy Blood brought from Palestine in 1150. Every year in early May the relic is carried in the colorful religious **Procession of the Holy Blood.** The **lower chapel** is a magnificent example of Romanesque architecture and a striking contrast to the upper chapel. Next to the chapel is one of the oldest and finest Gothic town halls in northern Europe. (For admission, ask the caretaker.) Its exterior turrets are quite striking, and, on the inside, the **Great Hall** has a magnificent vaulted fourteenth-century roof and nineteenth-century murals depicting the history of Bruges. The gold boss in the ceiling is original. If you have time, you might look through the adjacent eighteenth-century **Court of Justice** particularly to see the unusual black marble chimney piece in the Court Room, which was made in 1526.

After visiting these interesting buildings stroll a few yards along the narrow Breidelstraat back to the Market Place. When you have completed these two strolls, you will agree that Bruges is incomparable—a precious, enchanting, and beautiful heritage of Western culture.

VIII BRUSSELS

MODERN CAPITAL WITH AN OLD WORLD AIR

The Upper Town

Brussels, Belgium's metropolitan capital, has a genuine appeal for the tourist as well as the businessman or government official visiting this headquarters of the **Common Market.** Though it is an old city—more than a thousand years older than the country it governs—you will be struck by its modern, up-to-date air. Yet this mid-twentieth century vitality you sense as you stroll about Brussels hasn't spoiled those sections that are reminiscent of the late Middle Ages and the days of the Hapsburgs when the trade corporations were the center of the city's life.

In recent years this city of over a million people has been divided into an upper or newer, and a lower or older section.

You should start your walking tour of Brussels at the **Palais de Justice** in the upper town. Stroll over to the terrace from the square in front of this huge building. Here you have a good view over the lower town. You can use the automatic guide that for five francs presents a brief recorded talk in English on the city and its main buildings, such as the ancient **Town Hall,** that you see before you.

The **Palais de Justice,** called the Mammoth by local residents, is the largest building erected during the nineteenth century and covers a much greater area (five acres) than St. Peter's in Rome.

From the **Place Poelaert,** named for the Palais' architect, you follow the left side of the Rue de la Régence for about five minutes until you come to the **Rue des Sablons.** On the

BRUSSELS

ROUTE 1 ––––→
ROUTE 2 ·········→

100 50 0   100   200 YARDS 300

left is the **Place du Grand Sablon,** the center of the antiquar-
ians' district. You may feel like looking around some of the
antique shops that face the square. A flea market in antiques
takes place here in the open square on Saturdays and Sundays
from 9:00–2:00.

The pure Gothic Church of **Notre Dame du Sablon** on the
Rue de la Régence was founded during the fourteenth century by the guild of crossbowmen.

On the corner just across the avenue from the church is
the **Conservatoire Royal de Musique,** a fine museum of musical instruments (open Sunday 10:30–12:30; Tues., Thurs.,
Sat. 2:30–4:30).

The little park opposite the **Place du Petit Sablon** is one
of the most charming in Brussels and one of the most unusual
in Europe. Forty-eight bronze statuettes, representing the
various trading corporations of Brussels, rest on columns
which circle a delightful garden with box-hedged flower beds
and a fountain at the end. You will be fascinated to inspect
in detail the different figures of the ancient guilds—the fisher-
man, cobbler, saddle maker, archer, etc.

When you leave the park just above the fountain, have a
look at the interesting old house on the right-hand corner of
the square. Built in 1610, it is now a restaurant, **Au Roy
d'Espagne.**

Cross the street and enter the courtyard of the **Palais
d'Egmont,** a classical eighteenth-century mansion. You pass
under an archway and by keeping to the right come into the
attractive, wooded park which the palace faces. This is a
pleasant place to wander for a bit. The tower of the Palais
de Justice looms in the distance. You will notice **Beethoven's
statue** and recall his Egmont overture. Count Egmont was a
hero of the Low Countries' resistance to Spain.

Continue along the cobblestoned alley by which you entered the palace grounds and pass beside the ivy-covered
building in which there are studios, then go under an archway and through a large entrance doorway into the wide
Boulevard de Waterloo.

Turn left along this fine avenue with its attractive shops and in a few minutes you will come to a small square, the **Place du Trône.** The large classic building on your left is the Royal Palace. It stands in extensive grounds well back from the impressive entrance gates.

A left turn along the **Rue Ducale** will bring you to the front of the nineteenth-century palace which is landscaped with beautifully planted sunken gardens.

Now you should cross over to the **Parc de Bruxelles.** Belgium won its independence here in 1830. Earlier it was a hunting preserve of the Dukes of Brabant. Stroll down its broad tree-lined promenade, past the pond, towards the eighteenth-century **Palais de la Nation** which you can see facing you. It now houses the **Belgian Parliament** (open daily 10:00–4:00).

From the large pond in the park you follow the walk that will bring you out at the corner of the **Rue Royale** and the **Place des Palais.** Just across from the Rue Royale is the **Palais des Beaux Arts,** Brussels' cultural center, which is used for concerts and exhibitions.

A minute or two from this corner of the park is the **Place Royale.** This classic square, with the **statue of Godfrey de Bouillon,** leader of the First Crusade, in the center, is in eighteenth-century French style. The royal church of **St. Jacques sur Coudenberg** stands at the far end.

The **Musée d'Art Ancien** (open 10:00–5:00 daily except Monday) is on the corner of the square, its entrance facing Rue de la Régence. You should devote some time to visiting this outstanding art gallery, notable especially for its collection of Flemish and Dutch paintings.

When you come out of this museum, turn left along the **Rue du Musée** to see the charming **Place du Musée** on the left. The stately **Royal Library,** with its fine collection of engravings, medals and coins, faces the square. Its illuminated manuscript collection is well worth visiting (open daily 9:00–12:00; 2:00–5:00). You may also want to see Brussels' **Museum of Modern Art** across the square, which is mostly devoted to Belgian paintings.

From the Place du Musée it's only a moment or two to come out on the curving **Rue Ravenstein.** Art galleries and antique shops line this street but the most interesting building is just opposite, when you stand at the point where the street curves into the Rue Montague de la Cour. This red-brick turreted building is the late fifteenth-century **Hotel Ravenstein.** It is the only remaining patrician house of this period and has an attractive inner court.

A few steps further will lead you to the **Albertina,** a complex of buildings and exhibition halls that are built around a landscaped garden. Standing above the garden, you can see the spire of Brussels' **Town Hall.**

Continue on the Rue Ravenstein to the entrance on the left of the large **Galerie Ravenstein.** This is a huge modern office building with a circular glass dome in the central hall. You will pass various shops selling paintings and antiques, as well as a cafeteria, before you emerge on the far side of the building on Rue Cantersteen. A few steps to the right will bring you opposite Brussels' new glass skyscraper, the **Hotel Westbury.** There is a wonderful panorama over the city —both upper and lower—from the restaurant on the top of the hotel.

The Lower Town

You should commence your walk through the **lower town** and the older section of Brussels at the large **Church of Ste. Gudule,** only a few minutes along the **Rue des Paroissiens** from the Hotel Westbury and on the slope of the upper town. This Gothic church, dating from the twelfth century, possesses sixteenth-century stained glass windows and a fine carved wooden pulpit.

Walk down the **Rue Ste. Gudule,** in front of the church and then bear left on the Rue de la Montague past the gabled houses with their antique façades. Keep to the left after crossing the junction of several streets and continue along the **Rue de la Madeleine.** The houses on this street, one of the oldest in Brussels, are particularly attractive with their baroque façades, gables, and balconies. Don't miss the delightful little **Church of the Madeleine,** nor its eighteenth-century bell tower.

At this point turn right into the Rue Duquesnoy and at the Place St. Jean cross over into the **Place de la Vieille-Halle-aux-Blés** which is lined with old houses. You now bear right into the **Rue du Chêne.** A brick house on the left dates from 1697 and others are from the eighteenth century. If you look along the **Rue du Villiers,** on the left you will see part of the old city wall with a battlemented tower. Fifty yards or so on the right you will find an old courtyard in a patrician house. This is the office of the **Brussels Information Center** (open 8:30–6:00 except Saturday 8:30–12:00; closed Sunday). It's worthwhile stopping in to obtain useful pamphlets about the city or to make inquiries from the English-speaking staff.

The **Mannekin Pis,** Brussels' famous bronze statue of a small boy creating a fountain, is just ahead on the corner of the **Rue du Chêne** and the **Rue de l'Étuve.** More than three hundred years old this mascot of Brussels is regarded as its "oldest citizen." It has been stolen several times and was even broken up during the War of the Austrian Succession. But always it has been restored and put back in its place. The manikin has an entire collection of costumes with which he is dressed on special occasions. Nearby shops sell photographs of him wearing the various uniforms and suits of clothes.

Turn right on the Rue de l'Étuve and in a few yards you will come to an arch. The recumbent statue is of **Evrard T' Serclaes,** a fourteenth-century Brussels liberator. There is a story that if you touch the figure's arm or his dog's nose you will have good luck for a year—and then you have to return to Brussels for it to continue.

You now enter the heart of Brussels, the **Grand' Place,** one of the finest squares in Europe. Dominated by the tapering spire of the **Town Hall,** the square preserves the spirit of the ancient trade guilds. Although the original buildings had to be renewed after the bombardment of 1695 the Gothic and baroque character of the guild houses, with their picturesque gables, balustrades, statues and gilded decoration, has remained as a reminder of the trade corporations' central role in the history of Brussels. Be sure to return at night to see these dramatic buildings under floodlighting.

First look around the square to get an overall impression of the different buildings. Opposite the Town Hall is the large Gothic-style **Maison du Roi,** formerly called the House of the Bakers. This is of quite recent construction—the latter part of the last century. One of the finest corporation houses is the **House of the Archers** which dates from 1697. You can identify it by the portraits of Roman emperors which decorate its façade. Notice No. 6—**House of the Boatmen.** Its gable is in the form of the stern of a ship. Six houses on the southeast side of the square make up the **House of the Dukes of Brabant,** the home of various guilds. You will have a fascinating time just strolling around the square looking at the unusual details of these houses and browsing in the antique and lace shops. No. 10 is the **House of the Brewers.** Here you can visit a brewery museum and a reproduction of an old brewery (open 9:00–12:00; 2:00–5:00; closed Saturday and Sunday).

One of the finest restaurants in Brussels, **La Maison du Cygne,** is at No. 2 Rue Charles Blus in the **House of the Butchers** just where you entered the Grand' Place.

Before you visit the **Town Hall,** you will observe that the left side of the building which was built first (1412) is wider than the right side which was added in 1444. The tower was added later. The statue of Brussels' patron saint, the **Archangel Michael,** surmounts the spire. In the courtyard you will see Brussels' official distance marker. It is interesting to tour the Town Hall (open 9:00–3:00; Saturday and Sundays 9:00–12:00) to see the baroque **Great Council Chamber** and the **Salle des Mariages** where Brussels couples have their civil wedding ceremony performed.

Leave the Grand' Place by the side of the Town Hall on the **Rue de la Tête d'Or.** In a moment you will pass another of Brussels' odd fountains at the corner of the Rue du Marché aux Charbon and the Rue des Pierres, **le Cracheur** (the Spitter). Water pours from the man's mouth as though he were spitting. Now turn left on the Rue du Midi from the Rue du Marché aux Charbon—an old street—then right on the Rue du Lombard. Cross **Boulevard Anspach,** Brussels' main shopping street, then continue for about one hundred yards on the Rue des Riches Claires to the **Church of Notre Dame aux Riches Claires,** built of Spanish brick. You are now in the oldest part of the city.

From the rear of the church stroll left along the **Rue de la Grande-Ile.** In a few yards you will come to the **Place St. Gery,** named for the river island which was once on this site. Brussels was born on this spot in A.D. 580 when St. Gery built a little chapel here.

Now turn into Rue Jules van Praet and you will see Brussels' **Bourse** in front of you. Stroll to the left along the busy Boulevard Anspach. If you would like to visit the city's great fruit, vegetable and fish markets, take a short detour by turning left for one block at the **Marché aux Poulets.** You will note that many of the streets in this area are named for markets of one kind or another.

Cross the Boulevard Anspach and walk along the other side of the Marché aux Poulets and continue into the **Rue du Marché aux Herbes** which, as its name suggests, used to be a vegetable market in the Middle Ages. Along here you will discover little passageways off the street which are called "impasses." Down one of them is an excellent restaurant, **Bon Vieux Temps,** which has lots of atmosphere of days gone by.

About one hundred yards further along the Rue du Marché aux Herbes turn left into a narrow street, the **Petite Rue des Bouchers.** This section of the old city is full of intriguing little streets and restaurants. **Chez Vincent** is a colorful seafood restaurant on the Rue des Dominicains. Stroll along the Rue des Dominicains or turn from the Rue des Bouchers into a tiny passageway, the **Rue d'Une Personne** (just wide enough for one person).

After exploring these byways, a few yards further along the Rue des Bouchers will lead you to the center of Brussels' popular shopping arcades—the **Galerie du Roi** and the **Galerie de la Reine.** Here you will want to wander up and down these glass-covered arcades, lined with smart shops— a pleasant place to finish these walks through this modern capital with an old-world air.

IX PARIS

THE RIGHT BANK

Jeu de Paume to Place des Vosges

Paris' unique beauty and gracious charm take time to absorb. Walking is the ideal way to sense the mystique of this captivating city—a mystique which has exerted a magnetic attraction on visitors throughout the ages.

The river **Seine** flows through the center of Paris, dividing the city into the Right and Left Bank. A walk on the **Right Bank** will introduce you to various phases of Paris—modern and ancient, fashionable and simple. You will enjoy vistas that reveal the magnificence and splendor of the city. Also, you will discover out-of-the-way places where fascinating events in French history have occurred.

You will appreciate this walk more if you take it slowly and easily, with an occasional rest, perhaps at some agreeable café along the way or in one of several parks you will visit.

If you wish, divide this walk into several separate ones. Actually, the walk divides itself, since the route covers various aspects of Paris, some comparatively modern, some ancient, some elegant, some bourgeois or working-class.

Start in the morning at Paris' most magnificent square, the **Place de la Concorde.** The Seine flows alongside. Cross the vast Place de la Concorde, one of the largest squares in the world (the traffic makes it an adventure for nimble pedestrians, but perhaps you'll want to play it safe, hug the river, and go around the Place). Enter The Tuileries gardens by the steps near the **Orangerie,** the small building overlooking the river, where Claude Monet's famous murals *Les Nymphéas* are on view (open 10:00–12:00, 2:00–5:00, except Tues-

131

PLACE DE LA CONCORDE

PLACE VENDÔME

SQ.

AVE. DE L'OPERA

PALAIS ROYAL

RUE

JEU DE PAUME

RUE ST HONORÉ

TUILERIES GARDENS

START

ORANGERIE

DE

LOUVRE

RIVER

PARIS

THE RIGHT BANK

ROUTE ——————▶

METRO ●

100 50 0   100   200   300 YARDS

days). Stop for a few seconds on the terrace's balustrade facing the Place, and linger over the majestic scene: the seventy-five-foot granite **obelisk from Luxor** in the center (its companion may be seen in New York City's Central Park), flanked by spectacular fountains and, beyond it, Jacques Ange Gabriel's colonnaded twin mansions in the style of Louis XV. The recent cleaning of these buildings has made the Place lovelier than ever.

Before the Place was enlarged in 1854 by Jacques Ignace Hittorff, the site had already become famous. For here, between 1793 and 1795, during the French Revolution, the dreaded **guillotine** had ended the lives of Louis XVI, Marie Antoinette, Danton, Robespierre, and nearly three thousand others.

As you look down on this splendid square and along the expansive **Champs-Élysées,** note the five **Marly horses,** sculptured in marble, commanding the entrance to this avenue, which, broad and beautiful, climbs ever so slightly to the **Arc de Triomphe** at the **Étoile** more than two miles away.

You are now only a couple of hundred yards from the **Jeu de Paume,** the building along the terrace at the corner of the Place de la Concorde and the Rue de Rivoli, which houses one of the world's greatest collections of impressionist paintings. This treat should be saved for another occasion when you have an hour or more to do justice to this superb art gallery. The Jeu de Paume was so named because it was constructed for a royal tennis court in 1851. In 1920 it became an art museum.

Below the terrace midway between the Jeu de Paume and the Orangerie, are a spacious octagonal fountain, and nearby, attractive rose-bordered gardens. From here you can gaze along the tree-lined **Grande Allée** to the great **Arc du Carrousel,** and beyond it to the Louvre, originally a royal palace and now one of the world's greatest museums. A few yards from the fountain, on the side toward the Orangerie, you will find Aristide Maillol's statue of the *Femme Couchée,* erected in honor of Paul Cézanne.

Although formal in layout, the **Tuileries gardens** have a distinct charm because young children are usually to be seen playing along the graveled alleys, sailing boats among the goldfish in the round pond, riding on the merry-go-round, or sampling an ice at one of the stands under the trees.

When Jean Baptiste Colbert, Minister of Finance under Louis XIV, undertook the beautification of Paris in 1664, he commissioned André Lenôtre, designer of the great gardens of Versailles, as landscape-gardener of the Tuileries. The result of his efforts was so successful that Colbert favored reserving the gardens for royal use, but eventually he yielded and opened them to the public. Today, their sixty acres are much the same in layout as they were in Lenôtre's time.

Rambling along the gravel walk, past many statues of classical design, you will shortly find yourself in Lenôtre's flower gardens, whose borders of scarlet geraniums contrast effectively with the green lawns. Off to your left are the rounded leaden roofs of the six-story buildings along the Rue de Rivoli. When you stand in front of the Arc du Carrousel— a Napoleonic reproduction of the Arch of Severus in Rome— you may be surprised to notice that, although the vista before you appears to follow the laws of French architectural symmetry, careful checking will reveal that in reality the central wing of the **Louvre** is not in a straight line with the Arc de Triomphe at the Étoile, the Place de la Concorde, and the central walk in the Tuileries gardens.

Napoleon I reviewed his battle-scarred regiments near the arch. The nearby gardens and those between the two facing wings of the Louvre are on the site of the old **Tuileries Palace,** to which Louis XVI was taken by the mob in 1789, when he was brought from Versailles, and from which he left for the guillotine in 1793. Later, both Napoleon I and Napoleon III lived in the palace, which was finally burned by the Communards in the Revolution of 1871.

After turning left at the Place des Pyramides for a look at the gilded statue of Joan of Arc, you turn left again at the **Rue de Rivoli** and wander along one of Paris' most fascinating shopping streets. Note the uniform façades of the buildings facing the Tuileries. You will be lured by the many little stores under the arcades which run almost to the Place de la Concorde, with their infinite variety of wares: handbags, handkerchiefs, jewelry, hats, perfumes, china, and so forth. **Rumpelmayer's,** the fashionable *pâtisserie,* is at No. 226.

When you reach the corner of the Rue de Castiglione, turn right for a stroll around the splendid **Place Vendôme,** which you can see ahead of you beyond the Rue St. Honoré.

Much of Paris' charm is found in her many squares, some of which are huge, some tiny. They are representative of different periods in her long history. Most of them reflect the esthetic talent of the French, but none is more artistic than the one you have now reached.

The Place Vendôme, named for the Duc de Vendôme, illegitimate son of Henry IV, whose mansion was located here, was planned by the great architect Jules Hardouin-Mansart at the beginning of the eighteenth century. He laid out the octagonal Place and designed the harmonious limestone houses with their sloping roofs. These buildings are so treasured that they have now been declared historical monuments and no alterations are permitted to be made of the façades or roofs. The old-fashioned lampposts on the sidewalk lend an enchanting atmosphere, especially at night.

The **imposing shaft** in the center of the Place, modeled on Trajan's Column in Rome, although considerably higher, was erected by Napoleon I to commemorate his victories in Germany and Austria. The covering bronze bas-relief plaques, now weathered by time, came from captured cannon that were melted down after the Battle of Austerlitz. A **statue of Napoleon** as a Roman emperor surmounts the monument.

As you wander leisurely around the Place, on your left is the **Ritz Hotel** of world-wide reputation. You might stroll through its lobby and long corridors, noting the small but charming garden and looking in at its famous bar.

Return to the Rue St. Honoré and try a diverting brief detour by taking the first left, the Rue du Marché St. Honoré to browse among the many little shops—fascinating *épiceries, pâtisseries,* and *boulangeries* that make Parisian marketing such a colorful and delightful experience. The **Place du Marché St. Honoré** at the end of the street, now occupied by a parking garage, was formerly the old **Place des Jacobins,** a center of the French Revolution.

Back in the **Rue St. Honoré** you are following the route down which the tumbrels of the French Revolution rolled, carrying aristocrats on their way to execution. Today the street is characterized by many antique and leather-goods stores.

In a few minutes you reach the junction of the Rue St. Honoré and the Avenue de l'Opéra, where the **Place du Théâtre Français** is located. Joan of Arc was wounded in 1429 at this spot, then a gateway to Paris.

Cross the square and enter the Palais Royal at the far end of the square on the left, next to the **Comédie Française.** But first, perhaps you'd like to stop on the right and have an *apéritif* or *café au lait* at the **Café de la Régence,** where Napoleon once played chess.

The **Palais Royal,** built by Cardinal Richelieu in the seventeenth century, was later inhabited by Louis XIII and, for a short period, by Louis XIV. During the eighteenth century the gardens and the quadrangle's galleries were the favorite promenade of Parisians; after the Revolution gambling houses were established there. Today, however, the Palais Royal has an air of silence. The long symmetrical arcades on either side of the gardens, planted with elms and lime trees, extend from the **Galerie des Proues,** so named because it is decorated with prows of ships, to the **Théâtre du Palais Royal.** The recently cleaned Galerie des Proues, the remaining part of Richelieu's original buildings, gives the square a fresh appearance. Note the double colonnade between the **Cour d'Honeur** and the **gardens.** In the small shops along the arcade you can purchase old stamps or coins and other antiques.

At the far end near the Théâtre du Palais Royal, beyond the fountain in the center, is one of Paris' finest and most expensive restaurants, the **Grand Vefour.** It is among those exclusive Parisian restaurants where wealthy gourmets gather in historic surroundings for a quiet evening of serious eating and the finest of château-bottled wines.

A glass door midway along the colonnade on the right just opposite the fountain will lead into the Rue de Valois. Turn right and walk a few yards until you reach Rue du Col. Driant.

A couple of blocks east, just beyond the domed **Bourse de Commerce,** you come to **Les Halles,** since the twelfth century the city's famed central market and often called the "stomach of Paris." It's best to visit Les Halles in the early morning when the hectic distribution of produce is at its peak activity. Most of the halls with skylight roofs (which also cover streets in the market area) were built over a hundred years ago. Since the last war, the crush of produce trucks hauling food from all parts of France for redistribution in this small area in the center of Paris has been such a problem that plans are now under way for relocation.

If you decide to visit Les Halles before daybreak to get the true flavor of this hive of activity, you will want to drop in at one of the little restaurants nearby. In such gay spots as **"Au Chien qui Fume"** on the right, or **"Au Pied de Cochon"** on the left, you will enjoy the famous onion soup topped by a marvelous layer of melted cheese, or you may want to try escargots, if you can manage them at that hour.

Of course, if you visit Les Halles later in the morning, you will still find considerable activity as you wander through some of the twelve separate buildings. You will see butchers staggering under huge sides of beef or pushing handtrucks filled with cuts of meat; and porters wheeling great Swiss Emmenthaler cheeses or carting crates of Brie produced east of Paris and neatly packed in straw. As you enter the meat market on the left you will see hundreds of quarters of beef hanging on long spikes, ready for local butcher shops. The poultry market is on the right, and across the **Rue Baltard** you'll find dealers in eggs, cheese, fruits, vegetables, and fish.

Before leaving the area of Les Halles, stop in to see the high Gothic vaulting at the **Church of St. Eustache,** which is opposite the markets on the left. It is considered by many to be second only to **Notre Dame** in beauty among the churches in Paris.

Two short blocks to the east you reach the long **Boulevard de Sebastopol.** At this point you should turn right for five minutes or less along the boulevard to the **Place du Châtelet** to see the lovely Gothic **Tour St. Jacques,** an elegant Paris landmark built in the early sixteenth century and originally part of the **Church of St. Jacques-la-Boucherie.**

Retracing your steps along the boulevard to **Rue Rambuteau,** continue along this street crowded with stalls, food shops, and throngs of people from the neighborhood, to the old turreted buildings of the **Archives Nationales.** This museum contains magnificent mural paintings as well as France's great historical documents. It is worth stopping at the entrance from the Rue Rambuteau on the left to see the elegant court of honor of the **Hôtel de Soubise,** one of the finest architectural structures within the Archives group of buildings (open 2:00–5:00, except Tuesdays).

From here you enter **Rue des Francs Bourgeois,** with its many old mansions, in the **Marais district.** This quarter, now the center of hundreds of workshops producing millinery, costume jewelry, and piece-work for the stylish fashion houses, still maintains its traditionally cosmopolitan atmosphere. Its great period was during the seventeenth and eighteenth centuries, when its graceful mansions and palaces belonged to fashionable noblemen. In those days this was the center of Paris' artistic and cultural life. Now you can still search out many architectural gems of that day almost hidden by the present tenements.

Look up and down the narrow **Rue Vieille du Temple** as you cross it, and stop on the left at **No. 87** to see the little courtyard of the **Hôtel de Rohan,** also part of the Archives Nationales.

In a few minutes you will be at the **Musée Carnavalet,** a Renaissance mansion and since 1880 the **Museum of the City of Paris.** Its entrance is in the Rue de Sévigné around the corner to the left from the Rue des Francs Bourgeois (open

10:00–12:00, 2:00–5:30, except Tuesdays). Mme de
Sévigné lived here from 1677 to 1696, during which time she
wrote her well-known letters. Among its many other exhibits
the museum contains prints and models of old Paris (including some which show the evolution of the streets you have
just traversed), wrought-iron shop and tavern signs from the
fourteenth to the eighteenth centuries, and a collection of
seventeenth-, eighteenth-, and nineteenth-century costumes.

A couple of hundred yards farther on, across the **Rue de
Turenne,** you reach the oldest large square in Paris, the **Place
des Vosges.** Henry IV ordered that this first of the "Places
Royales," laid out in the early seventeenth century, be constructed so that the uniformity of the façades and the roofs of
the four-storied houses would create an architectural effect of
geometric unity, a sight rare in Paris. Today in the Place des
Vosges the faded rose-colored brick and peeling white stone
classical buildings, with their arcades and dormer windows
jutting out of slate roofs, are practically unchanged from the
days when Cardinal Richelieu lived at **No. 21.** About two
hundred years later Victor Hugo lived at **No. 6,** now a museum containing his drawings, as well as furniture he designed.

After the Revolution the square received its present name
for a reason rather remarkable in France. New taxes had
been imposed, and since the Department of the Vosges was
the first to pay them, its citizens were honored in this unusual
way.

As you stroll around this gem of the seventeenth century
it is easy to imagine the gay life led by the nobility in these
stately mansions.

This is the moment to drop in at a little café called **Ma
Bourgogne,** frequented by working people of the quarter, at
the corner of the Place and **Rue des Francs Bourgeois.** Here
you can get snacks, sandwiches and paté de campagne. If you
feel like lunching at an excellent, though moderately expensive, restaurant on the square, try the **Caconnas** in the opposite corner. While enjoying this respite after strolling through
the historic and fascinating Marais, you may find yourself

contemplating the present calm of the Place des Vosges, haunted with memories of the days when Louis XIII, more than three hundred years ago, reviewed splendid parades on horseback in this same square.

THE LEFT BANK

The Sacred Mount

This walk through the **islands in the Seine** and on the **left bank** will take you to some of the most fascinating parts of old Paris. As you will not want to be rushed while wandering around these out-of-the-way corners, it is advisable to divide this walk into two sections, perhaps one in the morning and the other in the afternoon.

In any case you should start at the east end of the Ile St. Louis by the **Pont Sully**—preferably in the morning. If, however, you are continuing the walk which finished at the Place des Vosges, you follow the Boulevard Henry IV from the **Place de la Bastille,** the site of the hated Royalist prison that was destroyed during the French Revolution. (Incidentally, the key to the Bastille is now in the United States, at Mount Vernon, having been presented by the Marquis de Lafayette.)

The **Ile St. Louis** resembles a small provincial seventeenth-century French town set down in the midst of Paris. It is a backwater of the busy city, with the sleepy air of an earlier age. After all, it is named after Louis IX, or Saint Louis, often called the Father of Paris, who was born in 1215, the year Magna Charta was signed.

Many artists and writers, as well as wealthy residents seeking quiet, have established themselves here in apartments, or sometimes even penthouses, in converted three-hundred-year-old mansions.

On setting foot on the island from the bridge, glance down the narrow Rue St. Louis-en-l'Ile in front of you. Now turn right along the **Quai d'Anjou,** which, shaded by tall elm trees,

OTRE
AME

EBELLO

QUAI D'ORLEANS

RUE ST. LOUIS

QUAI D'ANJOU

EN-L'ILE

CH.

GERMAIN

PONT DE SULLY

START 1

BLVD. HENRI IV

PARIS
THE LEFT BANK

ROUTE 1 ➤ ━ ━ ➤
ROUTE 2 ➤•••••••➤
METRO ●

100 50 0   100   200   300 YARDS

N

runs along the embankment above the Seine. The nineteenth-century artist and caricaturist Honoré Daumier lived at **No. 9.**

The first distinguished mansion you reach is the noted **Hôtel de Lauzun,** at No. 17, a typical nobleman's private residence, built in the middle of the seventeenth century and named after a fabulous Don Juan of the time who lived there. Two-hundred years later both the writers Théophile Gautier and Charles Baudelaire resided in this exquisite town house. Today it belongs to the municipality of Paris and is used to entertain distinguished guests of the city. (Permission to view it can be obtained from the Directeur-General des Beaux Arts de la ville de Paris, 14 Rue François-Miron, Paris 4.)

A few yards farther on, turn left along the Rue Poulletier and then right along the main thoroughfare, the **Rue St. Louis-en-l'Ile,** which bisects the narrow island lengthwise. Overhead on your left an old clock in the tower of the **Church of St. Louis-en-l'Ile** juts out above the street.

As you stroll past little shops and cafés you will be relieved to note the relative absence of motor traffic. Turn left at the next corner on Rue des Deux Ponts and shortly you will find yourself on the opposite side of the island, at the **Quai d'Orléans,** which is lined with gray and cream-colored houses.

The view of **Notre Dame** from the **Pont de la Tournelle** on your left is an artist's favorite. It is well worth stopping a few minutes to absorb the dramatic and memorable sight of the cathedral's famed medieval flying buttresses and towers.

As you saunter along the Quai d'Orléans, you see Notre Dame rising above the ivy-covered quay from a slightly different angle. If you should happen to be here at lunchtime, why not enjoy this fine view from a window table at **Quasimodo,** an excellent restaurant on the quay patronized by residents of the island.

From the Quai d'Orléans you cross the iron footbridge over an arm of the Seine to the park behind Notre Dame. To your right the lovely Late Gothic **Tour St. Jacques** rises above the stream. While you are walking through the little **cathedral park,** a group of black-frocked priests may pass on their way to Notre Dame, giving the scene an appropriate touch. Why not follow them under the trees and through the beautifully kept gardens along the side of this great cathedral of Paris, which was in process of construction for nearly two hundred years from 1163 to 1345. Its location has been a religious site since the time when a Roman-Gallic temple stood here. Pause in the gardens along the quay to look up at the glorious **towers,** the **rose window,** the **spires** above, and the characteristic **gargoyles.**

When you reach the front of the cathedral, continue to the **statue of Charlemagne** on the far side of the square, the **Place du Parvis Notre Dame,** to get a proper perspective of Notre Dame's magnificent façade and towers. The cathedral as we see it today owes much to Viollet-le-Duc, who restored it in the 1840's following the damage and deterioration it suffered during the Revolution and thereafter.

After examining the famous figures around the three **portals** decorated in wrought iron, you will want to spend some time (either now or later) studying the interior, especially the glorious seven-hundred-year-old stained-glass rose window over the main entrance, as well as those on either side of the nave. You may even wish to climb one of the bell towers to view old Paris and the Seine with its many bridges.

For another and perhaps lovelier view of Notre Dame, cross the **Pont au Double,** to the left from the cathedral's front, to the **Place Réné Viviani.** Walk across this tiny square, which boasts a locust tree well over 250 years old, to the twelfth-century **Church of St. Julien le Pauvre.** This is a delightful bit of the most ancient section of Paris. To your right you will notice the quaint old houses with their uneven roofs. Turn left into the picturesque **Rue Galande,** possibly the oldest street in Paris. You are now in the **Latin Quarter.**

Although you will be tempted to follow these narrow old streets indefinitely, continue on the Rue Galande to the juncture with **Rue Lagrange.** Cross this street and follow the Rue de l'Hotel Colbert. In about fifty yards turn right into the Rue de la Bucherie, then in a few yards go left on Rue du Haut

Pavé into the **Quai de Montebello,** where there are several good and moderately priced restaurants.

You leave the quay by turning right into the Rue de Bièvre, a narrow street almost opposite the **Pont de l'Archevêché.** After crossing the Boulevard St. Germain at the Place Maubert, turn slightly left into the **Rue de la Montagne Ste. Geneviève,** named for the earliest of Paris' patron saints. As you walk up the hill, known for ages as "The Sacred Mount," you are on the road, built originally by the Romans, that led from Paris to Lyons and Italy. Here, in the heart of old Paris, you may be entertained by a singer leaning over a decorative window box above a wrought-iron balcony. A golden horse head over an old house signifies a "Boucherie Chevaline" (shop for horse meat).

After crossing the Rue des Écoles, you bear right at a little square where several streets meet. Ahead of you, past charming old houses on either side of the street, is the **Church of St. Étienne du Mont,** a most attractive combination of Late Gothic and Renaissance architecture. Go in to see the beautifully carved sixteenth-century stone rood loft, the last one in Paris. It was used before the adoption of the pulpit.

In front of the church rises the dome of the Panthéon, the secular Temple of Fame where the "ashes of great men" have been enshrined since the French Revolution.

Hereabouts, practically every street (as you will note from the names) and many buildings and monuments are sacred to the memory of early Paris—including the **Paris of the Romans,** still preserved in the Roman baths in the park of the Musée de Cluny—and to the **Paris of scholarship** since the thirteenth century, when Louis IX's confessor, Robert de Sorbon, set up a theological college there, which was the origin of the Sorbonne.

A few hundred yards down the Rue Clotilde, flanked by the rear of the Panthéon and the **Lycée Henry IV,** you will come into the Rue de l'Estrapade, which you follow to the left for a few yards; then take a slight bend to the left on the Rue Blainville to reach a charming little square, the **Place de la Contrescarpe.** From this little square, surrounded by attractively weather-worn houses, five narrow streets stem in various directions. The most fascinating is the lively **Rue Mouffetard,** dating from the thirteenth century, which twists down a steep slope to the right and is usually jammed with working-class residents of the quarter darting in and out of the many shops—the greengrocer's with heaps of vegetables, a tiny bistro, and the bakery with long crusty *baguettes* and other inviting shapes of delicious bread and patisseries. Nearby a bearded student strums a guitar in a wine-shop-and-bar. The Rue Mouffetard is rich in local color and movement, with its market stalls and shops that give it the character of an Eastern bazaar. (The shops usually close from 2:00–4:00.)

Turn right in Rue Pot de Fer into the rather dull Rue Lhomond, then, after going through the little square, take a sharp right on Rue Clotaire to the **Panthéon.** Designed by Jacques Germain Soufflot in the style of Agrippa's Pantheon in Rome, the church was partially financed by the proceeds of three state lotteries. Inside are the tombs of Jean Jacques Rousseau, François Voltaire, Honoré Mirabeau, Victor Hugo, Émile Zola, Anatole France, and many other distinguished figures, both political and literary.

As you leave the Panthéon and stand on its front steps you can see, directly before you, down the Rue Soufflot to the Luxembourg Gardens with the Eiffel Tower in the distance. This is the quarter of the **Sorbonne.** The university buildings of the many graduate schools can be seen from the Rue Soufflot down the Rue St. Jacques to the right. These streets are usually crowded with students.

Entering the **Luxembourg Gardens** at the Place Edmond Rostand, turn right under the lime and chestnut trees to the lovely Médicis fountain, designed as an Italian grotto. The Italian influence pervades the **Luxembourg Palace** and gardens, named, however, for a French nobleman who sold the **Petit Luxembourg** (beyond the main building) to Marie de Médicis, the Florentine wife of Henry IV. The large palace, which she had constructed between 1615 and 1620 in the style of the Pitti Palace in Florence, is now the meeting place of the French Senate.

The Luxembourg's ornamental gardens, with their informal meandering walks, are located on the site of an ancient Roman camp. In front of the palace is a small artificial pond, surrounded by colorful flower beds. Spend a delightful half hour wandering around the gardens and end up by the **Orangerie** beyond the palace. You will be surprised to see palm trees growing outdoors in front of the Orangerie. This park, the largest on the Left Bank, is still a great favorite among the quarter's students and bohemians, as it has been since the seventeenth century. It is an animated and charming spot, with many children at play and many elders at ease.

If you have taken this stroll from the Ile St. Louis during the morning, by now you will probably be looking for a good place to lunch. There are many inexpensive restaurants around the Place Edmond Rostand where you entered the gardens. Or you can walk along the Rue de Medicis to one of several better restaurants in and around the **Place de l'Odéon.**

The Luxembourg to Sainte-Chapelle

Begin your second walk through the literary and artistic Left Bank in front of the **Luxembourg Palace** on the **Rue de Vaugirard,** the longest street in Paris. Turn right after a couple of blocks down the Rue Ferou to the **Place St. Sulpice** and **the church** of the same name, the second largest in Paris. Its organ is world-famous.

From here it is only a few hundred yards to the Boulevard St. Germain. You go along the narrow Rue des Canettes ("the Street of the Ducklings"), to the right as you emerge from the church. Then walk past the old houses on the Rue des Ciseaux just to the right and across the Rue du Four.

The Romanesque **Church of St. Germain des Prés,** the oldest in Paris, stands across the boulevard on the site of an eighth-century Benedictine abbey. Immediately behind the church and its graceful eleventh-century stone tower, on the Rue de l'Abbaye, you will notice remnants of the original abbey.

The two cafés on the opposite side of the square, **Les Deux Magots** and the **Café de Flore,** separated by a narrow street, are famous as centers of the existentialist movement and the meeting places of writers.

Walk right, along the Rue de l'Abbaye, then take the first street to the left, the short Rue de Furstenberg, which leads to one of the most enchanting miniature squares in Paris, the **Place Furstemberg.** Here in the shade of four magnolia trees and the square's antiquated, ornate lamppost there is a strange and quiet air. The nineteenth-century painter Ferdinand Delacroix had his studio at **No. 6.** You will be delightfully surprised to come upon several antique shops, among the most tasteful in Paris.

Leaving this lovely oasis, so near the bustling traffic along the **Boulevard St. Germain,** turn right into the twisting, narrow **Rue Cardinale.** Above you, rise picturesque houses in varying shades of gray and ocher, with window boxes beneath slanting roofs and crooked chimneys. Now turn left and cross the fourteenth-century Rue de l'Échaudé, and then left to the juncture of the Rue de Seine and Rue de Buci. Here you are in the midst of the neighborhood **market place.** Patisseries, grocery stores, vegetable stalls, and fish and meat markets cater to the many customers who crowd the street and sidewalks. Have a drink at the corner bistro while you watch the shoppers fight their way through the hawkers, and listen to the housewives, jamming the little streets, shout to the truck-drivers who are trying to get through with their loads of perishable foods. This is usually one of the gayest scenes in Paris.

Now stroll down the **Rue de Seine** toward the river. This street is a great center of **art galleries, bookstores,** and **print shops.** The art galleries feature not only the traditional artists, but especially the work of the younger generation who may well be the famous of tomorrow. Wander in and out, even if you are only browsing.

The end of the Rue de Seine turns into the quay. On your right is the imposing **Institut de France,** home of the renowned **Académie Française,** established by Cardinal Richelieu. Among other things, its forty scholars are charged with the responsibility for a dictionary of the **French language,** the first edition of which appeared in 1694. Four other academies— literary, scientific, political, and artistic—whose members are outstanding scholars, comprise the distinguished Institut. You should look around the inner courtyard of the seventeenth-century building, but also go upstairs to see the lovely old **library of Cardinal Mazarin,** Louis XIV's Prime Minister (open weekdays, 10:00–5:00).

Now cross the quay to the **Pont des Arts,** the only foot-bridge that crosses the Seine. From the center of the bridge there is an admirable view. To your right is the triangle-shaped Vert Galant at the tip of the **Ile de la Cité.** Above this little park rises the tapering spire of Sainte-Chapelle. To the left you'll see the figures and gargoyles of the **Tour St. Jacques.** In the opposite direction is the sweep of the **Louvre** and the graceful **Pont du Carrousel.** You will want to linger on this bridge for a while.

Returning to the quay, you'll be intrigued by the continuous rows of bookstalls with their paper books, prints, maps, and memorabilia of Paris. A few hundred yards left along the **Quai Conti,** across the stream of traffic, is the **Hôtel de la Monnaie**—the mint which houses a collection of French money since Merovingian days and is open to the public (Monday–Friday, 1:00–5:00; the workshops where modern coins are minted can be seen Tuesday and Thursday, 2:30–3:30).

Ahead of you is the **Pont Neuf** which, despite its name, is Paris' oldest bridge (dating from 1578), as well as its most popular. The Pont Neuf marked the beginning of bridges without houses. Cross it as far as the Ile de la Cité. There, under the statue of **Henry IV,** the famous seventeenth-century entertainer Tabarin, along with jugglers, songsters, and clowns, attracted crowds of Parisians to the swarming fairgrounds of the day. Their main locale was just to the right, the **Place Dauphine.** The first of the royal squares (built in 1607), it was one of the busiest market places in Paris until about a hundred years ago.

Before leaving the little **Place du Pont Neuf,** descend the steps behind Henry IV's statue to the park **Du Vert Galant,** a popular playground for little children. Stand for a few minutes alongside the hopeful fishermen at the point of the island under the shade of the overhanging trees. As you look downstream, from one bridge to the next, you will agree that this is one of Paris' most enchanting and peaceful spots.

Returning to the rose-colored brick and stone houses of the Place du Pont Neuf, follow the **Quai de l'Horloge** to the **Conciergerie,** the noted prison of the Revolution, which is still in use. During the Revolution its inmates included Louis XVI, Marie Antoinette, Danton, Robespierre, and hundreds of others before they were sent to the guillotine. Many of its medieval halls and cells are now open to the public (10:00– 12:00, 1:30–5:00, except Tuesday). At the corner is the **Tour de l'Horloge,** where the first clock tower in Paris was built in 1370. From here there is an incomparable view of the Tour St. Jacques against the sky.

After crossing the Boulevard du Palais, walk past the **Tribunal de Commerce** to the colorful central **Flower Market,** crammed with stalls and shops displaying cut flowers and plants of many varieties.

Return to the Boulevard du Palais by taking a right turn into the Rue Lutece, beyond the flower mart. This street runs along the building occupied by the **Prefect of Police.**

Now cross the boulevard and enter the **Cour du Mai** in the **Palais de Justice** to visit one of the truly glorious sights of Paris—**Sainte-Chapelle** (open daily except Tuesday, 10:00– 12:00, 1:30–5:00, –6:00 in summer).

This masterpiece of Gothic architecture was built by Louis IX (Saint Louis) between 1246 and 1248 to house holy relics he received from Baudoin, Emperor of Constantinople. They were later removed to Notre Dame. You enter the **Lower Chapel,** originally reserved for pilgrims. Its rather drab appearance only heightens the suspense until you climb the winding stone staircase to become dazzled by the brilliance of color and graceful lines of the **Upper Chapel.** This chapel, designed for the Royal Family, is world-famous for its magnificent **stained-glass windows** illustrating some fifteen hundred Biblical scenes. These windows are only rivaled by those in **Chartres Cathedral** for their radiant splendor and remarkable workmanship. The rich color of the dark reds and blues is extraordinary. To stand in the nave and see the sun streaming through the hundreds of glass panels (sixty per cent of the originals remain) is one of the great artistic experiences not only in Paris but in all Europe. Here is the perfect spot to end this walk through old Paris.

QUARTIER INVALIDES

To the Eiffel Tower

This is an afternoon walk that includes some of Paris' most interesting and scenic places. Its starting point is very accessible and the entire walk is located in the same general area of the city. You won't have any great distances to cover, so you can spend some time visiting the Musée Rodin and the Invalides. You will finish at the Eiffel Tower late in the day, in time to enjoy the wonderful panorama of Paris in the soft afternoon sunlight.

Start on the terrace of the **Palais dc Chaillot** at the **Place Trocadero.** From this vantage point a magnificent scene opens up before you. The view of the Eiffel Tower soaring to the sky is extraordinarily dramatic and beautiful. The **École Militaire** at the end of the green lawn seems framed underneath the Eiffel Tower. To your left you see the dome of the Invalides with the Panthéon in the distance. In a city where you are repeatedly carried away by so many superb vistas, this is surely one of the most moving.

Turn right along the **Avenue du Président Wilson** to the Place d'Iéna, and in a moment you will reach, on your right, the **Musée d'Art Moderne** (open 10:00–5:00, except Tuesday). Perhaps you would prefer to visit Paris' finest gallery of modern art when you can linger an hour or so. Its magnificent collection includes great works by Matisse, Maillol, Picasso, Braque, Rouault, Bonnard, Marquet, Dufy, Léger, and many others from the impressionist period to the present.

Continue on the Avenue du Président Wilson to the Place de l'Alma and wander along the **embankment of the Seine** in the direction of the Place de la Concorde. If it is springtime as you walk down the alley of carefully pruned chestnut trees on the Cours Albert I, the cone-shaped blossoms will be flowering through the green leaves. If it is midsummer, the trees will already be turning a slightly rust color. But in any season, the long vista of triple rows of chestnuts between the riverbank and the musty gray buildings will put you in the proper mood to savor the allure of Paris.

You will notice the *Bateaux-Mouches* moored to their wharves. They are glass-enclosed river steamers, on which you will probably want to cruise, preferably at night, between the **Ile St. Louis** and the **Bois** to see the many artistically illuminated monuments along both shores of the Seine.

As you cross the Place du Canada the golden horses of the Pont Alexandre III loom up on the right through the trees. The **Cours la Reine** that extends to the Place de la Concorde is also an avenue shaded by chestnuts. It was laid out by Marie de Médicis in 1616 so that she could display her Florentine import, the revolutionary sprung carriage that drastically altered seventeenth-century transportation.

On the far side of the Place du Canada return to the embankment so that as you walk you can study the elaborate *décor* of the Pont Alexandre III (built in 1900), that ex-

PARIS

QUARTIER INVALIDES

ROUTE ►--►

METRO ●

100 50 0   100   200   300 YARDS

presses so well in its fancy statuary and lamps the ostentatious style of the turn of the century.

Pause for a moment at the **Pont Alexandre III,** the only single-span bridge over the Seine. Then, as you turn right to face the bridge's gilded statues gleaming in the sunlight on top of the four stone pylons, there lies before you across the river the broad sweep of the esplanade in front of the domed Hôtel des Invalides.

In a few minutes you will come to the **Place de la Concorde.** Here you turn right at the fountain which splashes in front of the obelisk. Cross the **Pont de la Concorde,** which leads to the recently cleaned Palais Bourbon. There's a remarkable view from the bridge—**Notre Dame** on the left and the highly decorative and resplendent Pont Alexandre III on your right. Looking back toward the Place de la Concorde and its classic buildings, you see **the Madeleine** at the end of the Rue Royale. Note how architecturally harmonious with the buildings in the square the Madeleine is.

You turn right past the **Palais Bourbon,** where the Assemblée Nationale—the lower house of the French Parliament—meets. Its façade was designed during the Napoleonic period to balance the Grecian front of the Madeleine. Continue beyond the **Foreign Office** on the **Quai d'Orsay** and turn left on Rue de Constantine. Across the street is Paris' air terminal and, as you walk along, you'll see on the right the large Esplanade and the golden dome of the Church of the Invalides.

There is one of Paris' many pleasant little parks at the corner. Why not stroll by the flower beds and watch the children playing in the sand.

The **Musée Rodin** (open 1:00–5:00, except Tuesday) is a bit farther up, on the wide **Boulevard des Invalides,** just across the intersection of the Rue de Varenne. Formerly the eighteenth-century **Hôtel de Biron,** this sumptuous mansion with its extensive garden was Rodin's studio during the last ten years of his life. Some years before his death he agreed to leave his sculptures to the nation if the government would exhibit them in this building. You will want to spend a while studying the expressive marbles of this great master, especially such famous pieces as *The Thinker* and *The Kiss.*

On leaving the Musée Rodin, cross the Boulevard and take the first right from the Avenue de Tourville and walk to the front of the **Church of the Invalides,** where Napoleon's remains are enshrined in an **open crypt** under a sarcophagus of red porphyry, a stone used for burials in Imperial Rome. This is also the resting place of many of Napoleon's greatest generals, as well as the heart of Marshal Sébastian de Vauban, the fortress builder. Marshal Ferdinand Foch, Supreme Commander of the Allied Armies in World War I, is the only recent French hero to be buried in the Napoleonic crypt. The splendid interior of the church is elaborately decorated. To see several interesting personal **relics of Napoleon,** such as his sword and hat, go down into the crypt, where the Emperor's death mask is also exhibited.

Not far from the Invalides is UNESCO's unusual modern building, which has a particular appeal to those interested in contemporary architecture. To reach it you cross the Avenue de Tourville on leaving Napoleon's tomb and take the second left into the Avenue de Lowendal. You will see the **UNESCO Building** on the left at the Place de Fontenoy. It's worth taking a guided tour so you don't miss such unique features as the interior columns, which are circular at the base and square at the top, as well as the various conference halls designed and decorated by artists of each donor country. Also, see **Picasso's mural,** which has been quite controversial. Outside, there are such **contemporary works of art** as a mural by Joan Miró, a huge mobile by Alexander Calder, and a statue by Henry Moore. Be sure to look around Isamu Noguchi's delightful Japanese garden, which is not far from an extraordinary spiral cantilever staircase.

Now cross the street from UNESCO to the **École Militaire,** France's military staff college, founded by Louis XV, and turn left. Skirt this large building by taking the Avenue de Suffren to the right until you reach the Avenue de la Motte Picquet. Here you again take a right and you will be in the Place Joffre.

You now are facing the stately park of the **Champ de Mars** with the base of the gigantic Eiffel Tower spanning the width of its promenade at the far end. The Champ de Mars, originally an eighteenth-century parade ground, was the scene of popular demonstrations during the French Revolution. You will enjoy exploring the informal **gardens** on your right, for they are full of luxurious shrubbery and trees, as well as attractive flower beds. A small lake, cascades, and grottoes add to the charm. As in other Parisian parks, you will see little toy horse-carts provided for children at a modest fee.

When you reach the Avenue Joseph Bouvard, turn left across the main promenade lined with carefully pruned trees. On the far side, turn right into the second street, the **Avenue Charles Floquet,** to get an idea of the mansions, now mostly apartments, that were residences of stylish Parisians early in the century. A glance to your left will show that you are on the edge of an industrial, working-class district.

After a couple of blocks, turn right on the Avenue Octave Gréard, which will bring you to the base of the **Eiffel Tower.** You can take the elevator to one of the **three stages** (the top platform is 898 feet above ground). It's an exciting experience to watch Paris open up below you as the elevator ascends inside the framework of steel girders. If you don't want to go all the way up to see the tremendous panorama of Paris and its suburbs, the second platform commands an extensive view over those areas you are likely to visit and has the advantage of being close enough to the ground so that you don't have that remote feeling of being in an airplane. Then, too, you can pick out prominent landmarks more readily. A very good **restaurant** is on the first platform—a scenic spot to enjoy afternoon tea with Paris spread out at your feet.

MONTMARTRE

La Butte by Day

Almost every visitor to Paris goes up to Montmartre, and usually at night. You will probably dine in or near the Place du Tertre, wander about the many art galleries, and stop by at a cabaret or café. But you will find it more interesting, though perhaps not as gay or exciting, to walk around Montmartre by daylight. It is a delightful and very different little section of Paris—just a few blocks on the top of La Butte (or hill). Even though it may be "touristy" the winding little streets and byways off the Place du Tertre are fascinating and many are unspoiled. There's quite a bit to see and do in this picturesque village or commune de Montmartre.

The historical origin of the word Montmartre seems uncertain. Some stories ascribe the name to Mont des Martyrs where, according to tradition, three saints, including St. Denis, were beheaded. However, in its catalogue the Musée du Vieux Montmartre states that the word Montmartre comes from **Mons Martis,** because on this hill the Romans had built a temple consecrated to the god Mars.

A rural community until the last century, Montmartre was known for its plaster quarries, from which the phrase Plaster of Paris is derived. Artists and writers have been drawn to Montmartre for many years but around the turn of the century it became particularly famous as the haunt of the impressionist painters. Montmartre is still full of artists, as you will see when you wander about its nooks and corners. The old picturesque atmosphere abounds and even one of the famous Montmartre windmills has survived.

Start your walk through Montmartre at the **Place Clichy,** the famous locale of cabarets, cafés and the Moulin Rouge. Stroll along the **Boulevard de Clichy** into the **Boulevard de Rochechouart,** to the **Rue Dancourt.** Turn left along this

PARIS

MONTMARTRE

ROUTE ---->

100 50 0   100 YARDS 200

N

Avenue Junot

MOULIN

Rue Gir

Pl. Blanche

START

Bd. de Clichy

street and at the **Place Dancourt,** one of Paris' attractive small squares, go around the **Theatre de' l'Atelier,** which as the Theatre de Montmartre was one of the oldest in Paris, into the **Rue D'Orsel.** At the **Rue Steinkerque,** turn left and in a moment you will come to the old-fashioned funicular that will take you up the steep slope.

This in itself is an amusing experience. You are quite likely to find the car crowded with women and children from the neighborhood, all chattering at a great rate. As the car ascends, you will notice a small park on your right. In a few minutes you will be at the top, 328 feet above the Seine. Climb the steps to the terrace in front of **Sacré-Coeur.** A wonderful panorama of Paris unfolds below. Straight ahead you can see **Notre Dame** and the **Panthéon** just behind it, while to your right the **Eiffel Tower** pierces the horizon. (You are about on a level with its second landing.)

The white Church of Sacré-Coeur, one of the most familiar landmarks in Paris, was built in the Romanesque-Byzantine style between 1876 and 1914. You may wish to wander around its vast dark interior and look at the modern stained glass windows. One of the world's largest bells, **La Savoyarde,** weighing nearly nineteen tons, hangs in the tower.

From the basilica, turn right on **Rue Azais,** then right again on the **Rue St. Eleuthère** and left into the center of Montmartre, the **Place du Tertre.** This small square, similar to those in French provincial towns, is enclosed by old-fashioned gray, weather-beaten houses and restaurants. It is a great popular gathering place at all hours of the day and night. In warm weather the center of the square, under the trees, will be filled with tables where patrons of the adjacent restaurants are served. The narrow cobblestone street around the square is usually crowded with visitors, either watching the different artists at work or inspecting their paintings displayed on easels. A typical Montmartre painter may be dressed in beret, colorful blue jeans and a gray sweater, applying his paint with a palette knife. Just on the left you might see a bearded artist cutting out silhouettes with a scissors. At the corner of the square you will notice this somewhat faint red lettering on a gray building, "Commune Libre du Vieux Montmartre Mairie" an association founded by the artists in the quartier, which has a mayor and corporation but no legal significance. No. 3 was the first legal **town hall** of Montmartre (1790) and here Georges Clemenceaux, France's noted premier in World War I, was Mayor in 1871. In front of **La Mère Catherine,** the square's best known restaurant, you have a characteristic view of the domes of Sacré-Coeur.

Turn left from the square past the **Café La Bohême** into the Rue du Mont Cenis and on your right you will see the old parish **Church of St. Pierre.** Originally a Benedictine abbey, it is the third oldest church in Paris and an example of early Gothic architecture. The four Roman columns inside are ruins of the temple that was erected here. The choir's rib-vaulting is the oldest in Paris. Step out into the garden for a moment. When you are standing in the center, look up at the church's Gothic tower contrasted against the Byzantine-style dome of Sacré-Coeur.

Returning to the **Rue du Mont Cenis,** in about fifty yards you will come on your left to a tiny street or passageway, the **Rue Rustique.** Wander down here for a minute or two—it's a **Utrillo** scene come to life, so typical of Montmartre with its old-fashioned lampposts and window boxes overhanging the alley. Everywhere you turn there is a charming sight on this unspoilt street.

As you stroll along the Rue du Mont Cenis and the streets that run off it, you are bound to be attracted by the various art galleries. Some, of course, deal in rather inferior paintings but others are quite reputable though the prices are not as low as in certain parts of the Left Bank.

Walk to the end of the Rue du Mont Cenis and look down over the terraces below that lead to one of the main industrial quarters of the city.

Now turn back a few yards and right on the **Rue Cortot** (**Renoir** lived at No. 12) and again right on the **Rue des Saules.** As you go down the hill, you will pass on your right an amazing sight, a vineyard in the heart of Paris. The last of many that produced the wine of Montmartre, the terraces of **Clos Montmartre** are well tended. The picking of the grapes is an occasion for much festivity every year.

Turn right along the **Rue St. Vincent** past the vineyard and go into a garden on the right to visit the **Musée du Vieux Montmartre** (open 2:00–5:00 except Tuesday). This collection of memorabilia about Montmartre, in a house surrounded by trees and shrubs above the street, is well worth visiting. In addition to prints and posters, there are fascinating models of Montmartre and the section just below the hill. You will get a better idea of the distinctive character of Montmartre's history by spending a little time in this museum than any other way.

At the corner of the Rue St. Vincent and the Rue des Saules you will see a little two-storied brick cottage beneath a tree with a gnarled stump. This is the **Lapin Agile,** Montmartre's most famous cabaret (open after 11:00 at night except Monday). The sign above the door with the phrase "Poèmes et Chansons" depicts a rabbit balancing a bottle of wine on his arm and was painted by A. Gill, from which the cabaret took its name. At one time such noted artists as **Picasso** and **Utrillo** used to meet here. Come back in the evening to hear the entertainers sing songs of old Montmartre.

Continuing along the Rue St. Vincent you will pass, on the left, dilapidated cottages with old chimney pots. At the end of the street you will come to a little park on the right.

Now go up the hill and climb the steps on the **Rue Girardon.** After you pass a playground on the right, you will see a windmill above the building on the corner of the Rue Lepic. This is the **Moulin de la Galette,** a celebrated dance hall, the scene of Renoir's great painting. This windmill is the last of several that used to stand on La Butte a hundred years ago.

After you turn left along the **Rue Lepic** (**Van Gogh** lived at No. 54), you will notice weathered houses with red and gray shutters standing above little gardens. There's a little triangle of green on the right, the **Place J. B. Clement,** and to your left trees and a vine-covered wall rise above the street. Now you will pass more art galleries in the popular **Rue Norvins.**

Take a right turn into the narrow Passage Trainée for a couple of minutes until you come to the **Musée Historical de Montmartre** (open 10:00–12:00; 2:00–7:00; 9:00–11:00 daily). This is a wax museum where fourteen tableaux depict different periods in the history of Montmartre. Some scenes show Montmartre artists like **Toulouse-Lautrec,** others the period of the French Revolution with Danton and LaFayette, still others present the days of **Clemenceau.** Tours through this interesting museum are conducted in English.

Just opposite the museum you can enjoy a wonderful view of Paris over the typical slanted rooftops and chimney pots of the nearby houses.

Now return to the Rue Norvins and continue just a few yards to the **Place du Tertre** where you can watch the amusing street scene from a table in the square. From here you can pick up a taxi to reach the center of Paris.

X ROME

THE OLD CITY

In Ancient Rome

No visitor can do justice to Rome in a few days, for no other city in the Western world contains so much of historical interest or presents such an extensive view of Western culture.

Yet, unfortunately, your stay in Rome will probably be limited, so these walks have been planned to enable you to visit most of the interesting and important places, as well as to give you some variety. As you are likely to be there during the spring, summer, or early fall, when the weather is warm, the walks have been broken up as much as possible, so that you will not have to cover too much in any single stroll.

Two practical hints: The streets are often very narrow and the drivers speedy, so watch your step; ladies should be sure to wear low heels, as many of the streets are paved with cobblestones.

You can begin your acquaintance with the Eternal City with three enjoyable and instructive walks: one will introduce you to ancient Rome; the other two—both in the same general vicinity—will take you to some places that are not seen ordinarily by tourists. Since the latter two are relatively short, the three walks can be covered in a single day. However, if you decide on this plan, it is advisable to take a taxi from the point where the second walk ends to the beginning of the third walk.

Begin your walk in ancient Rome at the **Capitol,** set on a hill which has been revered since the days of the Etruscans. In the sixth century B.C. the **Temple of Jupiter** stood here near the site of the Tarpeian Rock.

You should approach the Capitol by climbing the flight of

166

steps from the **Piazza d'Aracoeli** to the **Piazza del Campido-
glio,** a few hundred yards from the **Piazza Venezia.** You will be
struck by the contrasting effects of the ancient brick **Church
of Santa Maria in Aracoeli** above you (built over the **Temple
of Juno)** and the ostentatious immensity of the marble **monument to Victor Emmanuel II** towering off to your left. As you
ascend the stairs, you pass through a delightful **garden** of
oleander, wisteria, palms, and pines. Take the path to the left,
below the top, to see the cage containing live wolves—the
symbol of Rome. Two large marbles of the **Dioscuri** dominate
the entrance to the piazza. You now are facing one of the
most beautiful and noblest small squares in the world, designed by Michelangelo. Right in front of you stands the
magnificent **equestrian statue of Marcus Aurelius,** an unusually well preserved second-century figure and one of the few
large bronzes of imperial Rome to have survived the ages.

The **Capitoline Museum** (open weekdays except Monday,
9:00–4:00; Sunday, 10:00–1:00) on the left contains one
of the world's oldest collections of **Greek and Roman statuary.**
You will want to return here to see such great sculptures as the
Capitoline *Venus,* the *Dying Gaul,* and *Cupid and Psyche.*
On your right is another fine museum, the **Palazzo dei Con-
servatori,** where you will find among many great works of art
the statue that more than any other is associated with the
founding of Rome, the Etruscan bronze of the *She-Wolf.* Both
these museums should be visited, either now or later, when
you can spare an hour or so.

Pause for a moment in this magnificently proportioned
square to study the lovely ocher-colored façade of the **Palazzo
Senatario** with its stately double staircase and graceful campanile. Today it is the Mayor of Rome's official residence. (You
should return here at night to see the square and buildings
illuminated.)

Now turn right to the terrace behind the Palazzo Senatario.
There before you lies the **Forum,** the center of political and
religious life in Roman days. As you gaze over this historic
place you will be able to identify several of its better-known

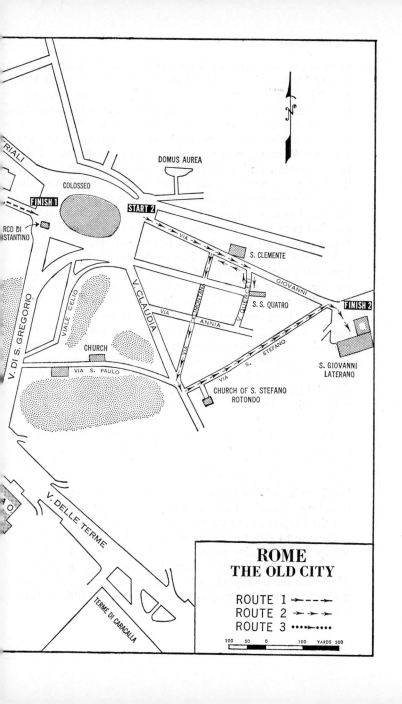

DOMUS AUREA

COLOSSEO

FINISH 1

RCO DI
STANTINO

START 2

VIA

S. CLEMENTE

GIOVANNI

FINISH 2

S.S. QUATRO

V. DI S. GREGORIO.

VIALE CELIO

V. CLAUDIA

VIA

ANNIA

VIA S. STEFANO

S. GIOVANNI
LATERANO

CHURCH

VIA S. PAULO

CHURCH OF S. STEFANO
ROTONDO

V. DELLE TERME

TERME DI CARACALLA

ROME
THE OLD CITY

ROUTE 1 →---→
ROUTE 2 →→→→
ROUTE 3 •••••→

100   50   0   100   YARDS 200

monuments—the Arch of Septimius Severus just below to the left, and the Arch of Titus at the far end of the **Sacra Via,** the Forum's major thoroughfare. You will see the Palatine Hill rising just to the right, and the Colosseum in the distance.

From the terrace, make your way down the curving road of huge cobblestones (perhaps the oldest in Rome), the **Via del Foro Romano,** past the colonnade of the **Portico of the Dii Consentes,** dating from the fourth century and one of the last monuments to the pagan religion. Now skirt the Forum (the marvelously decorated column of Trojan is off to your left) until you reach the Via dei Fori Imperiale on your left that runs along the park to the Forum's main entrance (open from 9:00 until one hour before sunset).

You can spend as much time in the Forum as will satisfy your thirst for knowledge of ancient Rome. In general only the foundations and several arches and columns have survived the destruction of the ages in their original form, yet the excavated area conveys a sense of the grandeur of ancient Rome. It is a fascinating experience to tread this historic ground and listen to a well-informed guide explain the significance of the ruins that lie all about you. For the purposes of this stroll, several of the more interesting sights will be mentioned here, but for details you should purchase a special guidebook and map of the Forum.

A good place to start your wanderings around the Forum is the great third-century **Triumphal Arch of Septimius Severus.** Not far away is the **Imperial Rostrum** from which orators addressed the populace. Just in front of the arch descend a few steps to the **Lapis Niger.** The tomb of Romulus is said to have been located beneath this black flagstone. The remains of the golden milestone measuring the routes throughout the Empire are to your left as you face the arch.

Be sure to visit the **Curia** where the Senate once met, the square brick building which Julius Caesar began in 44 B.C.

As you stroll along the Sacra Via lined with sanctuaries, which was the triumphal route of victorious generals, you will notice to your right three majestic Corinthian columns. They are the remains of the **Temple of Castor and Pollux.** Make your way closer to them so that you can observe the superb capitals of these splendid white marble pillars against the blue sky.

Pause for a moment to admire on the right the beautifully proportioned remains of the **Temple of the Vestal Virgins,** the guardians of the sacred flame which signified the perpetuity of the Roman state. Behind you are the ruins of the **House of the Vestal Virgins.** As you leave them, there is a fine view of the columns of Castor and Pollux.

The high arches farther along on the left as you go up a slight incline on the Sacra Via are the ruins of the huge **Basilica of Maxentius,** which was studied by Bramante and Michelangelo while they were designing **St. Peter's.** To your right there is a fine view of the umbrella cypresses, palms, and cedars on the crest of the Palatine Hill, the cradle of ancient Rome.

At the end of the Sacra Via you will come to the massive **Arch of Titus,** commemorating the capture of Jerusalem in A.D. 70. Notice the bas-relief under the arch which depicts the Roman soldiers carrying away the seven-branched candlesticks, the spoils from Solomon's Temple.

After touring the Forum, you should then turn to the right up the hill from the Arch of Titus to the **Palatine Hill** just above you. Settlement of the Palatine is known to date from the ninth century B.C. and it was here that Romulus and Remus are said to have founded Rome.

A stroll on the Palatine among the historic ruins shaded by umbrella pines, palms, and cypresses is one of the most romantic in Rome, so continue up the steps to the terrace of the **Farnese Gardens.** Stop for a few minutes on the main terrace just beyond. You will be enchanted by the striking panorama of the Forum beneath you. As you look out on this fabulous scene, pick out the ruins you found most interesting. In wandering around the picturesque gardens, remember that hereabouts beneath the olive groves were the homes of Cicero, Mark Antony, the orator Crassus, as well as the palaces of several Roman emperors. You should visit the decorative murals in **Casa Livia** ("the House of Livia"), now believed to have belonged to her husband, the Emperor Augustus. A small terrace nearby commands a fine view of St. Peter's dome and the Janiculum. From the House of Livia turn right and walk through the long vaulted underground gallery, known as the **Cryptoporticus,** which connected the palaces on the Palatine to Nero's Domus Aurea. You will see off to your right the remains of the huge **stadium of Domitian** and **Augustus' imperial palace,** before descending the hill along the **Barberini vineyard.**

Be sure to see the exciting *Son et Lumière* **performance** which is presented at the Forum most evenings. This dramatic presentation makes the days of early Rome live again and brings to life the ancient and historic ruins.

You leave the Forum by the gate just beyond the Arch of Titus. Now, you will see to your right the great **Arch of Constantine,** the last of the triumphal arches. Erected in A.D. 315 in honor of the Christian Constantine's victory over the pagan Maxentius, it was built from fragments of Flavian buildings. Inspect the reliefs and medallions, which commemorate scenes from the days of Trajan, Domitian, and Hadrian.

Dominating the square is the **Colosseum.** This massive monument has for centuries symbolized the eternity of Roman civilization, for it has survived earthquakes, fires, and vandalism. Even by today's standards the huge stone blocks in the three superimposed colonnades reflect the grandeur and magnificence of the Flavian emperors who built it between A.D. 72 and A.D. 80. You should go inside (open from 9:00 until one hour before sunset) and climb to the top gallery to see the remains of this enormous arena, where fifty thousand spectators could watch the gladiatorial combats and bloody acts of barbarism once performed within it. To get a good view of the Colosseum, which, incidentally, was named for the colossal **statue of Nero** that once stood near the site, walk up the path on the far side to the pleasant **Oppio Park.** Underneath this park are the remains of Nero's **Domus Aurea,** or "Golden House."

Here at the Colosseum is the fitting spot to end this stroll through the greatest monuments of Roman civilization.

Four Churches

The next two walks, each relatively short, will take you to some of the most fascinating **churches** in Rome—ones that many tourists miss. The second walk includes the only church in Rome (San Clemente), where you can see three centers of religious worship—dating from the second century to the twelfth—superimposed on one another at different levels in the same location. After visiting two other unusual churches, you complete the walk at the great Basilica of St. John Lateran. The third walk, which you should take in the afternoon, will bring you finally to the **Aventine Hill** at an hour when the soft golden glow adds much to the view you will have over the city.

The first stroll, to St. John Lateran, can be started at the **Colosseum,** if you have just visited the **Forum** and feel like continuing. If so, take the **Via di San Giovanni in Laterano** to the **Church of San Clemente.** Otherwise go directly (preferably by taxi) to the Church of San Clemente. (Open weekdays, 9:00–12:00, 3:30–6:00; Sunday at 10:00.)

This intensely interesting church of Byzantine design—from the days before the Emperor Nero to the Christian period more than a thousand years later—is unique. Here you can actually see the span of Roman history illustrated by four levels of construction on the same site. (When you go in, ask one of the Irish monks to take you around.)

The twelfth-century upper church, regarded as the finest example of a Christian basilica, was built directly on top of the lower fourth-century church. The discovery of the lower church was made in 1857 by Father Joseph Mullooly. His excavations also revealed the remains of a first-century building at a third and lower level. Later, from 1912 to 1914, it was found that a fourth **stratum** existed: buildings that were destroyed when Rome burned in A.D. 64 during the rule of Nero. The lowest level is sixty feet below the present entrance to the church.

So today you can descend from the **upper church,** with its decorative twelfth-century mosaic over the altar and its frescoes by Masolino, to the **lower church,** built at the time of Constantine over the **residence of St. Clement,** the third Pope after St. Peter. Fifth-century columns, ninth- and eleventh-century frescoes have survived. Go below to the remains of the second-century **Mithraic temple,** where you will see a bas-relief of the killing of a bull on the altar and also a bust of Apollo, the sun god.

After this exciting experience, turn right just beyond San Clemente into the Via Querceti and so on to the Via S.S. Quatro; then walk left up the hill and a few steps to the right to reach the entrance of the **Church of Santi Quatro Coronati.** Go into the courtyard and ring the bell to the left of the large green doors. A nun will come down and usher you into the lovely twelfth-century cloister. The graceful arches, the luminosity of the marbles, the fountain in the center, and the palm trees make this cloister one of the most romantic and beautiful in Rome. The bell tower adds a true feeling of the Middle Ages.

Return now to San Clemente and in a few yards turn left on the Via Celimontana. Continue for a few short blocks past a **military hospital** to a large square. At the end make a sharp left, keeping the hospital on your left, and about fifty yards farther you will come to **S. Stefano Rotondo.** (If the church is not open, ring the bell at the small door on the left of the entrance.) This is reputed to be the largest church in the world built in circular style. It dates from the fifth century. Two concentric circles of columns give its interior a most unusual and interesting architectural appearance.

Turn right when you leave the church and walk along the Via S. Stefano Rotondo until you reach the square dominated by the huge **Basilica of St. John Lateran,** the Cathedral of Rome, regarded by Catholics as their mother church. The Popes were crowned here until 1870. Although founded in A.D. 315, the church has been rebuilt throughout the centuries; the present building is largely the work of Borromini. The great **East Front,** with the statues of Christ and his Apostles above the Palladian-style portico, dates from the eighteenth century. In Holy Years the **Porta Santa**—the door on the extreme right—is opened. You will want to wander around the impressive interior and the **baptistry.** But be sure to visit the exquisite thirteenth-century **cloister** on the left of the nave. This is one of the loveliest and most serene corners of Rome. As you walk around this secluded cloister you will be enchanted by the superb twisted and plain columns inlaid with mosaics. A ninth-century wellhead stands in the center of the garden surrounded by green hedges and shrubs. Sit on a ledge in the far corner of the cloister and look above you to the upper cloister and its tiled roof against the great pile of the church. Nowhere in Rome will you find a more perfect spot for repose and meditation.

At this point, if you wish to continue to the third walk, you should take a taxi to the Church of Santa Maria in Cosmedin.

The Velabrum and the Aventine

Start the third stroll at the **Church of Santa Maria in Cosmedin** in the area know as the **Velabrum,** between the Palatine, the Tiber, and the Aventine. In ancient days this was the marsh where the shepherd Faustulus is supposed to have rescued Romulus and Remus. Later, Byzantines from the Eastern Empire settled in this section of the city.

The church is one of the finest medieval churches in Rome. Its Romanesque **belfry** is particularly beautiful. Just before you enter, be sure to notice on the left of the portico a large **marble mask** in the shape of a human face, known as the *Mouth of Truth.* In medieval times it was believed that when a person suspected of a crime put his hand in its mouth it would close if he swore falsely. The colorful interior of the church, largely the work of the twelfth century, reflects the original Byzantine influence of the eighth-century basilica. The Cosmati mosaic pavement, the varicolored antique columns, and the dark aura make this church particularly enchanting.

From the Church of Santa Maria in Cosmedin, go right a few steps, turning right again, into the wide Via dei Cerchi, and in a few yards turn sharp left into the **Via di San Teodoro,** noted for its tall narrow houses built during the Middle Ages. After two-hundred yards, go left into the Via del Velabro to the charming sixth-century **Church of San Giorgio in Velabro,** with its fine Romanesque tower. The rather austere interior is decorated by a beautiful mosaic pavement. Adjoining the church is the third-century arch of the money-changers, and almost opposite is the four-sided **Arch of Janus,** built in the fourth century—also a center for money-changers.

In the large square directly ahead you will see two small, graceful Roman temples, both unusually well preserved. The **Temple of Fortuna Virilis** with its fine Ionic columns is an architectural gem of beautiful proportions. Nearby, the lovely round **Temple of Vesta** was erected in the Greek style at the time of Augustus.

From here turn left past Santa Maria in Cosmedin into the Via della Greca. Then wind your way along the Clivo dei Publici up the quiet, serene **Aventine Hill.** As you walk up the road you will see below you the oblong Circus Maximus at the foot of the **Palatine Hill.**

The **Circus Maximus** was the largest arena built during the Roman Empire, 650 yards long and 150 wide, allowing three-hundred-thousand spectators to watch shows, races, and even mock battles (in A.D. 46 Julius Caesar staged one with a thousand infantry, six-hundred cavalry, and forty elephants). The rape of the Sabine women, in pre-Roman days, is believed to have occurred here.

At the top of the hill turn right into a small park. From the terrace at the far side you have a magnificent view over the **Tiber,** of the **Trastevere** section, the hill known as the **Janiculum,** and **St. Peter's,** as well as the domes of Rome's many churches. A little farther along the road you come to the **Church of Santa Sabina,** called the "Pearl of the Aventine." Continue another hundred yards to the **Piazza of the Knights of Malta.** On the wall of this square there are delightful bas-reliefs of musical instruments. The massive **gate** of the Maltese villa affords one of the most extraordinary views in Rome. If you look through the keyhole, you will see an artistically landscaped garden with the white dome of St. Peter's framed in a long avenue of cropped laurel trees.

Retrace your steps a few yards on the Via di Santa Sabina and turn right on the **Via di S. Alessio,** a street lined with stately homes. Oleanders, cypress, and palms in the spacious gardens add much color and beauty to this attractive residential section. Turn left a block or so before the street ends, and then turn right down the Via di Santa Prisca to the **Viale Aventino.** Here you can pick up a taxi or public transport to return to the center of the city.

THE RENAISSANCE CITY

To the Piazza Navona and Pantheon

These two walks take you through the **heart of Rome.** You will walk some of the narrow, old streets, hemmed in by massive *palazzi*. You will visit a few churches that are exceptional yet often by-passed, a magnificent square, the main shopping district, the Spanish Steps, and the lovely Pincian Gardens. By seeing such varied places, both interesting and beautiful, you will become aware of the many different civilizations Rome has lived through, and in particular, get a feel of Renaissance Rome. You will realize why Rome is indeed the Eternal City.

Start on the Via d. Teatro di Marcello at the foot of the **Capitoline Hill.** The majestic circular tiers of stone of the **Theatre of Marcellus** give you some idea of the huge edifice that the Emperor Augustus erected in 13 B.C. Twenty-two thousand spectators used to crowd it in Roman days. Andrea Palladio, an Italian architect of the sixteenth century, modeled his designs on its Doric and Ionic columns. You will notice private apartments built above the arches of the theatre.

Wander past the three superb **Columns of Apollo** by the arches of the theatre. The remains of the **Portico of Octavia** are now in front of you. Climb the steps from the theatre to the Via della Tribuna di Campitelli for an even better view of the Columns of Apollo.

Turn to the right along a narrow street to the tiny Piazza Campitelli, then go left along the Via dei Funari to the Piazza Mattei. Here is one of the loveliest fountains in Rome, the **Fontana delle Tartarughe** or **"Fountain of the Tortoises."** It's typical of Rome that in the midst of this rather poor area you should find such an artistic work in the center of a little square. Stand here for a few moments and look at this gem of a fountain with its four youths, each holding a tortoise and each with a foot resting on the head of a dolphin. The figures have been executed so skillfully that one senses a great feeling of life and movement.

On your right just before you reach the fountain is the **Palazzo Mattei,** one of Rome's oldest palaces, now the headquarters of the **Italo-American Association.** Go inside for a closer look at a Renaissance palace. In the first courtyard there are some fine bas-reliefs and friezes, and in the second a series of delightful terraced roof gardens above an ivy-covered wall. The **Palazzo Caetani,** still inhabited by the Caetani family, adjoins the Palazzo Mattei.

Keep straight ahead on the Via Falegnami, cross the wide Via Arenula, and you will come to the **Piazza B. Cairoli,** where you should look in at the **Church of San Carlo ai Catinari** to see the frescoes on the ceiling. Follow the colorful and busy Via d. Giubbonari for about fifty yards. Now turn

left at the Via dell' Arco del Monte to the Piazza dei Pelle-
grini. Just a few yards to the right on the Via Capo di Ferro
will bring you to the **Palazzo Spada,** built in 1540 and now
occupied by the **Council of State.** Paintings by Titian, Cara-
vaggio, and Rubens are on display (open 9:30–4:00).

Before you enter the palazzo, note Francesco Borromini's
façade. The great architect also designed the fine interior
staircase and colonnade which connects the two courts. The
large statue on the first floor is believed to be the **statue of
Pompey** at the base of which Julius Caesar was stabbed to
death (If so, the statue once stood in the senate house. This
is shown in the afternoon and on Sunday morning.)

By tipping the porter, you can see in the courtyard Borromini's unusual and fascinating trick in perspective. When
you stand before the barrel-vaulted **colonnade** you have the
impression that the statue at the end is at a considerable distance, yet it is actually only a few feet away. The sense of
perspective has been created by designing the length of the
columns so that those at the far end of the colonnade are
much shorter than those in front. The gardens of the *palazzo,*
shaded by a huge magnolia tree, are most attractive. The
courtyard is magnificently decorated.

From the Palazzo Spada you continue another block along
the Via Capo di Ferro and Vicolo de Venti to the imposing
Palazzo Farnese, begun in 1514 and considered by many to
be the finest palace of all. Michelangelo was the most distinguished of several noted architects who helped design it. Today it is occupied by the **French Embassy.** Its lovely seventeenth-century ceiling frescoes, as well as the huge guards
room with a tremendously high and beautifully carved
wooden ceiling, can be seen Sundays (11:00–12:00 noon).
Ask to see the modern tapestries of Paris and Rome designed
by Lurcat.

Directly in front of the palace along the Via d. Baullari you
will come to the **Campo di Fiori,** the famous site of executions
during the turbulent days of Renaissance Rome. Today, by
contrast it is a lively and colorful fruit, vegetable, and flower

market. To the left is the Palazzo della Cancelleria where the Cardinal-Vicar resides. Continue on the Via d. Baullari to the Corso Vittorio Emanuele, then turn right for a couple of hundred yards to the **Church of Sant' Andrea della Valle.** As you approach the church on the Via d. Baullari you are passing within yards of the remains of the **Roman Theatre of Pompey,** near which is believed to have been the place where Julius Caesar was assassinated. The dome of the church is, outside of **St. Peter's,** one of the largest in Rome. Opera lovers will be interested to learn that this church was the scene for the first act of *Tosca.*

At this point you cross the wide Corso Vittorio Emanuele II to the Palazzo Massimo alle Colonne with its interesting courtyard with frescoes above on the loggia. Then walk along the Corso del Rinascimento a couple of hundred yards, take the second left on the Via dei Canestrari to enter the splendid **Piazza Navona,** one of the truly glorious sights in Rome.

Your first impression of this elongated square with its three elegant fountains, its two churches that almost face each other, and its russet-colored buildings, is a sense of restful spaciousness—particularly welcome after wandering around the narrow and dark streets that you have followed since starting this walk.

The site of the oblong piazza is **Domitian's ancient stadium,** which was probably used for horse and chariot races. For centuries it was the location of historic festivals and open-air sports events. From the seventeenth to the nineteenth century it was a popular practice to flood the piazza in the summer, and the aristocrats would then ride around the inundated square in their carriages.

Giovanni Bernini's **"Fountain of the Rivers,"** in the center of the piazza, is built around a Roman obelisk from the Circus of Maxentius which rests on grottoes and rocks, with four huge figures, one at each corner, denoting four great rivers from different continents—the Danube, the Ganges, the Nile, and the Plate. The eyes of the figure of the Nile are covered, perhaps either to symbolize the mystery of her source or to obscure from her sight the baroque façade of the **Church of**

Sant' Agnese in Agone, the work of Bernini's rival, Borromini.

In the Piazza Navona there are many delightful cafés where you can sit, have a drink or lunch, and watch the fountains in the square. The scene before you is indeed theatrical and often appears in movies about Rome. Perhaps a street musician will pass to add that extra touch.

Take the Via di S. Agnese in Agone, next to the church and opposite the center of the square, then turn right after about two hundreds yards to reach the beautiful **Church of Santa Maria della Pace.** Inside you will find the lovely Sibyls painted by Raphael and a chapel designed by Michelangelo. The church's cloisters are among Donato Bramante's most beautiful creations.

Now return to the Piazza Navona and leave it on the opposite side by the Corsia Agonale; in a moment cross the Corso del Rinascimento. In front of you is the **Palazzo Madama,** once belonging to the Medici and now the **Italian Senate.** Walk by the side of the palazzo and after two blocks along the Via Giustiniani you will come to the **Piazza della Rotonda.** You are now facing the **Pantheon,** the largest and best-preserved building still standing from the days of ancient Rome.

This circular edifice, constructed by Agrippa in B.C. 27, was rebuilt in its present shape by the Emperor Hadrian. It was dedicated as a church in the seventh century. As you pause in the piazza by the Egyptian obelisk brought from the Temple of Isis, you will admire the Pantheon's impressive Corinthian columns.

The Pantheon's interior, still in its original form, is truly majestic and an architectural triumph. Its **rotunda** forms a perfect circle whose diameter is equal to the height from the floor to the ceiling. The only means of interior light is the twenty-nine-foot-wide aperture in the stupendous **dome.** Standing before the tomb of Raphael, the great genius of the Renaissance, when shafts of sunlight are penetrating this great Roman temple, you are once again reminded of the varied civilizations so characteristic of Rome.

As you leave the Pantheon, take the narrow street to the right, the Via del Seminario, a block to **Sant' Ignazio,** one of the most splendid baroque churches in the city. (Along the way there, about one hundred yards on your right, you pass a simple restaurant, **La Sacrestia,** where you can have the best pizza in Rome.) The curve of faded terra-cotta-colored houses in front of the church seems like a stage set. This is one of the most charming little squares in this part of Rome. One block along the Via de Burro (in front of the church) will bring you to the **Stock Exchange** in the old **Temple of Neptune.** A few yards farther, on the Via dei Bergamaschi, is the **Piazza Colonna.** The great column from which the square takes its name was erected by the Emperor Marcus Aurelius.

You are now at the **Corso,** though narrow, one of Rome's busiest streets. Horse races took place here in the Middle Ages.

If you have taken this stroll in the morning, and you have the time and inclination, walk to the right along the crowded Corso for half a dozen blocks to visit the fine private collection of paintings—mainly of the sixteenth and seventeenth centuries—in the **Palazzo Doria** (open Sunday, Tuesday, Friday, Saturday, 10:00–1:00). Turn right into Via Lata, then left in the square to the gallery's entrance. Here is your opportunity to see the inside of a palazzo where the family still lives. The sumptuous apartments are shown at 11 and at noon.

Otherwise, cross over the Corso and walk a block or so to the left. You will come to **Alemagna,** a delightful, though moderately expensive restaurant, which is particularly noted for its exceptional selection of ice creams and patisseries. Either here, or in one of the modest restaurants nearby, is just the place to end this first walk through the heart of Rome.

To the Spanish Steps

The second walk through the heart of Rome should be taken after lunch, so that you will reach the **Pincian Hill** when the soft light of the late afternoon is at its best.

Take a rest from sightseeing and have a look at the arcade of shops in the **Galleria Colonna,** opposite the Piazza Colonna. Then wander up and down past the attractive shops along the **Corso.** After this little expedition, walk left from the Galleria one short block on the Corso to the Via delle Muratte, and then left a couple of hundred yards to the **Piazza di Trevi.** You now see before you probably the best known and most ornate of all the fountains of Rome, the elaborate **Fontana di Trevi,** finished in 1762.

This great group of statues, among which are figures of Triton and Neptune, is brought alive by the tremendous flow of water (17½ million gallons a day) that pours from many parts of the huge monument. Its construction against the walls of the **Palazzo Poli** gives it the unusual appearance of a theatrical set.

Now go back to the Corso, turn right and continue your window-shopping in the direction of the Piazza del Popolo to the Via Condotti. The sidewalks of the Corso are extremely narrow and crowded but this adds a sense of adventure. Along the **Via Condotti** you will find many of Rome's most fashionable and luxurious stores, including the world-famous jeweler Bulgari. Other shops specialize in silks, ceramics, leather goods, and men's wear.

After strolling up and down the Via Condotti, walk a bit further on the Corso to the **Via della Croce,** where you will be tempted by the high-quality food shops. This entire area is filled with unusual and fascinating stores selling all those Roman specialties that make shopping here so exciting. You will find various kinds of Italian cheese in the food shops and stand-up bars in the wine shops. So why not wander around for a while? From the Via della Croce you can take the Via d. Boca Leone across the Via Condotti to the Via Frattina.

After this extensive shopping spree you will probably find yourself back in the Via Condotti in the latter part of the afternoon. This is the best hour to approach the **Piazza di Spagna** at the end of the street. The sun will be getting low in the sky behind you and its slanting rays will throw an almost unbelievably clear golden light on the glorious **Spanish Steps** and the striking **Church of Trinita dei Monti** which surmounts them. The combination of direct sunlight on the terra-cotta-colored church and the azure-blue sky against which it is silhouetted is without doubt one of the most thrilling and dramatic sights in Rome. Even though it's hard to find a spot along the crowded sidewalk to stand for a few moments, you should do so before you reach the piazza, for when you do you are so close to the steps that the magnificence of the perspective is lost.

Crossing the square to the foot of the steps, you will see the interesting **Fontana della Baracaccia**—shaped like a boat —in the center.

The glorious sweep of the double flight of steps is artistically divided into well-spaced landings. Here is one of the most popular **flower markets** of Rome, adding a fitting decorative note to the lovely scene.

As you climb the glorious curves of the steps, pause at the first balustrade and look around you at the reddish-yellow baroque houses. The poet John Keats lived and died in a house on the right, now a **Keats-Shelley Memorial House** (open 9:00–12:00, 3:00–5:00, except Saturday afternoon and Sunday.) Palm trees, oleander, and hanging vines decorate the different levels of the terraced gardens. From the top balustrade you can see to your right the uneven roofs and skylights of the **Via Margutta,** an interesting street inhabited by artists. There spreads before you one of the finest views over Rome. This is a place to linger for a while, cast your eyes over the panorama, and feel the pulse of Rome.

As you leave the terrace in front of the church and walk along the Viale della Trinita dei Monti, notice the attractive roof gardens on top of the houses below you. The palm, cypress, and olive trees along the road lend a romantic air to the scene.

The large palace on your right is the **Villa Medici,** the French academy for students of the fine arts. Its delightful **gardens,** extending from the lovely interior façade of the palazzo, are open from October to February between 2:00

and 4:00 on Wednesdays and Saturdays. Shortly you will come to a circular **overlook,** a favorite spot for artists.

Now cross the road and take the foot ramp to the **Piazzale Napoleone** in the **Pincian Gardens.** In Roman days this was the location of the villa of Lucullus, whose banquets were legendary. Today the gardens are a favorite park of Romans, and Punch-and-Judy shows and other games attract crowds of children. Nearby is the **Casina Valadier,** a delightful café with an outdoor terrace, named for Napoleon's architect, who laid out the Piazza del Popolo below. This is just the spot to enjoy an *aperitivo* while watching the sunset over the city and the Roman hills, with the great **dome of St. Peter's** silhouetted against the sky.

Piazza del Popolo to Castel Sant' Angelo

This is a walk that is right in the center of Rome, that is not very long and includes the Castel Sant' Angelo, the one place of unusual interest where you will want to spend a good deal of time. In addition, this stroll will take you to a street filled with antique shops that you might otherwise miss.

Let's start at the oval-shaped **Piazza del Popolo,** one of Rome's largest squares, just below the **Pincio Hill.** Pause here for a moment and look up at the shell-shaped fountains and the terraces covered with tall cypress, palms and pointed cedars—those trees that are so characteristic of Rome. When you stand near the massive arch and face the **obelisk** which **Augustus** brought from Egypt, you appreciate the vastness of the square. Water pours from the mouth of four statues of lions at the base of the obelisk. Straight ahead three streets, divided by two symmetrical baroque churches with lovely domes, spread in fan shape from the square's far side. In the **Church of Santa Maria del Popolo** adjoining the arched gateway, there are some outstanding works of art including frescoes by Pinturicchio. The church's **Chigi chapel** was constructed from a design by Raphael, Bramante was responsible for the apse and Bernini for some of the statuary.

As you face the twin churches from the Piazza, take the right-hand street, the **Via di Ripetta.** Now you must walk for four or five blocks down this rather uninteresting street lined with tall forbidding buildings until you reach the **Mausoleo Augusteo.** This huge circular mound covered with cypress trees was the tomb of the Emperor Augustus and his family. Dating from 28 B.C. it was one of the holiest monuments of ancient Rome. In those days this area was known as the **Campo Marzo.**

To your right you will find a stairway that leads to a temporary structure housing the reconstructed **Ara Pacis Augustae,** an example of the finest Roman art. This is an altar of peace erected in 13 B.C. and covered with bas-reliefs of the Emperor, priests, vestal virgins, and the populace. It was done in the style of fifth-century Greek art.

Stroll around the tomb of Augustus. On the side away from the Tiber, you will pass one of Rome's most famous restaurants, **Alfredo All' Augusteo.** Here the so-called "King of Fettucini" holds forth beneath the photographs of celebrities from all over the world, serving personally his own delicious recipe of fettucine with the "gold fork and spoon." Continue past the restaurant and beyond a tiny square. You will cross the Via Tomacelli on the far side of a lively outdoor food **market.** After pausing to enjoy this gay scene, walk along the **Via Di Monte D'Oro,** then turn right at the next street. In a moment you will be in a small piazza, the **Largo Della Fontanella Di Borghese.**

The **Palazzo Borghese,** one of Rome's late Renaissance palaces, is on your right. Shaped like a harpsichord, it belonged to Cardinal Borghese who became Pope Paul V. Walk through the front courtyard to the archway. Long vines hang on the walls from the grape arbor on the loggia above the arch. In the inner court there is a charming scene, typical of Roman palazzi: a fountain, the Bath of Venus, surrounded by a portico of many columns and statuary, plays in the garden beneath the high walls of russet-colored buildings. On top, you'll see delightful roof garden apartments with terraces.

When you leave the Palazzo Borghese, stop for a few

minutes on your right to browse about the **outdoor market** beneath the curving ochre-colored façade of the palace. Here you will find stalls filled with books, old prints, maps, and bric-a-brac—a fascinating collection of oddities.

Continue to the right on the **Via Clementino** and at the next corner, the **Via della Scroffa,** turn left. As you stroll along here you'll catch glimpses of fine palazzi, such as one on the **Via dei Portoghesi** on your right. When the street widens, make a sharp right, turning into the **Via di S. Agostino,** and after passing under an archway into a wide traffic-filled square, go straight across to the **Via de Coronari.** While crossing the square you'll notice the **Restaurant Passetto,** one of the best dining places in Rome, and through a narrow street on your left you'll be able to see the **Piazza Navona.** (This is included in an earlier chapter, The Renaissance City.) Don't miss the stone blocks and brick remains of the ancient stadium that occupied this site in Roman days. These are now preserved in the entrance to a modern building on your left.

The Via de Coronari, lined with Renaissance houses, is just what an antique enthusiast searches for in Rome. A narrow dingy street, it is crowded with tiny antique shops. Here is one dealing in furniture; there you'll see one specializing in brassware. If you are looking for paintings, glassware, lamps or china, you'll find them all in one little shop or another. Candelabras, basket ware and upholstery are also on sale along this street.

Shortly you'll come into the **Piazza of S. Salvatore** in **Lauro.** Turn right past a café into the square. Beyond the church you bear right into the Via della Rondinella to reach the **Lungotevere Tor Di Nona,** the broad tree-lined avenue that parallels the Tiber. On the other side of this busy thoroughfare, opposite the **Castel Sant' Angelo,** you have a fine view upstream of the twin towers of the **Villa Medici** outlined against the blue sky with the bushy cypress trees of the **Pincio** on the horizon.

Turn left and stroll along the promenade under the luxuriant sycamores whose branches hang below the retaining wall.

In a minute or two you will reach the **Ponte Angelo,** three of whose arches were built by the Emperor Hadrian in 136 A.D. The statues from Bernini's studio, which give the bridge such a decorative effect, were added during the sixteenth and seventeenth centuries.

Pause for a few minutes on the bridge to enjoy the view up and down stream and the massive circular **Castel Sant' Angelo** surmounted by the statue of a bronze angel after whom the castle was named in the eighteenth century. There is a legend that St. Gregory the Great, praying for a plague to end in 590 A.D., saw an angel sheathing his sword on top of the fortress, thus signalling the termination of the pestilence.

Actually, the Castel Sant' Angelo (open 9:30–6:00 in summer; 4:00 in winter) was originally the **tomb of Hadrian.** The Emperor built it in 135 A.D. He and succeeding Roman Emperors to Septimus Severus were buried in this great mound.

The mausoleum became Rome's fortress when Aurelian defended the city in the third century. Through the barbarian invasions, the citadel was the scene of bitter fighting. In the Middle Ages the castle was used as a prison. During Charles V's sack of Rome in 1527 Pope Clement VII took refuge here through an underground tunnel from the Vatican, which is still in existence. It was a state prison in Renaissance days. You can visit the old cells from one of which **Benvenuto Cellini** escaped by sliding down a rope of knotted sheets. It has been truly said that the Castel Sant' Angelo encompasses the entire scope of Rome's turbulent history in the dramatic events that have occurred here.

After entering the castle, to reach the museum you walk up a long spiral, tunnel-like **ramp** that dates from the Roman period. On the way up you will pass the **dungeons.** In the **museum** you will find an intensely interesting collection of ancient military weapons, as well as paintings and other art treasures in the apartments of the Popes which are decorated with elaborate frescoes, ceilings and stuccoes.

Stroll around the circular walk on top of the castle. You have a remarkable panorama of Rome. From each embrasure you get a different view over the rooftops, church domes, monuments, and hills of Rome.

Here on the ramparts of the Castle Sant' Angelo, where so much of Rome's exciting history took place, is an excellent place to end this walk in the Eternal City.

TO THE VIA VENETO

From the Esquiline to the Quirinal

This walk will introduce you to some parts of Rome that many visitors who only have a few days there aren't likely to explore. It's a walk that you might like to do one afternoon, for it ends up at the **Via Veneto** at a time of day when it's fun to sit at one of the attractive sidewalk cafés. Also, it includes some of the most interesting and beautiful **churches,** as well as pleasant **parks.** As a matter of fact, even if you are particularly interested in seeing churches, it's more sensible to stroll from one to another because you will find that you appreciate them more when you have a chance to see something different in between. Otherwise, by taking a bus or taxi, you will find yourself dashing from one church, or museum, to another so fast that they all become confused in your mind. This is just one of the advantages of walking, particularly in Rome.

This walk begins near the **Colosseum.** If you would like to start off early in the afternoon, why not lunch at the restaurant **Domus Aurea** on the **Oppian Hill.** Its terrace offers a dramatic view of the Colosseum.

Go down the hill to the **Via Nicola Salvi** just above the Colosseum. Whether you start at the restaurant or the Colosseum, follow this street to the Via di Terme di Tito and left

ROME
TO THE VIA VENETO

ROUTE →--→

100 50   0   100   200 YARDS 300

U.S.
EMBASSY

FINISH

VIA

VIA LUDOVISI

VIA VITTORIO

VENETO

VIA BARBERINI

PALAZZO
BARBERINI

VIA

VIA

QUATTRO

FONTANE

QUIRINALE

VIA

QUIRINALE
PALACE

BASE SOURCE E. VERDESI, ROME

for a couple of minutes to the square where you will find the **Church of S. Pietro in Vincoli,** founded as a shrine for St. Peter's chains in A.D. 442 (open 6:00–1:00, 2:00–7:30). You have come here to see the magnificent **statue of Moses** by Michelangelo, certainly one of the most remarkable and stirring works of the Florentine master. To stand here and study the details of the figure—the majestic posture, the powerful hands and arms, the strength of character shown in the face and eyes, so phenomenally expressed in stone—is indeed an unforgettable experience. You will probably wonder about the prophet's horns, which are explained as either representing rays of light or as a result of some mistranslation from Hebrew.

Outside the church, turn right into the narrow Via delle Sette Sale, which winds for a short distance over the **Esquiline Hill,** one of the highest of the Seven Hills of Rome. After a couple of hundred yards walk to the right into an attractive **park** with tall evergreens. Shortly you will come to a terrace that offers one of the best views of the Colosseum. Just beyond are the underground ruins of Nero's Domus Aurea, or **"Golden House."**

Returning to the **Via delle Sette Sale,** you walk between the high walls on either side. Olive and eucalyptus trees overhang the road. Continue a few hundred yards to a major traffic intersection where streetcars and busses run. Cross over and keep slightly right on the Via dello Statuto for another block to **Piazza Vittorio Emanuele.** Here is one of Rome's small, attractive parks that is relatively unknown but full of atmosphere. On the edge of the square there is usually a colorful flower-and-vegetable market. Wander around the park under the stately palms rising above ancient ruins. There are several fountains and a pond. You are likely to see a fun fair set up with ferris wheel, games, and the usual other entertainments. As in so many places in Rome, this park seems to be alive with cats.

You leave the park at the end where you entered and walk along the wide Via Carlo Alberto directly opposite for three blocks to the large **Church of Santa Maria Maggiore,** which you can see ahead.

This vast and impressive basilica, built in the fifth century, is particularly outstanding, not only for its architectural form, but especially for its unusual and fascinating **mosaics.** These extraordinary fifth-century works of art over the triumphal arch represent figures and scenes from the Old and New Testaments. Be sure to request that the special lighting be turned on so you can see the marvelous detail and color. The gold in the **ceiling** supposedly was brought from America by Columbus. The fourteenth-century campanile in front of the church is the tallest in Rome.

Now walk to the rear of the church and through the square, dominated by an obelisk. In a block or so, at the bottom of the hill, turn left on Via Urbana, walk for about fifty yards, and on your right you will see the small and charming **Church of Santa Pudenziana.** On this site below the level of modern Rome, it is said, was **Senator Pudens'** house, where Saint Peter is believed to have stayed while in Rome. The church itself, one of the oldest in the city, has in its apse **early mosaics** of the fourth century.

When you return to Via Urbana turn right and go a block or so on Via Panisperna, then right again on Via Milano. You now walk four blocks across the Via Nationale to **Via del Quirinale.** Here, a few yards on the right, is the elegant little church of **Sant' Andrea al Quirinale.** Bernini designed this baroque jewel in an elliptical plan. The ornate interior, with tall pink marble columns and angels in the dome, makes it one of the loveliest and most intimate of all the churches in Rome—a fitting tribute to Bernini's architectural genius. You are likely to find yourself wanting to drop in again just to absorb more of its exquisite beauty.

Now turn left and walk back along the Via del Quirinale to have a look at the **Quirinal Palace,** the residence of Italy's President, a couple of hundred yards farther on. Stroll over to the balustrade, from which, at this high point on the Quirinal Hill, you have an extensive view over the city, with St.

Peter's in the distance. The statues above a beautiful fountain in the center of the square are Roman copies of the Greek figures of Castor and Pollux. The palace, which years ago was the summer residence of the Popes, is open on Thursday from 2:00 to 5:00 and 3:30 to 6:30 in summer, but you must request permission in writing. Tickets are distributed at the palace attendant's office from 10:00 to 12:00 on Thursday, on submission of your passport.

Retrace your steps along the Via Quirinale. When you reach the corner where the **Via dei Giardini** begins, look above you to a delightful **roof garden.** A royal palm above a grape arbor sways in the breeze. Here is one of those amazing sights in the center of this great city that gives Rome such an unusual appeal. A few yards farther along you come to **Via Quattro Fontane.** At each corner of the intersection there is a small fountain and in each direction you have a fine view.

Turn left down the hill along the Via di Quattro Fontane. On your right is the **Palazzo Barberini,** one of Rome's most sumptuous. It is now the National Art Gallery (open 9:00–1:00, 4:00–6:00). Its collection of Italian paintings, including excellent examples of the great masters, is the finest in Rome. One of Raphael's marvelous portraits, *La Fornarina,* is here.

At the foot of the hill you will come into the **Piazza Barberini,** a busy traffic junction. At the far end of the square the wide and tree-lined **Via Veneto** winds up the hill. Before you turn into the Via Veneto, look at Bernini's **Fountain of the Bees.** (Bees were depicted on the heraldic device of the Barberini family.) At the top where the street curves to the left you will see the stately American Embassy on your right. Now you have reached the smartest couple of blocks in Rome for those who enjoy outdoor café life. Pull up a chair at one of the tables either at **Doney's** on your right or at the **Café de Paris** across the street and observe the promenade of people. One of the most entertaining experiences in Rome is to watch the different, and often exotic, types from all over the world as they pass here.

ACROSS THE TIBER

Trastevere and the Janiculum

This walk takes you across the **Tiber,** away from the main part of Rome to a section that many tourists don't visit in the daytime—**Trastevere.** (You probably will dine in the evening at one of its many restaurants that have such a gay, colorful air.) For generations this has been one of the poorest quarters of the city, an area with narrow streets crowded with people. Street vendors shouting their wares, the old houses, and the winding alleys give this section an atmosphere of the Middle Ages.

Start at the oldest bridge over the Tiber, the **Ponte Fabricio,** near the **Theatre of Marcellus.** Before you cross, wander along the embankment and look at the bridge's high and graceful arches. It's hard to realize that it is believed to date from the days of Julius Caesar. The Ponte Fabricio leads to the **Isola Tiberina,** a small boat-shaped island that has rather a pleasantly quiet atmosphere removed from the traffic that runs along the river. On the island to your right there's a large **hospital.**

Look to the left toward the gardens on the island with the **Aventine Hill** in the distance. Tall trees stand like sentinels at the tip of the island. Behind you on the embankment you will see the dome of Rome's **main synagogue,** in the old **Ghetto section.**

After crossing the **Ponte Cestio** from the Isola Tiberina to the far bank, turn left and walk along the stream for about fifty yards until you come to the Via dei Vascellari, which you follow to the intensely interesting **Church of Santa Cecilia.** Just before you reach the church be sure to notice on your left a most fascinating **house.** It's a remarkable building because so many different architectural styles are superimposed on one another. When you come in a few yards to the square

PZA.
COLONNA

PZA.
ROTUNDA

PZA.
POPOLO

PZA. NAV

CASTEL
SANT'ANGELO

CORSO VIT

PZA.
ROVERE

VIA CONCILIAZIONE

VIA PENIT.

FINISH

ST. PETER'S

BASE SOURCE E. VERDESI. ROME

TEATRO
MARCELLO

START

IS. TIBERINA

VIA FUNARI

VIA FALEGNAMI

VIA

VIA

GIUBBONARI

ARENULA

VIA ARCO MONTE

FERRO

VIA

TIBER

VIA D. VASCELLARI

SANTA
CECILIA

VIA S. MICHELE

VIA ANICIA

CH.

RIPA

VIALE

TRASTEVERE

SAN FRANCESCO

SANTA
MARIA
TRAST.

VIA LUC. MANARA

VIA SCALA

VILLA
FARNESINA

VIA

VEN.

VIA GARIBALDI

RIVER

SAN PIETRO
IN MONTORIO

GIANICOLO

LIGHTHOUSE

FRIO

PASSEGG.

PZA.
GARIBALDI

ROME
ACROSS THE TIBER

ROUTE ------►

100 50 0   100   200   300 YARDS

on your right, you will be entranced by the church's twelfth-century **campanile** leaning slightly above the medieval houses. Opposite is the popular and lively restaurant **"Da Meo Patacca,"** where you can dine outdoors and listen to strolling singers.

Ask a priest in the church to show you the **Crypt** (open 9:00–12:00, 4:00–7:00). Here you can look around the remains of several rooms of a first-century-B.C. Roman residence. In the third century A.D., when St. Cecilia lived here, an attempt was made to kill her by scalding, but she survived, only to be executed later. You can still see the steampipes of the period. But the **artistic treasures** are the ninth-century mosaics in the apse and the group of thirteenth-century frescoes in the ceiling of the sacristy. Don't miss the lovely statute of the saint below the altar. The fine **cloister** adjoining the church is the oldest in Rome.

Turn right from the front of the church down the Via di San Michele, turn right on the Via di Maddalena dell'Orto, then left on the Via Anicia to the **Piazza San Francesco d'Assisi.** Saint Francis stayed in the church in this square when he visited Rome in 1219.

At this point turn right along the **Via di San Francesco a Ripa** past typical Trastevere shops and cafés. Cross the broad **Viale Trastevere,** filled with market stalls, to the Piazza di Santa Maria in Trastevere. A fine fountain brightens the center of the square.

The façade of the twelfth-century **Church of Santa Maria in Trastevere** (open 6:30–12:00, 4:00–7:30) with its Ionic columns from Egypt and colorful mosaics is one of the most impressive in Rome. You will see other magnificent mosaics of the twelfth and thirteenth centuries over the apse and great arch as you walk about the interior.

When you leave, take the Via della Paglia on your left to the second turning on the right, the Piazza di San Egidio, then fork left on the **Via della Scala,** a delightful old street. You are now in a colorful old section of Trastevere. Continue on the Via Lungara beyond the arch to visit the **Villa Farnesina** on the right-hand side of the street at No. 230.

This graceful Renaissance villa (open 10:00–1:00, except Sunday and Monday) was built as a summer residence in the sixteenth century for the art patron and banker Agostino Chigi. His sumptuous fetes and banquets were famed for their luxury and gaiety. The quiet **gardens** planted with high cypress trees provide a suitable approach to the **gallery** where Raphael painted some of his loveliest **frescoes.** Here in the long gallery with the large windows is *The Story of Psyche,* designed by Raphael and painted by him and his pupils. You will be entranced by the remarkably lifelike figures of this superb fresco. In an adjoining room is the graceful *Galatea,* another exquisite fresco, which Raphael himself executed in 1514. There is a story—reputedly true—that Michelangelo, curious to see Raphael's work, slipped into the room in disguise and, when the guardian custodian was not looking, drew a lovely black-and-white charcoal head on the wall at the north end. It is clearly visible today on the right hand corner of the upper wall—one of the most unusual and valuable calling cards ever left. The large windows of the villa brighten the interior, so that these magnificent frescoes can be seen in the radiant colorings which have survived so remarkably more than four centuries.

Before leaving the villa, you should wander around the delightful gardens with their tall cypresses, oleanders, little fountain and hedges arching over a walk. Here is an ideal spot to rest for a bit.

After visiting the Villa Farnesina, you can return to the Piazza di Santa Maria in Trastevere to lunch at one of the square's moderately expensive bohemian *trattoria* (or informal restaurants), like the **Galeassi.** As you look out over the square, you will see the gay panorama of Trastevere life passing before you.

From here you wind your way out of Trastevere and up to the **Janiculum.** From the Piazza di Santa Maria opposite the

Galeassi follow the short street beyond the fountain for a few yards to the **Piazza di S. Calisto.** Continue straight ahead on **Via di S. Cosimato** and, after about one hundred yards, turn right on **Via Luc. Manara** for a few hundred yards to the wide **Via Goffredo Mameli.** At this point you follow the winding road up the hill. At the fork take a sharp left, cross the road, and go up the flight of steps to the terrace outside the **Church of San Pietro in Montorio.** It's a ten or fifteen minute walk from Piazza di Santa Maria in Trastevere.

Climb the hill and soon you will come to the **Church of San Pietro in Montorio.** Walk to the edge of the terrace for a breath-taking view over Rome. Now go into the small court-yard of the adjoining monastery to see **Donato Bramante's exquisite Tempietto** (open daily 8:30–12:30; 4:00–6:00). Ring the bell in the far corner for the English-speaking Franciscan monk to show you around. This tiny domed building of the early sixteenth century rests on sixteen Doric columns. Its circular construction is such a perfect example in miniature of the finest Renaissance architecture that it has been copied in countless churches, including the Chapel of the Sacrament in St. Peter's. The dome of the Capitol in Washington was also strongly influenced by Bramante's design. When you go inside, you will appreciate even more its graceful and classic detail, especially Bernini's decoration in the lower chapel.

From this point you continue along the Via Garibaldi to the large *Fontana Paola,* whose water is carried by the sub-terranean aqueduct built by the Emperor Trajan. On the right through a gateway you are approaching the crest of the Janiculum ridge. As you stroll along the path, under a double lane of sycamores, the sweep of the **Seven Hills of Rome** unfolds beneath you. Further along, palm and cypress trees shade the walk. In a few minutes you will reach the statue erected to the Italian patriot Garibaldi. Here you should pause at the terrace and try to pick out the more prominent features of the landscape—the **Capitol,** the **Pantheon,** the **Quirinal,** the **Villa Medici,** the **Pincian Gardens,** and the **Alban Hills** in the distance. If you happen to take this walk in the late afternoon, the effect of the sun behind you and the soft light falling on the ochre-colored buildings of the city is particularly dramatic. Rome seems more remote from the Janiculum than from the Pincio and perhaps for that reason more alluring. The view is more encompassing and the walk along the ridge more varied. Then, too, the vistas are frequently framed by the swaying branches of palms. The Eternal City seldom seems more artistic and beautiful than from the Janiculum.

Stroll a couple of hundred yards beyond the **Garibaldi Monument** for the finest view of all, just before you reach the **Lighthouse.** Now you can see to your left the glorious dome of St. Peter's.

If you don't wish to walk any further, you can pick up a bus at the Garibaldi Monument that will take you to the bottom of the Janiculum.

Otherwise you should continue beyond the Lighthouse and descend the steps on the right. From the terrace below you have a fine view of the **Castel Sant' Angelo** on the Tiber. Turn right into the Salita di San Onofrio, and after about fifty yards go down a long flight of steps on the right, the Via di San Onofrio, to the avenue along the river. Just to the left is the **Piazza della Rovere.** Cross over to the bridge. Here you have another striking view of the Castel Sant' Angelo. You should inspect it more closely another time, as suggested on page 190.

Return to the square and at the far side go under an archway into the Via S. Penetinzieri, then take a half right into Via Cav. S. Sepulcro to the wide **Via di Conciliazione.** A couple of blocks to the left you will be in the stupendous **Square of St. Peter's**—about a quarter of an hour's walk from the Piazza della Rovere. You will want to pay a special visit to St. Peter's, the **Sistine Chapel,** the **rooms of Raphael,** and the **Vatican Museum,** for these are among the greatest treasures in Rome and require at least half a day in themselves. Meanwhile, where could you find a more magnificent place to end this stroll than this spot surrounded by Bernini's majestic semicircular **colonnades?**

XI FLORENCE

JEWEL BOX OF ITALY

To San Miniato

Florence is perfectly suited to the visitor who tours the city on foot. The old section is small and compact. The major churches, art galleries, and museums are all close by, so you don't have to cover long distances to reach them.

The medieval and Renaissance area of historic and artistic interest is crowded into a relatively tiny area compared, for example, with **Rome.** Therefore, in Florence it's really essential to walk if you want to appreciate this treasure house of art and culture, for each turning reveals an enchanting church tower, house, or narrow street.

The walks suggested in Florence are arranged in an organized way so that you can visit its great treasures, for the essence of Florence lies in its marvelous works of art—its buildings, paintings, and sculpture—which are located in many different places throughout the city.

But before you walk through the heart of Florence, you should get a bird's-eye view from a magnificent vantage point overlooking the city, the **Piazzalle Michelangelo.** When you stand on this square above the **Arno,** with Florence at your feet, the plain beyond, and the **Apennines** in the distance, you should realize that here below you lies the city that, more than any other, is the birthplace and storehouse of Western art and has been the magnet for art lovers during the past five hundred years. Such an experience will provide you with an over-all view of the city before you begin to plunge into the breath-taking, artistic feast that Florence affords.

First, however, you might get yourself into the proper mood

to appreciate the masterpieces of painting, sculpture, and architecture, as well as the turbulent history of Florence. Start at the **Church of Santa Croce,** only a few blocks from the **Duomo,** or cathedral, the center of the city. If possible, take this walk in the afternoon when the soft golden light on the hills above will be especially dramatic.

Santa Croce, often called the city's Pantheon or Westminster Abbey, will, by reminding you of so many of Florence's world-famous figures in art, literature, astronomy, and politics, impress on your mind the magnificent pageant of learning and culture—and the struggles for worldly power—that are wrapped up in its history.

The largest and most beautiful of the Franciscan churches, Santa Croce has been described as the "recognized shrine of Italian genius." (Open 8:00–12:15, 3:00–7:00.) The striking white façade of this thirteenth-century church is inlaid with dark marble. Inside, you will find the **tombs of Michelangelo, Galileo, and Machiavelli,** three of the world's greatest figures in the fields of art, science, and politics. Here, too, is a memorial to another renowned Florentine, the poet Dante.

The artistic treasures in Santa Croce will whet your appetite for other masterpieces yet to be enjoyed. The series of **frescoes of the life of St. Francis** by the first great Florentine painter, Giotto, in the **Bardi Chapel** just to the right of the altar, are regarded as among his finest works, especially the death scene. Another outstanding example of Florentine genius is Donatello's remarkable sculpture, *The Annunciation.*

After leaving the church, be sure to visit next door the splendid **Pazzi Chapel,** Brunelleschi's lovely Renaissance building with terra-cotta decorations, in the upper walls by Luca della Robbia (open weekdays, 9:00–12:00, 3:00–6:00; Sunday, 10:00–12:00). The high campanile and the cypress trees in the first cloister are dramatic. The adjoining second cloister, with its tiled roof, is particularly peaceful, and the lovely green lawn adds to the tranquil air. Incidentally, the nearby **museum** has a superb crucifix by Cimabue.

It's only a step to the right from Santa Croce along the nar-

SAN MINIATO

PZA. G. POGGI

PIAZZALE MICHELANGELO

VIALE GALILEO

SERRISTORI

NICCOLO

LUNGARNO

VIA DEI RENAI

S. BORGO

VIA DI BELVEDERE

PTE.
RAZIE

TORRIGIANI

BELVEDERE

SH 1

BOBOLI
GARDENS

PALAZZO
PITTI

FINISH 2

S. AGOSTINO

A DEI SERRAGLI

URCH
ARMINE

FLORENCE

ROUTE 1 — – – →
ROUTE 2 •••••••→
ROUTE 3 →– →– →

100 50 0 100 200 YARDS 300

row Via Pinzochere to **Michelangelo's house** at the corner of **Via Ghibellina** and **Via Buonarroti,** where you will find several of the artist's works. (Open weekdays, 9:30–4:00; Sunday, 9:00–1:00.) The room containing Michelangelo's drawings is particularly interesting, for here are the original sketches for St. Peter's, the Sistine Chapel, and the Medici Chapel.

Now that you have been introduced to many of Florence's great masters, begin your walk to the Piazza Michelangelo by taking the Via B. S. Croce opposite Santa Croce for a few hundred yards past frescoed buildings to the Via de Benci, which, if you turn left, will lead to the new **Ponte alle Grazie,** rebuilt after World War II.

If you happen to be in Florence in the summer, you may prefer to take a bus to the **Piazzale Michelangelo** rather than climb the hill. If so, you can get the bus on the **Lungarno** on this side of the river. It will take you along the curving **Viale Michelangelo** to the Piazza.

However, if you would enjoy the walk in the late afternoon, cross the bridge, and as you do so, look downstream at the ancient Ponte Vecchio to your right.

On the opposite side, you are in the **Piazza de Mozzi.** There are several interesting palazzi here, among them, on the south side, the three thirteenth-century **Mozzi palaces** with overhanging tiled roofs. Just in front of them you turn left into the Via dei Renai and go past the **Serristori Palace,** once part of the city's walls. As you enter the Via d. Giardino note the old bell tower on your right. From here you continue on the Via S. Niccolo to the **Piazza G. Poggi,** where there remains a portico of the old city wall.

From this point you slowly wind your way up the ramp through the **gardens** above the square and up some steps to the Piazzale Michelangelo. Reproductions of the artist's famous **sculptures,** dominated by a large replica of his statue of David, decorate the square. Stroll leisurely along the balustrade to enjoy the superb panorama of the towers and roofs of Florence, the sweep of the Arno flowing into the distance, and the hills of Fiesole beyond the city. You can pick out **five bridges** over the river, the **tower of the Palazzo Vecchio,** the

campanile, and the **cathedral,** and to the left you see the remains of the **old city wall** on the cypress-covered hillside opposite. If you are fortunate enough to be at the esplanade in the late afternoon, the dome of the cathedral, the slender campanile, and the russet-colored medieval towers will be bathed in a soft golden light—an unforgettable effect so appropriate for this artistic city. This is just the moment for tea or a drink at the **restaurant** or one of the snack bars in the square.

After this refreshment you should continue up to the hill along the **Viale Galileo** to one of Italy's most beautiful Romanesque churches, **San Miniato.** About 150 yards along the viale you will come to a wide, double flight of steps that leads to this eleventh-century church, built in the basilican style (open 6:00–12:30, 3:00–7:30). Both its façade and interior are decorated with green and white marble in geometric designs creating a remarkably radiant effect, especially in the late afternoon sunlight. The beautifully painted ceiling and beams are most colorful. You should also see the lovely medallions by Luca della Robbia which adorn the ceiling in the **Chapel of the Cardinal of Portugal.** On leaving the church, pause on the terrace for another and even more extensive view over Florence. Don't miss the lovely old bell tower to your right.

On your way back down along the Viale Galileo, the slanting sun will throw a dimmer glow over the city and the Apennines will turn a deeper shade in the background. Turn left just before you reach the Piazzale Michelangelo and descend a long flight of steps under rows of cypress trees—the Via S. Salvatore al Monte—to the fourteenth-century **Porta San Miniato** in the old city wall. Keeping to the left along the Via S. Niccolo you will return to the Piazza Mozzi. When you reach the river, finish this stroll by sauntering along the **Lungarno Torrigiani** to the **Ponte Vecchio.** Across the Arno, to the right of the low mass of the **Uffizi Gallery,** rises the tower of the **Palazzo Vecchio,** but these you will visit on your walk through the heart of Florence.

Cradle of the Renaissance

Your walk through the **heart of Florence**—which although
filled with historic and artistic interest, will cover perhaps only
a mile at the most—should start at the magnificent cathedral,
or Duomo, and its graceful campanile. This walk will take you
to those palazzi and art galleries that every visitor to Florence
must see, even if he has only a few hours—the Bargello, Palazzo Vecchio, the Uffizi and Pitti palaces—as well as the
Ponte Vecchio. In addition to visiting these wonderful collections, you will be wandering through narrow streets and
past medieval buildings that will put you in the mood to appreciate all the more the many great works of art in Florence.

Second only to St. Peter's in size among Italian churches,
the **Duomo** was built mostly during the thirteenth century.
Its correct name is **Santa Maria del Fiore** (Saint Mary of the
Flower), which, like the lily in the Florentine coat of arms, is
derived from the tradition that the city, "Firenze," was
founded in a field of flowers. Before you enter the cathedral,
step to one side of the square to view its multicolored marble
façade, Brunelleschi's large and lovely **dome,** and, next to it,
Giotto's graceful **campanile,** an architectural triumph of perfect proportions. Michelangelo considered the dome such an
achievement that, more than a century afterward, when designing the dome of St. Peter's in Rome, he remarked that it
would be "larger but not more beautiful" than Brunelleschi's
in Florence.

You will be impressed by the immensity of the **interior** of
the Duomo, but even more by the **masterpieces** that fill it—
the unfinished *Pietà* by Michelangelo, **bas-reliefs** by Ghiberti,
frescoes by Uccello, and a fresco by Michelino of Dante ex-
plaining the *Divine Comedy*. It was here in the Duomo, incidentally, that Savonarola preached. If you climb to the summit
of the dome, you will be rewarded by a fine panorama of the
city. The ascent of the campanile, although nearly a hundred

feet lower, is a more satisfying experience, for from the stairway you will enjoy superb views of its classic design.

Opposite the Duomo stands the **Baptistry,** Florence's oldest building, dating from about the year 1000. Octagonal in shape, it is constructed of green and white marble in Romanesque style. Here, indeed, is one of the great artistic treasures of Florence, the world-renowned **bronze doors** with their gilded bas-reliefs. Ghiberti's **East Door,** which Michelangelo called "worthy to be the gate of Paradise" is a marvelous group of panels representing scenes from the Old Testament. This superb piece of sculpture took the artist twenty-seven years to finish (1425–1452). After you have absorbed the details of the Baptistry's unique doors, go inside to see the thirteenth-century pavement and fourteenth-century mosaics in the **cupola.**

Leave the Cathedral Square by the Via dei Calzaioli (named for the sixteenth-century stocking-makers). Just before you start along the street, notice the small building with the Gothic arches and the overhanging tile roof on the corner, the lovely **Loggia del Bigallo,** at one time the home of a Florentine benevolent society for abandoned children. After strolling down this extremely busy street for about two blocks, you will see on your right the towerlike **Church of Or San Michele.** Originally built as a grain market, the church is remarkable for the marble statues placed by the different trade guilds in the niches of the outside wall; they include works of such great Florentine sculptors as Donatello, Ghiberti, and Verrocchio. Wander around inside to see the great **Gothic tabernacle** by Orcagna.

Enter the narrow Via dei Tavolini almost opposite Or San Michele and continue along the **Via Dante Alighieri** to the **House of the Alighieri** at No. 2, where Dante is supposed to have been born. In a moment you will come to the Via del Proconsolo. On the other side of the street you will see the **Palazzo Pazzi Quaratesi,** one of Florence's finest fifteenth-century palaces. Now walk in the opposite direction for a short block to the medieval **Palazzo del Bargello** (open weekdays except Tuesday, 9:30–4:30; Sunday, 9:30–1:00). Its battle-mented thirteenth-century tower rises above an urban fortress, which successively as prison, execution site, and residence of the city's chief magistrate and later of the chief of police, has witnessed some of the bloodiest scenes in the history of Florence. It now is a national museum, particularly renowned for its unrivaled collection of Tuscan sculpture.

Enter the spacious **courtyard,** enclosed by a colonnade. To your left is a small room filled with the **works of Michelangelo.** Two, the young *David* and *Bacchus,* are especially outstanding. As you climb the **grand staircase,** notice the elaborate coats of arms of Florentine chiefs of police on the wall overhead. Giambologna's famous statue of Mercury is on the **Great Balcony.** In the adjoining **Great Hall** you will see some of the finest works of Donatello—especially his wonderful figures of the young David and St. George. On the other floors there are great Florentine **sculptures** by Michelangelo, Cellini, and Verrocchio, **terra-cottas** by the Della Robbias, and **frescoes** by Giotto in the chapel.

After reveling in this artistic feast, turn left into the square, then take a sharp right along the **Via Condotta** for three blocks. At the corner of the Via de' Cerchi look left for a fine view of the Palazzo Vecchio. Now cross the Via Calzaioli, and walk another block to the **Mercato Nuovo,** the city's main market place for flowers, leather goods, linens, lace, costume jewelry, and souvenirs—always a bustling, lively scene. Spend a few minutes wandering around the interesting stalls, then take the Via Vaccereccia to enter the splendid **Piazza della Signoria,** dominated by the fortresslike Palazzo Vecchio, Florence's best-known landmark.

The piazza was the center of the political and social life of medieval and Renaissance Florence. The bitter political struggles between the Guelphs and Ghibellines are associated with this square, and it was here that Savonarola was executed, as you will see from a bronze plaque in front of the **Fountain of Neptune.**

The **Palazzo Vecchio,** now the seat of Florence's municipal government, was the residence of the presiding magistrate during the Florentine republic and later was used by the Medici dukes. The bell in the **thirteenth-century tower** called citizens to arms or to conclave. As you look at the Palazzo's severe façade, embellished with coats of arms, you will perhaps reflect on the extraordinary contrast between the two great towers of Florence—the warlike Palazzo and the spiritual Campanile.

The great halls and sumptuous apartments, furnished with fine works of art, will give you an idea of the palace as it was in the days of the Medici (open weekdays, 9:00–6:00; Sunday, 9:00–12:00). Linger for a few moments in Michelozzo's beautiful **courtyard,** with its decorated ceiling, before you go in. On the upper floor, the huge **Hall of the Five Hundred** is one of the most splendid in all Italy.

Almost next to the Palazzo Vecchio are the three high semicircular arches of the **Loggia dei Lanzi.** Built in the fourteenth century as an assembly place for public meetings, the Loggia contains the greatest outdoor exhibit of **Renaissance sculpture** to be seen anywhere. Cellini's masterpiece *Perseus* and Giambologna's *Rape of the Sabines* are two of the great works that adorn this unusual open-air vaulted arcade.

Between the Loggia and the Palazzo Vecchio you will find the entrance to the narrow **Piazza degli Uffizi.** The **Uffizi Gallery,** containing one of the world's finest collections of paintings, will tempt you, but probably it should be saved until you have had a chance to absorb the rather intensive sightseeing on this walk. However, do not on any account fail to visit this gallery, with its Botticellis, Leonardos, Raphaels, and many other masterpieces of Italian art (open weekdays except Monday, 9:30–4:30; Sunday, 9:00–1:00).

Pass the Loggia and turn left into the Via Por. S. Maria to the **Ponte Vecchio.** This unique fourteenth-century bridge is the oldest in Florence. Silver and jewelry **shops** overhanging the Arno still line it as in the days of Florence's glory. Pause at various points on the bridge for **fine views** in both directions along the river. The **Cellini bust** in the bridge's piazzetta serves as a symbol of the Ponte Vecchio's association with goldsmiths, and, in fact, it has always had a goldsmith's shop. Don't miss the little balconies on the right above the statue. The **enclosed passageway** above the shops connects the Uffizi and Pitti palaces.

If you started this stroll in the morning, you will by now be looking for a place for lunch. There are many restaurants in the Piazza Signoria and near by.

The second part of this walk begins on the far side of the Ponte Vecchio. After crossing the bridge, follow the **Borgo S. Jacopo** to the right to the **Ponte S. Trinita.** From this new bridge, built since the war, you have a good view of the Ponte Vecchio. Now stroll along the **Lungarno Guicciardini** to the next bridge. At the Piazza N. Sauro turn left about fifty yards and right on the Borgo S. Frediano about one hundred yards. A sharp left will bring you into the **Piazza del Carmine.** Before you is the **Church of the Carmine** (open 6:30–12:30, 3:00–7:00). The purpose of this little excursion is to see the great masterpieces of Masaccio, who, as a forerunner of the Renaissance, revolutionized the art of painting by depicting three-dimensional form. By this innovation he deeply influenced Raphael and Michelangelo. Masaccio's remarkable series of early fifteenth-century **frescoes of the life of St. Peter,** in the **Brancacci Chapel,** rank among the finest examples of Florentine art. Be sure to request the priest to turn on the floodlights so you can see the frescoes properly.

When you leave the church, turn right along the Via S. Monaca, cross the Via dei Serragli into the Via S. Agostino, and continue to the end of the street. On your left is the massive **Palazzo Pitti** (open weekdays, 9:30–5:30; Sunday, 9:00–4:00). Although it does not have as great a collection as the Uffizi, the Pitti possesses a number of Raphael's works, as well as those of **sixteenth- and seventeenth-century Italian masters,** a gallery of **modern art,** lavish **Royal Apartments,** and a **museum** featuring fine works of silver, ivory, porcelain, and enamel.

Enter a gate to the left of the palace to enjoy the pleasant experience of sauntering leisurely through the famous sixteenth-century **Boboli Gardens** (open 9:00–6:30). Strolling about the hillside, you will discover many splendid fountains, fine statues, grottoes, and secluded nooks, as well as beautiful flower beds, formal terraces, and a profusion of oleander, ilex, tall cypress, and pines. The famous **May Music Festival** takes place here. As you walk to the **amphitheatre** beside towering hedges, you have a splendid view over the city. Other alleys of cypress are lined with classic statues and look out on the nearby hillsides. There is a little **café** in the gardens. Here, while enjoying a cooling drink, you have a fine view of the cathedral, its campanile, the Palazzo Vecchio, and the **hills of Fiesole.** This delightful park, with the artistic glories of Florence spread out before you, is an appropriate place to end your stroll.

In the Footsteps of the Medici

Florence is crowded with so many remarkable **works of art** that it would be foolish to attempt to see too much on any one walk. This stroll includes additional masterpieces of painting and sculpture that you should not miss while visiting the city; further, it provides a pleasant change by taking you through the fashionable **shopping district.**

Start on the opposite side of the **Duomo** this time and stroll along the **Via dei Servi**—a business and shopping street—for two long blocks to the **Piazza della Santissima Annunciata,** often considered the most beautiful square in the city. As you walk along, glance now and again into the courtyards that you pass.

When you arrive at the square, you will see two graceful arcades facing the piazza and its decorative fountains. But it is Brunelleschi's portico of the fifteenth-century **Hospital of the Innocent** (the first foundling hospital in Europe), on your right, that merits the closest inspection. Above the arches of the colonnade are Andrea della Robbia's lovely enameled **terra-cotta medallions.** The small cream-colored figures of babies in swaddling clothes against the exquisite light blue background are surely among the artistic gems of Florence.

Next, cross the square, and at the opposite corner take the Via Cesare Battisti to the **Piazza San Marco,** where you turn sharply to the left along the Via Ricasoli for a few yards to visit the **Accademia delle Belle Arti** (open weekdays, 9:30–4:30; Sunday, 9:00–1:00). Although this gallery houses a collection of thirteenth- and fourteenth-century Tuscan **paintings,** as well as several remarkable pieces of **sculpture** by Michelangelo, the masterpiece that you have come to see is Michelangelo's gigantic statue of David, fashioned when the artist was only twenty-five years old.

Leaving the Accademia, you turn right to the Piazza San Marco and cross to the far side to the **Museo del Angelico** in the monastery next to the **Church of San Marco** (open weekdays, 9:30–4:30; Sunday, 9:00–1:00). Enter the delightful cloister with its red-tiled roof, shaded by an old tall cedar tree. Upstairs, above the cloisters, Fra Angelico painted on the walls of the monastery's small cells his superb and incomparable **frescoes,** of which *The Annunciation* (at the top of the stairs) is generally considered the loveliest. Be sure to ask the attendant to loan you a magnifying glass so you can study the details of the paintings. The artist-monk passed nine years of his life here. Here too, Savonarola occupied a cell (the last one on the right at the end of the corridor) and in it you will see some of the Florentine reformer's personal belongings. Stop in also at the **Chapter House** off the courtyard to see Fra Angelico's large frescoe of the Crucifixion.

After leaving San Marco, cross the square and walk down the Via Cavour. At the end of the second block on your right you will come to the **Palazzo Medici-Riccardi** (open weekdays, 9:00–1:00, 3:00–5:30; Sunday, 9:00–1:00).

This forbidding palace, so reminiscent of the turbulent era of the Medicis, was built by Michelozzo in the fifteenth century for Cosimo the Elder and was later the scene of Lorenzo the Magnificent's brilliant court. Inside you will find many **relics** of Florence's great rulers, including Lorenzo's death mask, in the Medici Museum, as well as Gozzoli's admirable **frescoes** in the chapel.

But the Medici are remembered in the world of art more for their burial place than for their residence because Michelangelo adorned the tombs of the Medici with some of his greatest sculptures. To visit these extraordinarily expressive marble statues you turn right at the corner of the Medici Palace, go past an **outdoor market,** then turn left on the via del Canto de Nelli, and walk around the **Church of San Lorenzo** for one hundred yards to the entrance of the **Medici Chapel** in the **Piazza Madonna** (open weekdays, 9:00–4:00; Sundays, 9:30–12:30). Don't linger in the ornate chapel, but go on to the **new sacristy.** Here you will stand in awe before the remarkable male and female figures of *Day* and *Night* as well as those of *Twilight* and *Dawn.* These amazing pieces of **sculpture**—and that of Lorenzo in the posture of meditation—represent the height of Michelangelo's genius in portraying life in stone. On leaving you may wish to stop at the grandiose **Chapel of the Princes,** lavishly decorated in semi-precious stones.

From the Piazza Madonna, cross to the Via del Giglio directly opposite and follow it to the Piazza Santa Maria Novella. Across the square is the splendid green and white marble façade of the **Church of Santa Maria Novella** (open weekdays, 9:00–4:00; Sundays, 9:00–12:00).

This church of the Dominican order, begun in 1278, possesses some of the finest **frescoes and paintings** by Cimabue, Masaccio, Giotto, and Filippino Lippi, but it is especially noted for the wonderful Ghirlandaio frescoes in the **choir chapel.** After you have explored this art-gallery-in-a-church, stroll around the fourteenth-century green **cloisters** just to the right of the church's main entrance. The faded frescoes on the walls, the green and white vaulting in the roof, the tall cypresses, and the lofty campanile towering above combine to create an extraordinarily beautiful effect. As you wander around the cloisters, you can also see on request the remains of frescoes by Paolo Uccello in the refectory.

At this point you may want a rest from sightseeing, so why not cross the little park in the square in front of Santa Maria Novella and follow the **Via dei Fossi** on the opposite side for a shopping tour. This street is crowded with shops selling antiques, furniture, china, statuary, and so forth, where you can browse for a while.

At the far end of the Via dei Fossi you will come to the **Piazza Goldoni.** Turn left and stroll along one of Florence's leading shopping streets, the **Via delle Vigna Nuova,** where **elegant stores** feature such **Florentine specialties** as handbags, shoes, silk, jewelry, and leather handcrafts. (It's worth keeping in mind that shops in Florence, as in other Italian cities, close for the siesta between 1:00 and 3:00 but stay open late, often until 7:00 or so.)

The Via delle Vigna Nuova will lead you into the **Via Tornabuoni,** Florence's most fashionable shopping center. Directly across is the **Palazzo Strozzi,** a huge Renaissance mansion famous for its fine cornice and wrought-iron torch holders. Its forbidding exterior reminds you that fifteenth-century palaces were also fortresses. Now you should saunter along to Doney's famous café, the rendezvous of the leading Florentine families. **Doney's** is just the place to relax for a while and enjoy coffee or a drink, while you try to decide which of Florence's many artistic glories you want to revisit during your stay.

XII VENICE

BEWITCHING BYWAYS
In the Shadow of the Campanile

Every visitor looks forward to touring **Venice,** the fabulous
city of canals, by gondola. By all means enjoy the unique and
delightful experience of gliding in a gondola through the
labyrinth of the canals.

But to explore the many bewitching byways of Venice, and
feel a part of this extraordinary and little-changed community
built on more than **one hundred islands,** one must go on foot.
Venice, unlike any other city, is truly a world for the pedestrian, because all the streets are reserved for the walker.

Wandering along the alleys or lingering by a bridge over a
back canal away from the crowds, you will discover fascinating bits of the old city. Wander where you wish, take your
time, lose yourself in the spirit of Venice. You will not be
harassed by traffic noises as in almost every other city; in
Venice the sounds you hear are mostly those of the padding
of feet on the flagstone pavements, voices from an upper balcony, the lapping of water against the stone buildings.

Here are **three separate walks,** none particularly long because Venice is compact. The first will take you through
"classic" Venice, with its splendid historic monuments and
churches as a background for its present workaday life. The
second supplements the first and leads to Venice's fabulous
Fish Market across the Rialto and to its **museum of contemporary art.** The third is on the **other side of the Grand
Canal,** where lovely baroque churches, the **Accademia,**
Venice's famed art gallery, and sumptuous palazzi express
the mood of Venice.

VENICE

ROUTE 1 → – – – →
ROUTE 2 ••→••→•••→
ROUTE 3 →→→→→

100   50   0   100   YARDS 200

Just strolling about this fascinating city for a few hours is a pure delight. Even in midsummer the weather is not too hot for walking. The strong Italian sun beats down only in relatively few piazzas and campos; the streets and alleys are so narrow that most of the time you are in the shade.

Perhaps the best time to set out is about 4:00, when life in Venice resumes after the long midday siesta. Start at the center of Venetian life, the **Piazza San Marco,** but before commencing your walk, look around the renowned square. The sparkling mosaics above the doorways of **St. Mark's Church,** together with its bulbous domes, cast an Oriental atmosphere over the square, recalling Venice's traditional ties with the East. This lavishly decorated basilica, embellished with more than five-hundred columns of marble—mostly oriental—was designed in the form of a Greek cross and rebuilt during the eleventh century on the site of a former church. Perhaps it is the unusual combination of **Oriental and Gothic styles**—the colorful Oriental domes and mosaics and the Gothic pinnacles adorned with stone figures—that makes St. Mark's so enchanting.

Over the **main entrance** stand the famous **four gilt-bronze horses,** Greek workmanship of the period of Alexander the Great. To study these lovely pieces of sculpture, climb up to the porch by the stairs inside the church. From here you have also a striking view of the square.

The **interior** of St. Mark's is so filled with marvelous early Byzantine mosaics and rare marble that it defies description. The magnificent golden **altar screen** of the tenth century, with its six thousand jewels, is merely one of many dazzling works of art.

A few yards from the square, on the **Piazzetta** beyond the campanile, is the **Doges' Palace,** one of the finest and most beautiful secular buildings in the world. The creamy, pink and white marble façade, above the graceful upper and lower Gothic arcades, presents a remarkably harmonious, massive yet delicate, architectural picture. It was originally built in the twelfth century but reconstructed in its present style almost two hundred years later. The sumptuous **ducal apartments** and **council chambers,** decorated with lavish paintings by the great Venetian artists, should be visited when you have an hour or more at your disposal (open in summer, 9:00–5:00; in winter, 10:00–4:00).

The **two columns** in the Piazzetta, close to the water, are noted Venetian landmarks and were brought from Constantinople. The symbol of Venice, the Lion of St. Mark, surmounts one, and on the other you see Saint Theodore and his crocodile.

Opposite the Doges' Palace in the Piazzetta is Sansovino's sixteenth-century **library,** which contains an archeological museum. Next to the library is the Marciana collection of rare books and manuscripts.

Returning to St. Mark's Square, you see, directly opposite, the Renaissance **Torre del'Orologio**—the clock tower over an arch beneath which runs the **Merceria,** Venice's main shopping street. (You can climb the tower from an entrance at the beginning of the Merceria.) This tower is one of the loveliest sights in the square. Its great clock face in gold and enamel bears the Signs of the Zodiac and shows the phases of the moon. Above the dial, and below the golden **Lion of St. Mark** —resplendent against a decorated blue field—Roman and Arabic numerals show the hour. On top, the famous two bronze Moors have been striking the hours with heavy hammers for five hundred years.

Now pass beneath the towering **campanile.** (An elevator will take you to the top for a panoramic view of **Venice,** the **Lido,** and adjacent **islands.**) On either side of the square are arcades, beneath the old **Law Courts** on the right and beneath the **Correr Civic Museum** on the left. Napoleon's **Fabbrica Nuova** ("New Building") at the end completes the magnificent piazza.

At the northwest corner of the square a passageway leads to the **Bacino Orseolo.** This small open space of water, opposite the **Albergo Cavalletto,** is often filled with gondolas bobbing up and down in silence while the gaily dressed gondoliers await customers.

Follow the crowded street alongside the **Rio Orseolo.** You will brush past porters with crates of tomatoes on their heads. Cross the bridge (there are about four hundred in Venice) and walk down the Calle Goldoni to the **Campo San Luca.** Cross the square and take the last turn on the right—the Calle Sanhuca. Turn left on the Calle dei Fabbri to reach the Grand Canal. From the quay you have perhaps the best view of the Rialto Bridge on your right and down the canal to your left. Make your way to the famous **Ponte di Rialto.** Designed by Giovanni da Ponte in 1588, the approaches to this great stone landmark spanning the Grand Canal rest on some twelve thousand poles. Its high arch was designed to permit clearance of an armed galley. Twin rows of little shops crowd the sides of the center walk.

Pause for a moment while crossing the Rialto and look down the **Grand Canal,** teeming with ferries, launches, motorboats, and gondolas. The spectacle is diversified and exciting. On either side of the canal stretch the lines of great palazzi, those ornate private palaces of Venetian nobility and wealth.

From the Rialto, staying on the same side of the Grand Canal, walk about fifty yards or so straight ahead to the Campo S. Bartolomeo. Turn left along the busy **Salizzada del Fontego dei Todeschi** alongside the central post office.

You now keep straight ahead on the **Salizzada S. Zuan Crisostomo** (to the right of the russet-colored church is an excellent moderately priced restaurant **"Da Nane Mora"**) over two bridges, and shortly you will be in a square opposite the **Church of Apostoli.** Now turn left into the wide **Via 28 Aprile.** A few hundred yards farther on, you turn left to the **Ca' d'Oro,** an exceptionally splendid old brick palace of a Venetian nobleman (open 10:00–5:00 in summer; until 4:00 in other seasons). Wander around the elegant tiled courtyard, then through the stately entrance hall to view Franchetti's **art collection,** including Titian's noted *Venus with the Mirror* and, in the chapel, Mantegna's *San Sebastian.* Be sure to go out on the charming portico for the view over the Grand Canal with the campanile of St. Mark's in the distance. Now retrace your steps to the Church of the Apostoli and cross the little bridge.

You will have noticed that all the Venetian bridges have steps leading up and down, for they have all been constructed to clear large barges. Pushcarts are specially designed with a small set of front wheels to negotiate the steps.

A hundred yards or so on the Calle Dolfin will bring you back to the Salizzada. Here in the Campiello Flaminio Corner by an open market you turn left on the Salizzada S. Canciano to the **Church of S. Canciano,** then right and left into the Campo Santa Maria Nova. Immediately over the bridge before you is the **Church of Santa Maria dei Miracoli,** a gem of Venetian Renaissance architecture built at the end of the fifteenth century (open 9:30–12:30, 4:00–6:30). This little building standing off by itself (one side washed by the canal) is an example of perfect design and exquisite ornamentation. Porphyry and serpentine (the first a dark red and purple stone, the second a mottled green) highlight its **outside decoration** of white and colored marble. Inside, the walls of the nave are covered with precious marbles; the beautiful sixteenth-century carving at the base of the columns by the altar and the vaulted ceiling of painted wood are equally fine. No other Venetian church is like this one. Ask the attendant for a mirror, so that, without straining your neck, you can study the **painting of St. Francis** in the ceiling to the left of the entrance.

Return over the bridge you crossed from the **Campo Santa Maria Nova** and immediately beyond, to the right, you will come to a graceful iron-railed bridge. This is one of those inimitable corners in which the city abounds and which gives Venice its painting-like quality. It is characterized by russet-brownish houses and ivy-covered terraces. To your left, red awnings overhang a tiny tree-lined garden. Behind you is a stone bridge and the Church of the Miracoli. Below in the canal lie barges filled with freight. A lavishly decorated gondola with a gay wedding party may slip by.

A few minutes walk over two bridges brings you to the **Church of SS. Giovanni and Paolo,** before which stands the famous **equestrian statue of Bartolommeo Colleoni** by Verrocchio, considered by some critics to be the greatest of its kind. The dynamic figure of the fifteenth-century *condottiere* on his battle charger, apparently about to prance from the pedestal, expresses arrogant defiance. As you stand at the base of the statue, look at the stone *trompe-l'oeil* bas-reliefs at the entrance to the **Ospedale Civile** next to the church. There's a striking view of the statue against the sky from the front of the Ospedale.

This is a good time to sit down at the café on the square, have a cooling drink, and study the details of the militant and arresting statue. Also notice in the square the sixteenth-century well, one of the finest in Venice.

Now stroll alongside the large Church of SS. Giovanni and Paolo, known as Venice's Pantheon because so many doges are buried there. Just beyond the end of the square, turn right along the Calle dell' Ospedaletto, then veer right into the shopping street of the Calle Lunga S. Maria Formosa to the large **Campo S. Maria Formosa.** The church and its campanile provide a dramatic backdrop for the lively and colorful **fruit-and-vegetable market** in the spacious square.

Walking down the Ruga Giuffa Santa Maria Formosa at the left end of the square, you are on your way to the little **Church of San Giorgio degli Schiavoni** to see the marvelous paintings by the late fifteenth-century Venetian painter Carpaccio. (This is one of those frequent occasions in Venice when you can easily take the wrong turning. But, even if you do, you may well come upon a fascinating scene that you probably could not find if you tried. The safest rule to follow when you are uncertain is to go with the crowd.) Walk to the end of the street, and, keeping to the left, cross a bridge to the Calle d. Preti, then another to reach the **Calle Lion,** which leads to the church. Stop for a moment on one of the bridges and watch how a city that moves by water carries on its daily life.

The **Carpaccio masterpieces** were painted in panels fixed to the walls of this small building, originally an institution for Dalmatian seamen. The series on Saint George is particularly famous; it is entertaining and colorful and with superb artistry presents the detailed life of the period.

After enjoying the Saint George and the other series Carpaccio painted here, return by the Calle Lion. Cross the next bridge, then turn left along the canal to the Fondamenta dell' Osmarin. At the Campo S. Provolo make a turn to the right and follow the Salizzada S. Provolo to the **Campo S. Filippo Giacomo.** This is one of those charming little squares crowded with open market stalls, selling fruit, clothing, and souvenirs, that make Venice so appealing and vivacious. Just before you reach the Piazza San Marco you will cross the canal behind the Ducal Palace, from which you have a fine view of the **Bridge of Sighs.**

A turn to the left will bring you to **Jeshurun,** the fine lace-and-embroidery establishment, where you can see the work in process.

Late in the afternoon is the perfect time to relax at **Quadri's,** one of the liveliest cafés in the piazza. Listen to the music as you watch the golden sunlight illuminating the brilliant multicolored mosaics over the **portals of St. Mark's** and bathing the entire Byzantine façade in its soft glow.

Along the Back Canals

This walk in Venice will take you through another section of the city to charming squares, past leaning campaniles, over the Rialto to Venice's fabulous markets, and finally to its outstanding gallery of modern art. And, of course, you will constantly be crossing the myriad of bridges over the network of canals—a never ceasing source of fascination, interest, and amusement.

Start at the **Piazza San Marco** and wander along the arcades to the far end—the side closest to the **Grand Canal.** Go under the archway and follow the **Salizzada S. Moise** past attractive shops until you find on your left the dramatic baroque façade of the **Church of S. Moise.** Cross the wide bridge and shortly you will see on the Calle 22 Marzo the sign of the **Antico Martini** (one of Venice's finest restaurants). Turn right along the Calle delle Veste for a few hundred yards and over a couple of bridges until you reach **La Fenice Theatre** on your left in a small square. La Fenice is one of the most exquisite opera houses in the world. It was the scene of the young composer Verdi's most spectacular triumphs. If the theatre is closed, ask at the excellent **restaurant (La Fenice)** next door where to find the caretaker so you can see the delightful interior, with its frescoes by Giovanni Domenico Tiepolo and its charming candelabra lighting. You will want to return to La Fenice, one of the best restaurants in Venice, to enjoy your favorite Italian specialties served under a picturesque grape arbor.

Return to the Calle 22 Marzo and continue to the **Campo S. Maria Zobenigo.** The façade of the seventeenth-century church gives the square a distinguished air. But, as so often in Venice, there is also a touch of simpler forms of beauty. Look at the colorful flowers on the roof of a nearby shop.

From here you follow the signs on the buildings pointing to the Accademia. They will lead you through another square and then, in a few moments, to the large **Campo Morosini.** Keep to the left to the Campo S. Vidal and pause just in front of the **Accademia Bridge.** On your right are two of the most charming small houses that you will see in Venice. Not only are the russet and gray houses themselves attractive, but they are set back in a lovely garden full of oleander bushes. Just opposite is the **Palazzo Cavalli,** now a bank. Go in for a minute for an interesting view of the Grand Canal.

Now return to the large square—the Campo Morosini—and straight ahead you will see the Gothic **Church of S. Stefano,** with its fourteenth-century façade. Notice the **Renaissance campanile** to the right of the church. It leans more than any other in Venice. Beyond the church you keep straight ahead through the Campo S. Angelo and enter the **Calle de la Mandola,** a narrow street filled with enticing market shops. Over the next bridge is the Campo Manin. Just a bit farther, when you reach the Campo San Luca, you turn left down one of Venice's many narrow alleys to the Grand Canal. As you wander along here you have a fine view of the Rialto Bridge. Perhaps this is a good moment to sit at an outdoor table facing the canal, have a refreshment, and gaze at the passing crowd.

Now you are about to plunge into one of the most exciting corners of Venice—the site of the main **food markets.** Cross the Rialto and on the other side you will find yourself in a street crowded with shoppers. Any weekday morning you will see people gathered before one open stall after another selecting from the fascinating displays of fruit, flowers, vegetables, meat, chicken, and every conceivable variety of Italian cheese. You will have lots of fun just wandering from one shop to the next, inspecting the food, checking over the prices, and watching the excitement—so typical of Italy—generated both by the shopkeepers and customers.

But the most colorful scene is yet to come. Turn right under the arcade, and after zigzagging for a hundred yards or so (in fact, go left, then right, and left again), you'll reach the city's **Fish Market.** On the way, more street merchants will be shouting, even singing, their wares. Under the building's high arches are countless open tables, each with a different kind of seafood. You will find mussels, snails, shellfish (*scampi*), octopus, squid, and all the local fish. It is certainly one of the most amusing and colorful scenes in Venice. As James Morris graphically describes it in his excellent book, *The World of Venice* (which, incidentally, you should read while you are there): ". . . a glorious, wet, colorful, high-smelling concourse of the sea . . . its stalls are lined deliciously with green fronds, damp and cool; and upon them are laid in a delicately-tinted, slobbering, writhing, glistening mass, the sea-creatures of the lagoon."

From the Fish Market, walk along the Grand Canal to the

end of the quay, cross the bridge, turn left into the Calle dei Botteri, and then right at the Calle dei Cristi. After about one hundred yards look for the sign pointing the way to the **Ca' Pesaro,** the **Galleria d'Arte Moderna.** Finally, you approach the palace which houses it along a small canal.

The home of the international gallery of modern art exhibits works by nineteenth- and twentieth-century artists of Europe and America (open weekdays, 9:00–1:00, 2:30–6:00; Sunday, 9:00–1:00). You also will find here many works that have been shown in the **Venice Bienalle exhibits.** If you are interested in contemporary painting and sculpture, you will find the exhibit at the Ca' Pesaro stimulating and perhaps a welcome change from the old masters shown in the other Venetian galleries.

When you leave the palace, why not return to San Marco on a *vaporetto* (Venice's **water bus**)? To reach the dock, cross the bridge outside the palace and turn right to the Grand Canal. On the other hand, perhaps it's time for lunch. If so, return to the markets and there you will find quite a good, little inexpensive restaurant, the **Peoceto Risorto,** in the **Calle della Donzella.**

Across the Grand Canal

Although the part of Venice that lies across the **Grand Canal** from San Marco is a lesser-known section, it is intensely interesting. In it is one of the city's great landmarks, the Church of Santa Maria della Salute; as well as the famous Accademia art gallery, the Palazzo Rezzonico; the Scuola San Rocco, noted for its wonderful paintings by Tintoretto; and the Church of the Frari with its great painting by Titian.

Start at **San Marco,** but instead of taking a vaporetto from the dock just below the gardens that face the lagoon, step aboard a *traghetto,* a **public gondola** which ferries Venetians across the Grand Canal from the **foot of the Calle Vallarezza.**

When you land, walk past the **Church of the Salute,** which dominates this end of the Grand Canal, to the **Dogana,** or

"Customs House," at the end of the quay. This seventeenth-century building is rather fine itself, and its position at the juncture of the two canals overlooking the lagoon is quite exceptional. From this point you have a marvelous view of the **Doges' Palace,** the **campanile,** the **harbor,** and the **Island of S. Giorgio** to the east.

Returning to the Church of the Salute, which Longhena designed in the baroque style during the seventeenth century, go up its stately steps and inside to see the paintings by Titian (especially the three in the ceiling, which are examples of his mature period), as well as a fine work of Tintoretto.

Walk along the side of the church and the old abbey opposite to the **Ponte della Salute.** After crossing this bridge you turn sharply left down a narrow alley, the Calle del Squiero, to the **Zattere,** the embankment along the Canal della Giudecca. This is an interesting stroll because ships so frequently pass here. It becomes even quite dramatic if you happen to be on the Zattere when one of the large **Italian liners** is arriving from New York, for its appearance seems to overwhelm the Venetian scene. As you walk along, you will notice Andrea Palladio's **Church of the Redentore** across the canal in **La Giudecca,** the old "Ghetto" of Venice. Continue to the baroque **Church of Santa Maria dei Gesuati,** where there is a fine altarpiece by Giovanni Battista Tiepolo.

At the **Fondamenta Nani,** just beyond the church, turn right along a small canal. If you walk down the near side of this canal to the last bridge you will get an unusual glimpse of one of the large palaces, with the Grand Canal beyond. A little farther on, turn right into the **Calle Gambara** to reach the **Accademia,** one of the leading art galleries in Italy and certainly the finest in Venice (open 9:00–1:00, 3:00–6:00). Naturally, most of its paintings are of the **Venetian school;** they range from the earliest period to the eighteenth century. The Bellinis, Carpaccio, Piero della Francesca, Giorgione, as well as Titian, Tintoretto, and Tiepolo, are some of the masters whose great works are on exhibit in this remarkable collection. Be especially sure to see such treasures as Giorgione's *Tempest* and Carpaccio's *Legend of St. Ursula,* but don't overlook Gentile Bellini's fascinating scenes of Venetian life about 1500.

From the Accademia turn left on the Calle Gambard and watch for blue signs marked **"Ca' Rezzonico."** These will lead you to the **Campo S. Barnaba.** Cross the next bridge and turn right along the **Fond. Alberti** to Longhena's majestic late-baroque palace, built in the seventeenth century (open 9:00–12:30, 2:30–6:30). Considered by many to be the most splendid patrician residence in Venice, Ca' Rezzonico contains an exceptional collection of eighteenth-century paintings, furniture, and tapestries. On the second floor is a series of colorful and amusing **frescoes by Giovanni Domenico Tiepolo,** moved from his own villa. The English poet Robert Browning died in his apartment in this palace. The extensive **exhibitions** of costumes, porcelain, and curios and an old chemist's shop will give you an idea of eighteenth-century Venetian life.

From the Ca' Rezzonico to the **Scuola San Rocco** you will wander through some of Venice's charming byways, over little bridges with views, down sleepy canals, through local markets, and past neighborhood cafés. This is an area where you encounter few tourists. But just when you feel you have been transplanted to the Venice of centuries ago, you will suddenly encounter a modern shop in an old building displaying the latest electrical appliances—a reminder that modern civilization is encroaching even in the most ancient parts of Venice. Still, Venice has been spared the noise of motor traffic, and it is this fact, perhaps more than any other, that enables you to sense in the byways and corners of this city the spirit of its old civilization.

Walk along the canal from the Ca' Rezzonico to the Calle de la Boteghe, then turn right to the Calle del Capeler and across a small square to the Calle Foscari. After crossing the bridge, the street widens. Go straight ahead, then down a narrow alley, Calle de Dona Onesta, then cross another bridge, turn left, then right in Calle Stretta Lipoli to the **Campo dei Frari.** (If these directions seem too complicated, simply ask a shopkeeper for Chiesa dei Frari.)

On reaching the back of the large **Church of the Frari,** go left a few yards to the entrance of the **Scuola San Rocco** (open 9:00–1:00, 3:30–6:30). This Renaissance building, formerly one of Venice's six great schools for the education of poor girls, contains a large number of **paintings by Tintoretto.** The great sixteenth-century artist's huge canvases on the walls and ceilings, depicting scenes from the Old and New Testaments, are one of the most extraordinarily dramatic and imaginative series of paintings in Venice.

Across from San Rocco is the tall brick campanile of the Church of the Frari. Go around to the front of the Gothic church, the largest in Venice, and inside you will find Titian's *Assumption* over the altar, a lovely Donatello of St. John the Baptist, and, in the sacristy, a fine triptych by Giovanni Bellini. Also stop in to look around the **cloisters** with their white stone arches and russet-colored walls.

When you leave the church, you should walk to the **Rialto,** less than fifteen minutes away. To do so, you simply follow the red signs marked "Rialto" which you will notice just after crossing the bridge on the other side of the square from the Frari. As is common in Venice, the route will wind in and out of narrow streets and alleys, but wherever it leads you, you will discover some new phase of this lively and fascinating city. The last part of the route before you turn right to the Rialto is along the **Ruga S. Giovanni.**

On reaching the Rialto, you can take a vaporetto back to San Marco. Or, if you wish to do some shopping, return to San Marco by the **Merceria,** Venice's leading shopping street, specializing in silks, leather goods, and glassware. To get to the Merceria from the Rialto, you turn right into the Via 2 Aprile and in a hundred yards or so, by the **Church of S. Salvatore,** you turn left. At the end of this crowded street, you will pass under the famous clock tower into the square of San Marco.

Now, having discovered the enchantment of Venice, it is

time to take a gondola and, as you slip through the narrow canals, ruminate over the ages-old fascination of this unique city, less changed since its days of glory than almost any other you will visit in Europe.

XIII VIENNA

BAROQUE BEAUTY ON THE DANUBE

In Alt Wien

Your first walk in **Vienna** should be in the oldest part, the **inner town.** Here, you will find winding streets and obscure little squares; you will peek into bewitching courtyards and old baroque palaces; and you will see the rooms where Mozart composed. Not only will you visit famous St. Stephen's Cathedral, which dominates the old quarter, but you will also explore less-known but still fascinating old churches. In this way you will absorb the spirit of *"Alt Wien."*

Start at the world-renowned Vienna **State Opera House,** the center of the city's cultural life. You can tour this magnificent and modern (reconstructed in 1955) opera house—a most worth-while experience—with a guide in July and August at 9:00, 10:00, 11:00, 1:00, 2:00, or 3:00. The Opera House is located on the **Opera Ring,** a section of the wide boulevard which circles the inner city on the site where its ancient walls once stood.

Saunter along **Kärtner Strasse,** Vienna's main shopping street. Join the crowd now gazing at the tempting windows, now browsing in and out of the stores. But in a moment or two you will leave this bustling scene of present-day Vienna and immerse yourself in the atmosphere of two hundred years ago by simply turning right off this up-to-date thoroughfare, a few hundred yards from the Opera into **Himmelpfort Gasse.** Down on the right at No. 8 you will come to the majestic **town palace of Prince Eugene of Savoy,** one of the greatest

235

SCHOTTEN GASSE

MÖLKERBASTEI

SCHOTTENHOF

DR. K. LUEGER RING

UNIVERSITY

TIEFER GRABEN

SA.

TEINFALT STR.

FREYUNG

FINISH 1

HERREN GASSE

AM HOF

CH.

NEW CITY HALL

BANK GASSE

BURG THEATER

START 2

DR. K. RENNER RING

VOLKSGARTEN

PARLAMENT

KOHLMARKT

CHURCH

G.

HELDEN PLATZ

SCHWEIZERHOF

CH.

NAT. HISTORY MUSEUM

BURG RING

NEUE HOFBURG

SPI.

ALBERTINA

BURGGARTEN

FINISH

ART MUSEUM

OPERN RING

STA.

C.

VIENNA

ROUTE 1 >– – –>
ROUTE 2 >••••••>

100 50 0   100   YARDS. 200

military leaders of the seventeenth century, who helped save Vienna from the Turks and later became Marlborough's ally against Louis XIV. This baroque building, now the **Ministry of Finance,** was designed at the end of the seventeenth century by the great architect Fischer von Erlach. Before entering, inspect its impressive façade. (Open Saturday and Sunday, 3:00–5:00. On other days you probably will be allowed to look around the entrance hall and stairway.) The ceiling painting over the stairs, the rococo plaster figures, and the ornamental balustrading will give you some idea of its elaborate interior.

Retrace your steps a few yards and turn right on the narrow, typically medieval Rauhenstein Gasse and again right on winding Ball Gasse until you reach little **Franziskaner Platz.** This old square with its little fountain faces the gray walls of the **Franciscan monastery and church,** built in a combination of Late Gothic and Renaissance styles. Notice the lovely baroque houses around the square before you turn left into the curving Singer Strasse. Just beyond Blut Gasse on the right you will come to the **Hall and Chapel of the Teutonic Knights** (open May 1–September 30: Tuesday, Wednesday, Saturday, 10:00–12:00, 3:00–5:00; Sunday, 10:00–12:00). The church, dating from the fourteenth century, contains flags and coats of arms of the Knights of the Holy Roman Empire. On the second floor you will find a most interesting collection of religious plate and armor. On leaving the church, turn right along Singer Strasse a short distance until you return to Kärtner Strasse.

Cross over to see the **Stock im Eisen,** a strange relic rather inconspicuously attached to the corner of a large building. During the fifteenth century, locksmiths, inspired by an old legend, used to drive a nail into this old stock or stump for good luck. Now, some five-hundred years later, you see the remains of the tree trunk covered with nails.

You are now facing **St. Stephen's Cathedral,** one of the great Gothic cathedrals of Europe and the spiritual center of Viennese life. Its slender spire against the sky is an inspiring sight. Before crossing the Stefans Platz to visit the cathedral, saunter along the **Graben,** one of the city's main shopping streets. Perhaps this is the moment to stop in for Viennese coffee *mit schlag* (with whipped cream) at one of the attractive **cafés** on the Graben.

Stefans Platz, in front of the cathedral, used to be the scene of the **Passion Play** centuries ago. When you enter the cathedral, notice the giant door dating from 1230 and built in the Romanesque style. After you have spent a while wandering about this historic shrine and looking at its artistic treasures, take the elevator to the bell tower. The **view over the city** from this high vantage point is quite exceptional. Here you will see the huge new bell, or **Pummerin.** The new Pummerin was made after World War II from metal taken from the famous old Pummerin, which had been fashioned from Turkish cannon captured at the liberation of Vienna, but which was damaged during the recent war.

At the back of the cathedral you will discover a little passage under an arch that leads into **Dom Gasse.** Here, at No. 5, is **Figarohaus,** Mozart's home from 1784 to 1787 (open weekdays except Monday, 9:00–4:00; Sunday, 9:00–1:00). You should climb the steps in this old building to visit the rooms where the great composer wrote *The Marriage of Figaro.* It's exciting to realize that Mozart played chamber music with Haydn and Beethoven in this apartment. The little museum has many Mozart souvenirs and manuscripts on display.

Retrace your steps through the archway, and on your right you will find another little passageway at No. 6 Stefans Platz, opposite the cathedral. This will lead into Wollzeile. Cross over and continue through a similar alley at No. 5. The alley is called a *Durchhaus,* and was standing in the days when Turkish cannon balls were raining on the city. You might like to stop in at a little *Weinstube* here for a refreshing glass of Heurige, the famous Viennese wine.

At the end of the passage you will come out in **Bäcker Strasse,** right in the heart of medieval Vienna. Look into the picturesque, ivy-covered courtyard at No. 7, then turn right and go to the square at the end of the street—Dr. Ignaz Seipel Platz. This is the **old university quarter;** the large building on the left in French classic style is known as the Aula, or Assembly Hall, of the old university. Go in the Jesuit church built in baroque style to see the ceiling paintings and fine marble columns. A few yards along Sonnenfels Gasse turn right into the narrow and winding **Schönlattern Gasse,** typical of old Vienna. At the **Basilisk House,** No. 7, there is a plaque commemorating the legend of the gallant apprentice who in 1212 killed the hideous basilisk, or monster, who supposedly lived in the well of this house and poisoned the neighborhood with its fumes.

Just beyond this house you encounter one of those surprising retreats in the middle of the city. On your left is the **Heiligenkreuzerhof,** the winter residence of the monks from the Holy Cross Monastery in the Vienna Woods. This large building facing an oblong courtyard has been in the possession of the abbey since 1206. You can still see the wine casks stacked in the right-hand corner. Leave by the archway at the far side, walk along the Grashof Gasse, then turn right on Köllnerhof Gasse, and go to the **Fleischmarkt.** One of the most ancient streets in Vienna, this street of the Butchers Guild—the center of the Greek and Armenian trading community—was called by its Roman name, the Via Carnorum, until about a century ago. Next to the **Greek Orthodox Church** is **Griechenbeisl,** a typical old Viennese restaurant with a reputation for the best beer in Vienna. It is said that the ballad "Ach, du lieber Augustin" was written here. The balconies over the tiny courtyard give it a delightful air. If you started this stroll in the morning, by now you will probably feel ready for lunch, so why not stop in either here or in the restaurant **Zur Linde,** a famous guest house founded in 1435 and a favorite of the composer Johannes Brahms. It is just around the corner from the Fleischmarkt on the **Rotenturm Strasse.** Here you can enjoy your favorite Viennese dish in a pleasant garden.

After a leisurely lunch, cross the Rotenturm Strasse and

continue along the Fleischmarkt up a flight of steps to **Juden Gasse.** This section, the old **Ghetto,** still retains some of its former character. Turn right and go about twenty-five yards to the **Ruprechtskirche,** built on the old walls above the **Danube Canal.** This is the city's oldest church and dates from the thirteenth century. Just to the right of the little square you will find the **synagogue** at No. 4 Seitenstetten Gasse.

Return along Juden Gasse, past the street merchants selling old clothing, into the **Hoher Markt.** This is the oldest section of the city and was the center of the medieval town. Underneath the present busy square are the ruins of the Roman settlement, **Vindobona.** You can visit these **excavations** at No. 2 Hoher Markt. (Open Tuesday, Thursday, Saturday, Sunday, 9:00–1:00; Wednesday, Friday, 3:00–7:00). At one end of the square you will notice a colorful clock, the **Ankeruhr.** Historical figures associated with Vienna parade across its face when the noon hour strikes.

Leaving the Hoher Markt at the far end, turn right into **Marcus Aurelius Strasse** (the great Roman emperor died in Vienna), and then left along Salvator Gasse. On your left, at No. 5, is the Early Renaissance portal of the old Town Hall Chapel. Just a few yards farther along, you will come to the lovely fourteenth-century **Maria am Gestade,** the Church of St. Mary, which overlooks the Danube Canal. As it was so close to the river, fishermen and boatmen used to worship here during the Middle Ages. To get a good view of the church and its high tower, it's worth while descending some of the steps below to the place where in the earlier days boats were moored.

Return past the church a block to **Stoss im Himmel Gasse** (literally translated "thrust in Heaven Lane," the name is associated with a Viennese legend) on your right to **No. 3,** a beautiful baroque house. About fifty yards farther on the left on Wipplinger Strasse the **old City Hall** faces the former Bohemian chancellery, now the **Law Courts,** a building also designed by Fischer von Erlach, at the beginning of the eighteenth century. Cross the street and walk along the short Fütter Gasse to Juden Platz. On the opposite side of this square wander down the curving Pariser Gasse into the **Schulhof,** a little square where you will find at No. 2 Vienna's **Clock Museum** (open Tuesday, Wednesday, Saturday, 10:00; Tuesday, Saturday, 3:00), where thousands of clocks made during the past eight-hundred years are on display.

You are now in one of the most enchanting corners of Vienna. Just ahead is the rounded back of the **Church of the Nine Choirs of Angels.** A tiny watch shop has been built right in between the buttresses. Here one can sense the characteristics of old Vienna: the juncture of four streets so narrow only one car can go down them, the cobblestone paving, an old house (the **Pfarhof**) dating from about 1600 on the corner of **Steindl Gasse,** and the high walls of the church. Pause for a few minutes, look in at the watch shop, and just stroll around this secluded spot. Then walk along Seitzer Gasse beyond the church and turn right on Bogner Gasse to **Am Hof,** a wide square which was the site of medieval tournaments. As you walk around the square, you will find fine baroque façades at No. 7 and No. 12. No. 10, a good example of an eighteenth-century building, used to be Vienna's arsenal. A Turkish cannon ball, a souvenir of Vienna's critical years, is lodged over the doorway of No. 11.

Leaving the square by the Heidenschuss, directly across from Bogner Gasse, you come into the Freyung, an area so named because fugitives could find sanctuary here. No. 4 on the left is the handsome late-baroque **Kinsky Palace.** Just across stands the massive **Schottenhof.** Its tree-shaded courtyard, which you enter by **Schotten Gasse,** is another good place for some refreshment. The first monks in the twelfth century were Scottish (hence the name) and Irish, but their addiction to sports and dances, in addition to their habit of selling religious objects for profit, led to their replacement in the fifteenth century by the more suitable German Benedictines. On the opposite side of this street, at No. 3, you can walk through a small courtyard to visit the deep cellars of the **Abbey of Melk.**

Proceed a few yards farther on the Schotten Gasse, turn left, and climb the steps to the Mölkerbastei, built on the old fortifications. On the corner is a delightful rococo house known as the **"Drei Maderlhaus"** (named for the three girls from Schubert's *Lilac Time*). Around the corner, to the right, at **No. 8** on the **Mölkerbastei,** is the lovely house where Beethoven lived on the fourth floor. (Open weekdays except Monday, 9:00–4:00; Sunday, 9:00–3:00.) At the foot of the ramp turn right a few yards to the Oppolzer Gasse, which will bring you out on the **Ring**—the end of this walk through old Vienna. From here you can take a streetcar or taxi back to the Opera.

The Grandeur of Imperial Days

The second walk in Vienna includes many of the city's sights that are most interesting from a historical and artistic point of view. The places you will visit are largely associated with the Hapsburgs, and the Holy Roman and Austro-Hungarian Empires, which they ruled successively until the end of World War I.

Start at the **Burgtheater,** or national theatre, on the **Ring** just opposite Vienna's large **City Hall,** built in the Gothic style during the nineteenth century. Just across from the theater, on the same side of the Ring, you enter the beautifully landscaped **Volksgarten,** a park laid out on the site of the old fortifications. In summer the formal rose garden and semicircular rose beds throughout the garden are particularly attractive. Just to your right, across the Ring, you will see the **Austrian Parliament** building, designed in the classic style nearly one hundred years ago. Under the trees in the park are two delightful outdoor **cafés,** providing an enjoyable spot for a drink or a light lunch.

When you leave the Volksgarten you will face a large open square, the **Helden Platz.** Directly beyond stands the massive

Neue Hofburg, the newer section (late nineteenth century) of the **Imperial Palace.** The great sprawling block of buildings to the left is the **Alte Hofburg,** the main part of the Hapsburgs' royal residence. The Hofburg is quite a mixture of styles and shapes, because throughout nearly five hundred years of the Hapsburg reign in Vienna there were frequent alterations, reconstructions and extensions.

Go through the entrance on the left of the Helden Platz, into the great central court. There are many parts of the palace you can visit, especially the state rooms, including the **apartments of the Emperor Franz Joseph I.** (Open weekdays, 9:00–4:00; Sunday, 9:00–1:00.) But the most interesting section is the **Schatzkammer,** the collection of religious and lay treasures which you reach by entering the oldest section of the palace, the Schweizerhof, which dates from the thirteenth century (open Monday, Wednesday, Saturday, 9:30–3:00; Tuesday, 2:00–7:00; Sunday, 9:00–1:00; closed Friday). Here you will be fascinated to find the **Hapsburg crown jewels,** especially the crown of the Holy Roman Empire, set with precious stones. It is believed to be nearly a thousand years old. You will be excited to see **Charlemagne's own prayer book,** as well as ancient swords, orbs, and scepters of the Holy Roman Empire and the Hapsburg dynasty. The crown jewels, coronation garments, vestments, and insignia comprise an unusual display.

Right nearby is the entrance to the **Burgkapelle,** or Imperial Chapel, where the noted **Viennese Choir Boys** sing on Sunday morning at 9:30 Mass as their predecessors, including such great musicians as Haydn, Mozart, and Schubert, have done for 450 years.

Returning to the central courtyard, take the passage on your right to Michaeler Platz. Just across the small square is the **Michaelerkirche,** one of Vienna's oldest churches, a combination of Romanesque and Gothic architecture.

From the church turn left along Reitschul Gasse, and in a moment, on the right, you reach the famous winter riding school and its majestic riding hall. No visitor to Vienna should miss the magnificent spectacle of the **Spanish Court Riding School's** white Lipizza stallions being put through their paces by their trainers with balletlike precision, just as has been done for nearly three hundred years. Even today the riders never begin a performance without saluting the Royal Box with its picture of Emperor Charles VI—an illustration of the Austrians' ingrained respect for the imperial tradition. (The school is closed during July and August. During the rest of the year inquire for tickets from the concierge of your hotel.) Across the street from the school is the Stallburg, the stables.

Walk under a passageway on this street and you will come into the **Josefs Platz,** an impressive baroque square. The **National Library,** which possesses an outstanding collection of books, maps, and manuscripts, occupies one side of the square. Just a few steps beyond the square on Augustiner Strasse you will find on your right the noble **Augustinerkirche** where Napoleon was married to Marie Louise in 1810.

At the end of the street, on your right, is one of Vienna's finest art collections, the **Albertina,** including a remarkable group of **drawings by Albrecht Dürer.** (Open Monday, Tuesday, Thursday, 10:00–2:00; Wednesday, Friday, 10:00–6:00; Saturday, 10:00–1:00.) The **Music Collection** of the National Library is also here.

Now turn left, on the other side of a small square, along Tegetthoff Strasse to visit the **Imperial Crypt,** the burial place of the Hapsburgs beneath the Kapuzinerkirche. It's an extraordinary experience to descend into the vaults and find lead or copper coffins of 141 Hapsburgs all laid out in rows. At the end is the decorative double sarcophagus of Empress Maria Theresa and her consort. (Open, 10:00–12:00.)

Retrace your steps along Tegetthoff Strasse to the **Opera House.** This may be just the moment to drop in at **Sacher's,** Vienna's most famous hotel, and try the delicious Sachertorte at one of the outdoor tables. After leaving Sacher's, walk a block past the front of the **Opera** to the **Ring.** Now go down the stairs to see how excellently, in recent years, the Viennese have developed pedestrian underpasses below major traffic centers. You will find snack bars and shops attractively planned with many stairs and escalators leading to the different streets and bus and train stops.

There is one art collection which you must visit—at the **Museum of Fine Arts**—undoubtedly one of the finest in Europe and the fourth largest anywhere (open weekdays except Monday, 10:00–3:00; Sunday, 9:00–1:00). Just walk right, along the Opern Ring, for four blocks. On your right you pass the attractively landscaped **Burggarten,** in case you feel like strolling through another of Vienna's parks. When you reach the museum on the left, go to the first floor to see the paintings. In the extensive collection are outstanding examples of such **Italian masters** as Raphael, Giorgione, Titian, and Tintoretto, great Dutch artists like Rembrandt, leading **Flemish painters** like Van der Weyden and Pieter Breughel, and the **Spanish school** including Velasquez. It's fitting to end your walks through this city, renowned for its culture, among such superb works of art.

XIV MUNICH

ART, MUSIC AND BEER
Within the Sound of the Glockenspiel

Munich, more than any other German city, will impress you as one of Europe's leading centers of art and culture, not to mention gaiety. As you walk through this city of more than a million people, you will be struck by its beautifully laid out, spacious streets and squares, its attractively landscaped parks and gardens, and its classic atmosphere. Despite tremendous war destruction and subsequent rebuilding, Munich has preserved its prewar old-world elegance and kept its appeal for those who love painting, music, and learning. Its cultural reputation is maintained by its renowned **university** with thirty thousand students and its magnificent **art galleries** and **museums.** And, on the lighter side, its open-air **beer gardens** are unmatched in their ability to spread a sense of relaxation and good fellowship, especially on warm summer evenings.

Your first walk in Munich should be in the **older section.** Start in the morning at **Max-Josephs-Platz** and walk past the **National Theater,** the home of the **Bavarian State Opera,** and a block or so along Maximilian Strasse until you reach Am Kosttor on the right. Turn down here about a hundred yards and you will come to a little square known as the **Platzl.** On your left is the typically nineteenth-century building of the famous **Hofbrauhaus** or court brewery, owned by the State of Bavaria. You will want to return here in the evening for a stein or two of *helles* or *dunkels* either in the great banquet hall upstairs, where you will be entertained by a lively brass band, or in the more plebeian beer hall on the ground floor. Four million people visit the Hofbrau every year and con-

247

MUNICH

ROUTE 1 »----»
ROUTE 2 »••••»

100 50 0   100   200 YARDS 300

sume about thirty-six thousand pints a day of the famous beer.

Just across the street is the **Platzl Inn.** This is a lively restaurant featuring typical Bavarian singing and dancing— a gay spot for an evening's entertainment. Continue along Orlando Strasse past the Hofbrauhaus one block to Lederer Strasse, where you turn right, cross Sparkassen Strasse, and go through an archway. Now wander into the **Alter Hof,** the ancient residence of the Dukes of Bavaria, which dates from the thirteenth century. Its old-fashioned courtyard, with the only surviving towered Gothic building, still retains its historic atmosphere.

From the Alter Hof saunter along **Burg Strasse,** one of Munich's most ancient streets. In a moment you will come to Munich's **oldest house** at **No. 5.** Inside the Gothic entrance you will find the **Weinstadl,** a charming wine inn, where huge wine casks add color to the tavern's original furnishings. Another interesting house is **No. 11,** where the great rococo architect François de Cuvilliès lived. Burg Strasse, probably more than any street you will see in Munich, conveys the flavor of the city's early history.

Turn right at the end into **Marienplatz,** the center of Munich and a busy square, in front of the new (1865) City Hall. If you started your stroll in the morning, you should reach here in time to see the entertaining performance of the **musical clock,** a great Munich attraction, which children particularly find a great treat. At 11:00, after the hour strikes, colorful figures appear: knights jousting as in a tournament. and dancers performing to melodious tunes. Every day, crowds of people congregate in the square to enjoy this gay spectacle.

From this point stroll beyond the square into **Kaufinger Strasse,** one of Munich's most popular shopping streets. At the second block turn right a few yards to get to the **Frauenkirche,** the city's most famous and popular church, built in the Late Gothic style and nearly five hundred years old. The massive twin brick steeples (328 feet high) have been for centuries a Munich landmark, just as they were a symbol of the wealth of the burghers who built them in the fifteenth century. Although the church's interior seems somewhat bare today as the result of heavy war damage, you will be impressed by the vastness of the nave and the height of the roof. An elevator in the south tower will carry you to the top, where in clear weather you can see the Alps.

Returning to Kaufinger Strasse, walk along a little farther to **St. Michael's Church,** an excellent example of German Renaissance architecture and a symbol of the influence of the Jesuits in the late sixteenth century. Cross the street and do a bit of window-shopping on your way back to Marien Platz. Then take a sharp right in the Rosen Strasse, continue in the narrow Pettenbeck Strasse, and make a left turn into Rosental Strasse. This will bring you into the Victualien-markt or **Food Market**—a most interesting and colorful sight. Here you will find dozens of open stalls displaying all kinds of provisions. In one corner of the square is the fish market, with live fish swimming about in huge tanks of water. Prices for trout, eels, etc., are chalked up on a blackboard. Not far away is the vegetable section ("Munich's quality vegetables fresh daily.") where potatoes are separated according to size and quality. Across the road you will find the egg and fruit markets. Each stand is fascinating not only for the variety of products but for the attractive manner in which they are presented for sale. There is a real country touch in the market, and indeed many of the vendors are farmers. Nearby you will find a great variety of flowers, and just opposite there are stands selling all kinds of dried fruits, cheese, nuts, and bottled jams. Great tubs are full of different sorts of pickles and raw sauerkraut. At **Münchener Bratwurstglöckel** you can try a weisswurst, a favorite sausage among Müncheners.

Just a block away you will see the cupola of **Peterskirche,** the oldest parish church, which dates from the end of the twelfth century. A few steps beyond the church will bring you back to Marien Platz. Now turn right and on the far left side of the square you will see the surviving part of the Old Town Hall, the **Alte Rathaus.** The building stands astride the main street. Traffic moves from Marien Platz to the Tal under vaulted archways. Walk down the Tal and in a block or two turn around for a fine view of the towers of the Frauenkirche. Shortly you will come to the **Isartor,** the only old gate to the city whose main towers are still standing. Although built in 1314, it was renovated and a fresco was added early in the nineteenth century.

You continue through the **Isar Platz** and along Zweibrucken Strasse to the **Isar River.** Cross the first bridge and on your right is the **Deutsches Museum,** one of the greatest scientific museums in the world, specializing in the development of technology in industry. For the layman the great attraction of this museum is the remarkable way in which the exhibits demonstrate the operations of modern industry. For example, you visit a coal mine perfectly reproduced in life size. Not far away you stand on the bridge of a ship facing a **scene in Hamburg Harbor.** Scale models of power stations and steel mills show exactly how they function. Many of the experimental models can be operated by pushing a button. In addition, the museum contains one of the greatest collections anywhere of original scientific apparati and technical machinery. No visitor to Munich should fail to spend a considerable time in the Deutsches Museum, and for children it is an eye-opening educational experience. (Open 9:00–5:00.)

From the Alte Pinakotek to the English Garden

The second walk through Munich covers mainly the newer and more spacious section of the city, whose planning was largely influenced by King Ludwig I of Bavaria (1825–1848), a devotee of the classic tradition. As you walk around this well-laid-out part of Munich, you will encounter a world-famous art gallery, the Alte Pinakotek, as well as the delightful English garden.

Begin at the **Lenbach Platz,** one of Munich's most attractive squares. At the far end, the decorative **Wittlesbach Fountain** (named for one of **Bavaria's** oldest ruling families), with its terraced design, creates a splendid effect. The adjoining square, **Maximilians Platz,** has such a quiet appealing air, with its chestnut trees and gardens, that you should walk through it before turning left on Max Joseph Strasse to **Karolinen Platz.** The tall obelisk in the center is a memorial to the Bavarian soldiers who died in the Russian campaign of 1812. **Amerika Haus,** the office of the U.S. Information Agency, including a large library, stands on the left.

A block ahead along **Brienner Strasse** you come into the broad **Konigs Platz,** a monument to King Ludwig the First's passion for Hellenistic art. Here he tried to recreate the spirit of the Grecian period by constructing a neoclassic marble gateway based on the **Propylaea** in Athens. The **Glyptothek,** also in the Greek style, is on your right. Go past the Propylaea and on the corner of Luisen Strasse, on your right, you will come to the lovely **Villa Lenbach,** originally the home of the nineteenth-century German painter Franz von Lenbach. Now it houses the excellent **Municipal Modern Art Gallery** (open weekdays, 9:00–4:00). The **Kandinsky collection** is outstanding, but you should also look around the other rooms in this rather intimate gallery. Outside the ocher-colored building there is an attractive garden with statuary and a fountain.

As you leave the Villa Lenbach, turn left on Luisen Strasse, walk one block and then turn right on Gabelsberger Strasse pass the **Technische Hochschule,** Munich's technical university, to the **Alte Pinakotek** (open daily, 9:00–4:30; Tuesday and Thursday, until 8:00). It is set back from the street facing a large lawn.

This magnificent **art collection,** the finest in Munich, is another of the great European galleries. It comprises all the leading schools of European art but is particularly distinguished for its masterpieces by Raphael, Titian, Dürer, Rembrandt, and Rubens. If you are an art lover, you will want to spend considerable time here, either now or later, viewing these wonderful paintings.

On leaving the Alte Pinakotek, take Barer Strasse for one block to return to Brienner Strasse at Karolinen Platz.

As you saunter along this street, you will pass many attractive and fashionable shops. In two blocks you will come to an open square, the end of Maximilians Platz. Now cross Brienner Strasse and take the street on the right that leads to Salvator Platz. On the other side of this small square you will be in **Kardinal Faulhaber Strasse.** Stop at No. 7 to view the ornate façade of the **Archbishop's residence,** one of the most elegant private houses still standing in the city.

Next, retrace your steps a few yards and make your way through the arcades of one of Munich's typical postwar buildings to Theatiner Strasse. The use of arcades and passageways with stores on the inside as well as on the street is a hallmark of the architectural design of much of the city's recent business and shopping construction.

On **Theatiner Strasse** there are many smart shops and delightful cafés. On your left in the next block toward Brienner Strasse you will come to the grand **Theatinerkirche,** the most imposing baroque church in the city. This huge yellow seventeenth-century edifice with the twin towers set the style for many of the baroque churches throughout Bavaria. Its white rococo interior, splendid ornamentation, and fine paintings create an impressive effect. When you stand in front of the church, you will see the **Feldherrnhalle** just to the right facing the large **Odeons Platz.** This is another creation of King Ludwig I and is copied from the Loggia dei Lanzi in Florence.

Now cross the square and enter the **Residenz,** before the war the most luxurious group of buildings in Munich. It used to be the residence of the Dukes (later Kings) of Bavaria. Again, Ludwig I was responsible for much of this lavish palace, largely destroyed by air attacks during the war. Some rooms have been restored and you can see many of the movable objects which were saved. Perhaps the most interesting museum is the **Treasure Room,** or Schatzkammer, which you enter from Max-Josephs-Platz. (Open weekdays, 9:00–5:00; Friday, 8:00–10:00; Sunday, 10:00–1:00.) Here is an unusual **collection of jewelry and silver,** including royal crowns, **gold work** from Charlemagne's period, Late Gothic and Early Renaissance **precious stones,** and a lovely **statuette of Saint George.**

The other exceptional building in the Residenz is the exquisitely restored **Cuvilliès Theater** (open 2:00–5:00; Sunday, 10:00–5:00).

Return to Residenz Strasse and at No. 1 you will find the theatre's entrance, off a large oblong interior courtyard whose entire façade has been rebuilt in a baroque design. The theatre's interior is one of the most enchanting examples of elaborate rococo style to be seen anywhere.

From the Residenz stroll along Odeons Platz for a hundred yards and turn right opposite Brienner Strasse into the pleasant **Hofgarten.** There are several cafés here where you can enjoy a drink by the flower gardens. While crossing to the far end of the Hofgarten, you should turn around for an interesting view of the towers of the Theatinerkirche. The large bombed-out building ahead of you, a block or so away, is the former **Army Museum.** When you emerge from the gardens, walk a short distance and make a half right onto Prinzregenten Strasse. Just across this broad street you will see the **Haus Der Kunst,** or House of Art. The part of the building before you contains the permanent collection of the former **Neue Pinakotek;** at the far end there are temporary exhibits of modern art and sculpture.

Just beyond the House of Art you can enter the **English Garden,** one of the most attractive and natural parks in any European city. The middle path along the canal is one of the pleasantest. The combination of fine trees, meandering walks, open meadows, waterfalls, and a lake, as well as a Chinese pagoda, makes this extensive park unusually appealing. At the **Chinese pagoda** you will find a **café and restaurant.** This park is just the place to wander or simply sit in a pleasant nook at the end of your day's walk.

XV GENEVA

THE OLD TOWN

Vistas and Courtyards

Geneva has been one of the crossroads of the world ever since Julius Caesar passed through it during his campaign against the Gauls in B.C. 58. Today, the city maintains this status, drawing diplomats to the **UN** and **ILO,** as well as international businessmen and just ordinary tourists. For the visitor, Geneva has a special allure—it occupies a beautiful position at the end of Lake Geneva, it has a truly cosmopolitan air, and it has the attraction of a French-speaking community. On clear days, snow-covered **Mont Blanc** rises majestically in the distance, providing an exciting sight from the lake-front promenade.

Walking is by far the best way to see Geneva. It's not a large place; the population only about 165,000. As you walk about the city, you sense its intimacy and small-town atmosphere. The **main shopping district** comprises only a few blocks on both sides of the river. The **promenade and parks** along the lake front are most inviting. In particular, the small, **old town** on the heights—the most appealing part of Geneva —just cannot be seen properly except on foot.

This is the section to visit first, so let us start in the morning at the **Place St. Gervais** and cross the bridge over the **Rhone,** which divides the city, to the island in the middle. It is believed that this is the site of the first bridge over the Rhone, built even before the time of Caesar. There used to be a thirteenth-century castle here (later a prison), but all that remains is the tower with the clock—the **Tour de l'Ile.** This is a historic spot for the liberty-loving Swiss, because here in

257

GENEVA
THE OLD TOWN

ROUTE - - - →

100 50 0 100 YARDS 200

LAKE
GENEVA

WATER JET

QUAI GUS. ADOR

FINISH

PONT DU MONT BLANC

PONT DES BERGUES

QUAI DU RHONE

QUAI DES BERGUES

RUE GRAND

RUE CONFÉD.

RUE DE LA CORRATERIE

RUE CITÉ

START

QUAI

PLACE NEUVE

RUE CALVIN

RUE GRAND

RUE DES GRANGES

CATHEDRAL

PL. BOURG DE FOUR

RUE L'HOT. DE VILLE

PROMENADE DE TREILLE

PROMENADE DES BASTIONS

REF. MONUMENT

UNIV.

ART & HISTORY MUSEUM

N

1519 Philibert Berthelier was beheaded for his defense of freedom. Wander around the little island with its attractive houses. On Wednesday and Saturday mornings there is a gay street market dealing in fruit, vegetables, and cheese along the Quai des Moulins.

Cross to the other side of the stream, turn right into the Place Bel Air and at its far side take the wide **Rue de la Corraterie.** After a few blocks along this busy thoroughfare you will reach the **Place Neuve,** Geneva's finest square. The **Musée Rath** on your right holds temporary art exhibits. Just beyond it is the **Grand Theatre,** a smaller edition of the Paris Opera.

On the opposite side of the square you come into a pleasant park with broad walks. Here, on your left, is the impressive **Reformation Monument,** separated from the gardens by a small moat and a fountain. The monument is actually built into the old wall which the Reformers under John Calvin constructed as a defense of the city. The one-hundred-yard-long memorial, dedicated in 1917, commemorates the great leaders of the Reformation. Larger-than-life statues of the four great Reformers, including Calvin and Knox, occupy the center of the monument. **Bas-reliefs** show the major events in this religious revolution that occurred in different countries. Americans will be interested in the **inscription from the Mayflower Compact,** carved in stone, and the scene depicting the **Pilgrim Fathers,** whose leader is clasping the Geneva Bible.

The buildings of the **University of Geneva** stand back in the park on the opposite side from the Reformation Monument.

Leave the gardens at the gate beyond the monument and turn left on **Rue St. Leger.** After passing below an archway, you will start to climb the hill to the old town. On either side of the winding street you will pass interesting old houses. On the left is an attractive **bookshop,** appropriately called "La Joie de Lire." And don't miss the decorative doorway at **No. 35** opposite. You are now coming into the lower level of the **Place du Bourg de Four,** Geneva's most enchanting square. There is a tiny shaded garden just ahead below the wall that supports the upper part of the square. Many interesting shops line the street. Above them you will notice the signs of old inns that formerly stood here. The street veers to the left, circling the park, and leads you into the main square, with its eighteenth-century fountain. Pause for a few minutes and just look around. Five streets meet in this unspoiled **center of old Geneva,** which still preserves so much of the spirit of an earlier age. This was a crossroads in Roman days. The gray buildings, with their gables, uneven roofs, and chimney pots, will remind you of a corner of Paris. The antique shops and art galleries, many bursting from open cellars under acacia trees, add a Bohemian flavor to the spot. Why not stop at the delightfully gay café **La Clemence** on the corner facing the square and watch the life go by? There's an attractive clock on the wall just overhead, and it may indicate that it is late morning, just the time for an apéritif at an outdoor table behind the grillwork. You will probably finds lots of students, artists, and local residents here, basking in the sun. Overhead huge elms shade a side of the square. Before you leave this spot, teeming with local color, browse about the shops a bit. The bakery, pharmacy, hairdresser, and butcher all contribute to the animated scene.

From the square turn right into the Rue des Chaudronniers. In a block or so you will come to a large building on your right, the **Musée d'Art et d'Histoire** (open daily except Monday, 10:00–12:00, 2:00–6:00). Although the gallery includes ancient sculpture and decorative arts, you should concentrate on its painting collection on the first floor to see a good selection of impressionists, as well as works by Corot and artists of the Italian and Dutch schools.

Return to the Place du Bourg de Four and on the far side take the **Rue de l'Hôtel de Ville.** In a few yards turn right into the **Rue de la Taconnerie.** You will pass some attractive houses (note the heads in relief over the store at **No. 6**) before reaching the lovely little **Place de la Taconnerie** in the shade of a huge elm. At the left of the square, up a few steps, you will find a **statue of Jeremiah.**

The **Cathedral of St. Peter,** which dominates the square, was built between the tenth and thirteenth centuries on the site of a **Roman temple** and became a **Protestant church** in 1536 (open 9:00–12:00, 1:30–6:00). The interior is rather simple, but one interesting relic is the chair said to have been used by John Calvin. If you feel so inclined, you can climb to the top of the tower for a wonderful panorama of Geneva, the lake, and the Alps. In any case, be sure to walk behind the cathedral to a terrace where you have quite a good view over the city. Opposite the front of the cathedral and in the small square to the right there are some beautiful **patrician houses.** The large one with masks on the façade was built in the style of Louis XV by one of the architects responsible for Versailles. Follow the short Rue St. Pierre away from the cathedral, then turn right at a little fountain, one of the oldest in Geneva and decorated with geranium pots, and immediately left into the **Rue Calvin.** There are several stately houses in this block—one of the most noted is **No. 9** where Madame de Staël lived. **Calvin's house** at **No. 13** was rebuilt early in the eighteenth century. Just pull open its wooden door to see the typical courtyard and façade of this fine building.

Now return to the entrance of the Rue Calvin and turn right on **Rue du Puits St. Pierre.** On your right, at No. 6, you pass the fifteenth-century **Maison Tavel** with its circular tower. Just ahead at the next corner stands the ancient **Arsenal** with a few old cannon. It is the arcaded building with a wooden beam roof directly opposite Geneva's **Hôtel de Ville,** or Town Hall. Aside from a delightful courtyard, the most interesting feature of the Town Hall is the sixteenth-century inclined ramp with stone vaulting that leads to the upper floors. You can ask the doorkeeper to show you the **Alabama Room** where the first Red Cross convention was signed in 1864.

Continue beyond the Town Hall along the Rue Henri Fazy past the Tour Baudet—dating from 1455, where the **Geneva Council of State** meets—to the **Promenade de la Treille,** the oldest terrace in Geneva. This broad terrace, shaded by chestnut trees, commands a fine view of the mountains. Retrace your steps a few yards and turn left into the **Rue des Granges** for a glance at several of the magnificent mansions which look over the Promenade de la Treille and the Place Neuve below. At No. 10 go through the alley and on to the terrace above the old city wall. The courtyard at No. 6 is also quite impressive.

Take the Rue du Cheval Blanc from the Rue des Granges into the **Grand Rue,** probably the finest of these old streets. Jean Jacques Rousseau was born on June 28, 1712, at **No. 40,** which has since been rebuilt. You will get an idea of the hidden attractions of these houses if you enter No. 29–31 and go along the passage to an iron grilled gate, and then climb a few steps. Through a window you see a most picturesque courtyard in front of an ivy-covered Spanish-style house with a tile roof and balcony. The wooden stairs from the cobblestoned court, the gay flower boxes in the windows, and the statues in the flower beds make an unusually striking scene. At No. 11, the **house of the French Resident,** Napoleon gave audiences when passing through the city in 1800.

If you should be here about lunchtime, **Au Plat d'Argent,** at No. 4 Grand Rue, is an excellent moderately priced restaurant with an atmosphere in keeping with the old town you have been visiting. In the adjoining square, the **Place du Grand Mézel,** there is a charming fountain. From here continue down the hill into the Rue de la Cité, then turn right into the busy Rue de la Confédération. Just beyond the large church in the **Place de la Fusterie** you should turn left into an arcade, a lively **shopping center** with an enticing food shop and other tempting stores. Geneva's most up-to-date café and restaurant, **Movenpick,** is in the Place de la Fusterie. It's an excellent place to enjoy anything from a patisserie or salad plate to a full-course meal at moderate prices. After leaving Movenpick, you turn right along the **Rue du Rhône,** a main shopping street. In a couple of blocks you will reach another of Geneva's old towers, in the **Place du Molard.** Walk a short block to the **Grand Quai** along the lake and cross over to the gardens. Here is Geneva's decorative **floral clock.** As you end your stroll along the lake front in this delightful park, you will see the **Jet d'Eau,** which from May to September hurls a stream of water nearly five-hundred feet into the air. It is reputedly the world's highest fountain—a dramatic finish to this walk in old Geneva.

THE LAKE SHORE

To the UN

The European headquarters of the **United Nations** is one of the principal sights in Geneva and well worth visiting. One way to get there is a delightful walk, mostly through parks along the lake, from the center of town, which should not take much more than an hour and a half.

If you take this walk to the UN immediately following the first walk, which ends at the lake-front promenade, you will enjoy crossing in one of the little launches that goes from the nearby quay to **Paquis.** After landing, turn right along the broad walk along the **Quai du Mont Blanc.** On a clear day you have a magnificent view, through a soft bluish haze, of snow-covered Mont Blanc about one-hundred miles away. Excursion boats leave the wharf for tours along the lake.

This stroll along the flower-bordered promenade, with the lake on your right, the hills of **Cologny** beyond, and the **Alps** in the distance, is probably the most dramatic in Geneva. The sailboats and small craft in the anchorage on the lake shore add a gay touch.

At the end of the Quai du Mont Blanc you veer to the left into the **Quai Woodrow Wilson** and soon pass the original building of the **League of Nations,** where a tablet commemorates President Wilson.

In a few minutes you will come to the large and beautifully kept park that runs along the lake front. The **Perle du Lac** restaurant, a short distance farther on, is one of Geneva's

FINISH

UNITED
NATIONS

ILO

AVENUE DE LA PAIX

AVENUE DE FRANCE

REST.

LAKE

GENEVA

N

QUAI W. WILSON

PALAIS
WILSON

GENEVA
THE LAKE SHORE

ROUTE — – – –

100 50 0   100   200 YARDS

START

QUAI DU MONT BLANC

best. It occupies a superb position overlooking the water to distant Mont Blanc. Keep on the path that skirts the lake and, after you pass a promontory from where you have a fine view, you will come to the building of the **International Labor Office** (open 9:00–12:00, 2:15–5:30, except Sundays in winter).

Cross the square in front of the ILO into the interestingly landscaped **Botanical Gardens,** and then take the **Avenue de la Paix** to the entrance of the UN building (open weekdays, 9:30–11:30, 2:30–5:30, until 4:30 on Saturday; Sunday, 10:30–11:30, 2:30–4:30). It is well worth while to take the guided tour through this fine building, constructed in 1937 for the League of Nations, to see, in particular, the impressive **Political Council Room,** where major international conferences are held. The **terrace and gardens** overlooking the lake are especially attractive. Stroll down to the **bronze globe** decorated with the Signs of the Zodiac, an artistic **memorial to Woodrow Wilson.**

You have now experienced the scope of Geneva—a scope which spans the centuries and encompasses the varying atmospheres of the old town on the heights and the UN on the lake, the pulpit of John Calvin and the international forum inspired by Woodrow Wilson.

XVI ATHENS

RUINS OF ANCIENT GREECE

To the Acropolis

Though **Athens** is a sprawling modern metropolis of almost two million people, covering a huge area, the important ruins of ancient Athens, the cultural source of Western civilization, are close together and can be visited in a single walk. This stroll, then, will take you to these exciting and dramatic remains of ancient Greece but you will want to revisit certain places, especially the Acropolis, for a more leisurely inspection. The world-renowned Acropolis is so much the focal center of any visit to Athens that you should engage an English-speaking guide (available at the entrance or in town) to explain the details of the great monuments you will see there.

You should make this tour your **first walk** in Athens because it will introduce you to the most interesting and significant places. The only important exception is the **National Archeological Museum,** the greatest collection of excavated treasures from the days of Greek antiquity to be seen anywhere. You should devote at least an hour or two to these fascinating exhibits (open 8:00–2:00; 3:00–6:00 daily except Monday; in winter 9:00–4:00; Sundays 10:00–2:00).

Start this stroll at **Constitution Square,** the center of Athens. Directly across this busy square is the old **Palace.** Built in 1834 in Bavarian style (King Ludwig I of Bavaria laid the first stone), the old Palace has housed the Greek Parliament since 1935. On the terrace just below the building, you will see the Tomb of the Unknown Soldier, guarded by the colorfully uniformed and kilted Evzones.

After you have looked at this rather austere monument, turn right along Leoforos Amalias for about one hundred yards to an entrance of the **National Gardens.** This delightfully landscaped park, filled with temperate and semi-tropical flowers, plants, and trees, provides a welcome haven on warm days. Stroll generally to the left along the tastefully planted walks and in a few minutes you will come out on the broad avenue Vasilissis Sofias. (If you ever become lost in Athens, remember that an amazingly large number of people speak English.)

At the corner of this wide avenue and Koubari Street you will find the **Benaki Museum** (open 9:30–1:30; 4:30–7:30 daily except Tuesday and Sunday afternoon; 1 Jan.–28 Feb., 9:30–2:00). This interesting private museum, founded by Anthony Benaki, comprises a fine collection mainly of Greek art from prehistoric times to the present day as well as modern Greek popular art including colorful Greek costumes plus minor arts and crafts from Eastern Mediterranean countries. In addition, there is a fine exhibit of Chinese porcelain. The district to the left of the museum's entrance along Koumbari Street is the fashionable residential area of **Kolonaki.** Modern apartment houses line the streets in this smart section of town.

If you are particularly interested in Byzantine art, you should continue for four blocks along Vasilissis Sofias. At Loukianou Street cross the street and in the middle of the block you will be at the **Byzantine Museum** (open 9:00–4:00; Sunday 9:00–1:30; Monday 2:00–4:00). The lower floor of the museum is largely devoted to Byzantine sculpture with painting and other arts on the upper floor. There is a hall of iconography in the garden.

Returning along Vasilissis Sofias to the National Gardens, you turn left for three blocks on Hirodou Attikou and then you will see the **Royal Palace** on the left—an attractive, unostentatious building secluded from the street in pleasant gardens. This has been the king's residence since the restoration of the monarchy in 1935.

Cross over from the Royal Palace and have another stroll through the attractive National Gardens. There is a café for

MUSEUM

GRAND BRETAGNE HOTEL

GEORGIOU ST.

START 2

START 1

LEOFOROS VASSILISSIS SOFIAS

MUSEUM

OLD PALACE

Constitution Square

OTHONOS ST.

TOMB OF THE UNKNOWN SOLDIER

FILLELINON ST.

NATIONAL GARDENS

IRODOU ATTIKOU

ROYAL PALACE

LEOFOROS AMALIAS

ZAPPEION

LEOFOROS OLGAS

HADRIAN'S ARCH

THE OLYMPIEION

STADIUM

ATHENS

ROUTE 1 ●●●●●●●●➤
ROUTE 2 ――――➤

100 50 0   100   200 YARDS 300

refreshments if you feel like a rest. Or just have a seat on a bench under a cypress tree. If you keep to the left you will come in a few minutes to a large exhibition building, the **Zappeion.** From the terrace in front of the building, there is a fine panorama. On your left you will also see **Mt. Hymettos.** The **Acropolis** is off to your right and the waters of the **Saronic Gulf** straight ahead beyond Piraeus. Behind you rises the sharp summit of **Mt. Lykabettos.**

Turn left from the front of the Zappeion and leave the park at the junction of several main avenues. On the opposite side you will see the **Stadium.** This huge outdoor arena (70,-000 seating capacity) built in 1895 for the first modern Olympic games, is located on the site of the stadium that was used in ancient Athens for the Panathenaic games.

A few moments to the left along Leoforos Olgas will bring you to one of Athens' most monumental ruins of the Roman period, the tall Corinthian columns of the Temple of Olympian Zeus. It's a most impressive sight to look up at these majestic columns against the blue sky. You can still see the drums of the columns dating from the sixth century B.C. used in an earlier temple. Hadrian completed the great temple in the second century A.D.

You will see **Hadrian's Arch,** erected at the time the Emperor came to Athens to dedicate the temple. Go closer and read the inscriptions which reflect Hadrian's pride in his contribution to the city. On the side towards the Acropolis there is in Greek, "This is Athens, the old city of Theseus." But on the side towards the Temple of Olympian Zeus Hadrian had ordered this inscription: "This is the city of Hadrian and no longer that of Theseus."

From here you turn left along one of Athens' busiest thoroughfares, **Dionysiou Areopagitou.** Five or ten minutes walk along this street will take you just below the Acropolis to the **Theater of Dionysus.** This is the most famous theater in Greece. The first drama was presented here by Thespis in 534 B.C. and later the great Greek classical drama flourished here with the initial performances of plays by Aeschylus,

Sophocles, Euripides, and Aristophanes. About 17,000 people could be accommodated in the theater. So many alterations have been made over the centuries that one can only identify the different periods of the theater's construction with the greatest difficulty, but in general the present dimensions date from about 330 B.C. Much of the existing decoration, paving, and seating are remains of the Roman days.

The Roman Theater of **Herodes Atticus,** built in A.D. 161, lies just below the entrance to the Acropolis as you continue up Dionysiou Areopagitou.

By now, if you have started this walk in the morning, you will be ready for luncheon. There is an excellent restaurant which you can see from the main road and is just a few yards on the left—the **Dionysus.** Its huge glass windows look out on the Acropolis opposite. Be sure to return here in the evening when you can dine while watching the Acropolis under floodlighting.

After a good luncheon and a rest, you will be ready to visit the **Acropolis** across the way. But before you do, you ought to stroll for five minutes or so to the left to the **Pnyx.** You keep to the right to reach the top of this hill. From here you will have one of the finest views of the magnificent buildings that crown the Acropolis. The Pnyx was the meeting place of the peoples' assembly and the scene of great orations by Pericles, Themistocles, Demosthenes, and other leaders of Athens during the fifth and fourth centuries B.C. Now spectators watch "Son et Lumière" performances from here. It is a moving experience to stand on the Pnyx, look out over the light green pines and tall dark cypress to the Parthenon with Mt. Lykabettos in the distance. Only the singing of birds interrupts the quiet beauty of this memorable scene.

After viewing the Acropolis from a distance, you make your way down the hill across the avenue and up the winding road that leads to its entrance. Although the natural Klepsydra spring has attracted men to the Acropolis since the Neolithic age (about 3000 B.C.) the first ramparts date from the Mycenean period about 1500 B.C. The glories of the

Acropolis that we admire today are the inspired buildings and temples erected under the direction of Pericles a few years after 449 B.C.

Even though you may decide to tour the Acropolis more thoroughly on another occasion, you may wish to stroll about now and obtain an overall impression. Go through the entrance gate to the **Propylea** or monumental gateway. As you climb up the stone steps through the Propylea you will have your first full close-up view of the majestic colonnade of the Parthenon, one of the architectural masterpieces of all time. The architect Iktinos designed the building which was begun in 447 B.C. The famed sculptor Phidias supervised all the sculptures, such as the metopes, pediments and frieze. But before you approach the Parthenon, turn right to visit the exquisite little **Temple of Athena Nike** which dates from 421 B.C.

Enter the **Parthenon** through the far end, which in ancient times was the front of the building. Be sure to stroll up and down the colonnades on both sides and at the end. Notice that the columns are wider at the bottom than at the top. There are many optical illusions in the Parthenon's construction. For instance, the slight inclination of the columns inwards gives the impression that they are at right angles at their base.

About fifty yards from the front of the building on your right is the intensely interesting **Acropolis Museum** (open 9:00–4:00 daily, except Tuesday, 12:00–4:00; Sunday 10:00–2:00) where you will see many of the most important portable objects found on the Acropolis since 1834. In addition to the marvelous sculptures from the pediments and frieze, there are also exhibited here the remarkable statues of the famous **Korai,** or sixth century B.C. maidens. Don't miss the small exquisite marble of the goddess Nike loosening her sandal. This was a segment of the balustrade that surrounded the Temple of Nike.

From the museum, walk to the belvedere or terrace at the

east end of the rock. Here you have a magnificent view over the city of Athens and the mountains that surround it.

Now stroll along the north side of the Acropolis to the **Erechtheion,** the temple with the famous porch of the maidens. One of the finest examples of Greek architecture, the Erechtheion was built between 421–406 B.C. as a major part of Pericles' plan of the Acropolis. After admiring the graceful figures that still stand on the temple's porch, make your way back to the entrance of the Acropolis.

From the car park in front of the gate, you keep to the right. The low hill on your left is the **Areopagus** where the council of nobles and Athens' highest court met. Now you continue along the path that skirts the Acropolis. Take the first left down the steps, then wind your way down the hill, keeping the open excavated Agora area on your left. Turn left at the far corner of the **Roman** (or smaller) **Agora.** Then go left at the end of the street and you will see the entrance to the ancient Agora on your right (open 7:30–6:00 every day).

The **Agora** was the focal center of community life in ancient Athens, the popular meeting and assembly place and one of the most important points in the city. Habitation on this site has been traced to 3000 B.C. In the midst of the excavated ruins one beautiful temple has survived the ages. The **Hephaisteion** formerly called the **Theseion** on the far side is the best preserved example of a Doric hexastyle (six columns in front) temple of the fifth century B.C. in Athens and the most perfectly preserved relic of the Periclean age in Greece. It is older than the Parthenon.

The long two-storied building with the colonnade to the right of the entrance to the Agora is the reconstructed **Stoa of Attalos.** The present building, reconstructed by the generosity of John D. Rockefeller, Jr., and other American donors, as a faithful copy of the original second century B.C. structure, contains the **Agora Museum** (open 9:00–6:00 daily; 9:00–1:00 Sunday). This collection includes many fascinating exhibits such as ballot tokens used by ancient juries, Neolithic vases, mycenean relics, fine pieces of Greek sculpture, and various amphoras dating from the fifth century B.C. to the fifth century A.D.

A few minutes' walk from the Stoa will bring you to **Ermou Street** where you can find a taxi or bus to return to Constitution Square.

PLAKA—THE BAZAAR QUARTER

This is a walking tour through an unusual section of Athens, **Plaka,** the fascinating old quarter of the city less than half a mile square between **Syndagma** or Constitution Square, the city's center, and the Acropolis.

Although little of it dates from the Greek War of Independence (1821–27), and most was built just over a century ago, Plaka is the oldest inhabited part of Athens. The name appears to be derived from the Albanian word "Pliaka," meaning old.

It has the air of a country town—completely unplanned— in the heart of a bustling city. There are narrow, winding, cobble-stoned streets, low whitewashed houses with flower-filled inner courtyards, tiny shops displaying bizarre Oriental wares, hawkers selling bread or vegetables from baskets astride little donkeys, numerous tavernas where in the evenings, while sampling typical Greek dishes and local wines, you will hear Greek songs to the accompaniment of a type of guitar, a *bazooki.* Here you sense the days of the Turkish occupation, the Athens that Byron knew, even the influence of Byzantine civilization in the many churches.

You should begin your walk to Plaka at **Constitution Square.** Starting from the Grande Bretagne Hotel, circle the broad esplanade, which is shaded by pepper trees and crowded in good weather with tables and chairs for patrons of nearby cafés. At noon and late in the day Constitution Square is so jammed with people it seems like a giant beehive.

On the far side you turn right along Mitropoleos Street in the business district. After a couple of blocks the street opens into a large square. Directly ahead is the rear of the **New Cathedral of Athens** built between 1840 and 1855 from previously used material of seventy demolished churches and chapels. Although you may wish to look around the cathedral, the real treasure in this square is the **Little Metropolis** just to the left on the far side of the Great Metropolitan Church.

This tiny twelfth-century church, a little gem, set just below the level of the square and surrounded by grass and shrubs, is the finest example of Byzantine architecture in Athens. Built entirely of marble which has turned a golden color, it is a cruciform church with a dome only 39 feet above the floor. Look carefully at its fourth century B.C. frieze which depicts the twelve signs of the zodiac, representing the major festivals and seasons of the year—an Attic calendar in pictures. Each month is illustrated by a man dressed according to the temperature of the month. Byzantine bas-reliefs are also set in the church's façade. An amusing modern touch is the telephone just inside the entrance.

Leave the square by passing in front of the New Cathedral to enter Evagelistrias Street. After one block, a left turn on busy Ermou Street past up-to-date stores, will lead to the **Kapnikarea Church.** Surrounded by offices and shops (some in Byzantine style), this small eleventh-century church stands like an island beneath two tall cypress trees in the center of busy Ermou Street. Built of unevenly cut stone and brick, it has a dome of fine proportions and a spacious interior. King Ludwig of Bavaria was responsible for saving it in 1834 when town planners wanted to pull it down. Today it is considered one of the finest of the Athenian churches.

From the church take Kapnikarea Street for two blocks to **Pandrosou Street,** Plaka's most colorful thoroughfare. Vendors may be selling roasted chestnuts or sesame-seed rolls in the street. Perhaps an accordion player will be adding to the gaiety of the scene. Athenians seem to spend much of their time in the streets, and crowds at all times of the day are quite usual. You may wonder where all the people are going and why. In Plaka there are more pedestrians than cars and the pedestrians always seem to be dodging traffic in the narrow streets.

Turning right into Pandrosou Street, you will pass shops selling twine and cloth. The street narrows and suddenly becomes an Oriental **bazaar**—shops selling brass, copperware and bric-a-brac. Here is a cobbler making shoes. Dozens of pairs are hanging in bunches inside the shop and out. Another nearby shop displays antique ikons and silverware. A few doors away is a shop with all types of Greek national costumes. Gay embroidered blouses or bright scarves, red-and-black leather sabots with pompons make attractive souvenirs for the tourist. Stop for a moment and watch craftsmen, sitting at their workbenches, laboring over jewelry or silverware.

Martinos, at No. 50, is one of the more reliable antique dealers. This shop features handmade silverware produced by its own craftsmen. Old Greek coins of the fifth century B.C.—the age of Pericles—may also be on sale.

Perhaps you will want to buy a lekythos—a small antique Greek vase (about six inches high) used for perfume in the sixth century B.C. Permission to take these antique pieces out of the country usually requires two or three days.

At the end of Pandrosou Street on the left is the **Museum of Decorative Arts** (open 9:00–2:00 except Wednesday) located in a former eighteenth-century Turkish mosque. The museum's collection includes a fine exhibit of embroidery of the second century A.D. Coptic cloths as well as contemporary work from the islands, Greek jewelry, Byzantine pottery, ikons, gold, and silverware.

Return along lively Pandrosou Street, then turn right into Eolou Street. **Hadrian's Library** (open 8:00–sunset) is about ten yards on the right. Not much remains of this Roman building except portions of the wall, a few façades and several columns. After wandering about the ruins, you might like to rest on a bench under the trees in the delightful little square opposite. About fifty yards further along Elou Street you will see the marble **Tower of the Winds** in the Roman Agora (open 8:00–sunset). This is one of the most interesting remains of the Roman period. Built in the first century B.C., it is a water clock, sundial, and weather vane.

This octagonal tower was erected so that each side faces a cardinal point of the horizon from which the wind blows. Each wind is represented by a figure carved in stone. For example, Boreas, the north wind, is depicted as a bearded man dressed in heavy clothing blowing into a conch shell. Zephyr, the west wind, is shown as a youth throwing flowers into the air.

The water clock is believed to have operated by the flow of water into a cylinder. The changing water level showed the passage of the hours. The tower itself is one of the earliest architectural examples of an octagonal plan.

From the Tower of the Winds you should walk around the area occupied in ancient days by the Roman **Agora.** Keep it on your right until you are on a curving street above it. Follow this for about fifty yards, then turn right into a very narrow street between whitewashed houses. The first little street to the left will lead, after a short distance, to a flight of steps just below the Acropolis. A palm tree sways in a garden to the right of the steps.

Just along here, right beneath the precipitous rock, is one of the most rural bits of Plaka. A goat may be grazing on bits of grass along the rocky slope or chickens are likely to be feeding outside a shack. There is an interesting little church here by the steep cliffs, the fourteenth-century **Metamorphosi.** As you follow the hillside you will shortly come to a narrow winding street. On the left there's an orange tree on a terrace and just above, a grape arbor decorates a white house.

After climbing a flight of steps on the right, a left turn leads past one of Plaka's popular **tavernas.** A bit further along is an open slope. A small olive grove nestles against the sloping hillside. At this point you will find yourself just below the observation terrace at the northeast corner of the Acropolis.

The first narrow street to the left, **Thespidos,** goes down the hill to a lively vegetable market on the corner a block or so below.

At this point turn left into **Tripodon Street** and wander past fascinating little shops to Flessa Street. A right turn here and then another right at the corner where five streets intersect will bring you into **Adrianou Street.** This is one of the principal thoroughfares of Plaka, usually crowded with people and throbbing with much going-and-coming in and out of its many and varied stores. From one comes the strong aroma of coffee. In another, you will see fish and sea food fresh from the Aegean. No. 96 Adrianou Street is believed to be one of Athens' oldest houses. Outdoor market stalls add to the tumult.

At the end of Adrianou Street, you will find the marble monument of **Lysicrates,** a wealthy Greek citizen, in a small garden, a bit further along on the right. It dates from the fourth century B.C.

The circle of six graceful Corinthian columns once supported the bronze tripod which the chorus under the patronage of Lysicrates won in a musical and dramatic competition.

Almost opposite the monument is the thirteenth-century **Church of Haghia Ekaterini.** It is in a sunken court beneath palm trees. Stop in to look at the ikons. After passing this square on the left, a couple of minutes along Lisikratous Street will bring you to **Leoforos Amalias,** the broad avenue opposite Hadrian's Arch and the Olympieion. From this point you can catch a bus or taxi and in a few minutes be back in Constitution Square.

XVII BARCELONA

BARRIO GOTICO

Mons Taber to Picasso

The popularity of Spain's **Costa Brava** in recent years has brought many more tourists to **Barcelona,** the capital of Catalonia. The more discerning have discovered that Barcelona is full of historic and artistic interest. It is a city to visit, not just pass through.

One of the largest port cities on the entire Mediterranean shoreline, Barcelona is a dynamic metropolis—the chief industrial and commercial city of Spain. Barcelona's history goes back more than two thousand years to the time when the Phocaeans from Greece settled here. The Romans, after capturing Barcelona from the Carthaginians, made it an important center of Roman Spain. You will see many remains of the Roman period.

There are really two cities in Barcelona—the old and the new. The new city, just as impressive as Madrid, boasts broad, stately avenues like the **Paseo de Gracia** and the **Avenida de Franco** crowded with imposing modern office and residential buildings.

But it is old Barcelona—a small area near the port called the **"Barrio Gotico"** that will attract you the most. Full of character and crammed with interesting places this section can be covered easily on foot in half a day. Few cities offer the tourist such a wealth and variety of sightseeing within a few hundred yards as you can find in the quarter around the **Cathedral.**

Let's start this walk through old Barcelona at the city's main square, the **Plaza de Cataluña.** Stroll from this wide esplanade, with its handsome fountains surrounded by flower

279

beds, into the **Avenida Puerta del Angel.** A noisy street fair
with music blasting from loud-speakers may be under way.
The Puerta del Angel narrows just beyond a large department store on the right. Take the left fork for a hundred
yards or so. You will pass on your left a fine modern building with huge glass windows and an unusual stone façade—
quite a contrast to the ancient Cathedral across the **Plaza
Nueva.**

Located on a site that dates from the early Christian era,
Barcelona's distinguished Gothic cathedral was built mainly
during the fourteenth century. You will be struck by its high
vaulted arches and particularly by the shafts of light which
brighten the otherwise dark, mysterious air of its interior.
After looking around the many chapels and beautifully carved
choir stalls, go out through the door near the high altar into
the narrow **Calle de los Condes de Barcelona.**

Immediately on the left you enter the **Museo Marés** (open
10:00–2:00; 4:30–8:30) located in the sixteenth-century
Viceregal Palace. You may care to inspect the Marés collection of religious art but far more interesting are the Roman
remains in the **Museum of the History** of Barcelona which
you reach by descending to the **underground excavations.**
Here you will see the ruins of a second century Roman forum,
the remains of a fourth century Christian basilica and foundations of a Roman palace and homes. It's fascinating to
wander around these subterranean excavations—all extremely
well lit and marked. Some are directly under the Cathedral
itself. At the far end you will find a model which shows the
relation of the Roman ruins to the later buildings.

After climbing the steps marked *Salida* (Exit), you should
ask the guard to show you the **chapel of St. Agatha,** a fourteenth-century Gothic church that belonged to the Kings of
Catalonia. Just beyond is the huge **Salon de Tinell,** the reception hall of the Royal Palace, with its original stone arches
and wooden roof beams. Ferdinand and Isabella received
Christopher Columbus in this hall in 1493 on his return from
his first voyage to America.

You can leave the Barcelona Historical Museum by descending a stone stairway in the courtyard into the Calle del Verguer. A few feet to your right and you will be in the impressive **Plaza del Rey.** Pause for a few minutes to admire the ancient walls surrounding the small square, the wide staircase, and the lofty lookout **tower of King Martin** with its five tiers of round arches. This is one of the most impressive corners in old Barcelona.

Wander into the courtyard next to the Plaza del Rey. Here is a quiet, peaceful spot in the midst of a metropolis— a beautiful stone staircase, an arched cloister and a bubbling fountain in the center of the court.

Go out the far side of the court to the rear of the Cathedral, then stroll to the left for a couple of minutes along the Calle Freneria. From here you have an unusual view of the Cathedral's tower rising above the old houses with their iron grill balconies.

Returning to the Cathedral, you now take the narrow street directly behind the apse to the left, the **Calle del Paradis.** Just before it turns right a few yards ahead, you go left into the courtyard of a medieval house and you will see an arrow that points to the four Corinthian columns of a Roman temple. They mark the summit of **Mons Taber,** the highest point in Roman Barcelona. Note the old millstone embedded in the street just before you cross the threshold. In all these little streets around the Cathedral you'll find many antique shops; why not have a break from sightseeing and enjoy a look around?

A moment or two along the **Calle de la Piedad** to the left will bring you to the Cathedral's **cloisters.** The high Gothic vaulting of the arches and the various guild chapels are two outstanding features of these delightful cloisters which surround a garden patio planted with palms and magnolias. Don't miss the flock of geese, traditionally associated with Barcelona, that live in the gardens. Pause for a moment while walking around the cloisters for a view through the arches or the palm leaves of the Cathedral's bell tower and Gothic spire.

Go out on the **Plaza de Garriga** and then a few steps to the right. On your left you'll see the delightful patio of the Romanesque **Archbishop's Palace.** Opposite a magnificent stone staircase a fountain bubbles beneath a terrace and arched galleries. This is one of the most artistic patios in Barcelona.

Another attractive little patio is the **Casa del Arcediano** on the left of the Calle Santa Lucia and opposite the Cathedral. A moss-covered fountain plays in the patio which is color- fully decorated with old blue-and-yellow tiles.

Returning to the Plaza del Garriga, turn right along the **Calle Montjuich del Obispo.** This leads to a small square, the **Plaza de San Felipe Neri,** with a fountain in the center. The house on the left displays a coat of arms (1740) of shoes, boots, and shoelaces over the beautiful wrought-iron grill bal- cony because it belongs to the Guild of the Shoemakers. At this point wander off to your right. Here is a maze of old houses with attractive balconies, narrow cobblestone streets. Don't miss the little shrine with an inscription on colorful tile which is built right into the façade of a house.

After turning left along the Calle Felipe de Neri, you will pass more antique shops along the Calle San Severo before reaching on your left the entrance to the **Church of San Severo.** Have a look at its baroque interior.

A right turn from the **Plaza del Garriga** will take you along the Calle del Obispo Irurita. Straight ahead you will see a modern **Gothic bridge,** between two buildings. The façade of the building on the left (Disputación or Provincial Council) changes its style from Baroque to Renaissance to Gothic.

In a moment or two you will be in the large **Plaza de San Jaime,** Barcelona's historical and administrative center. A sharp right turn will bring you into the **courtyard of the Dis- putación** (open 9:00–2:00; 4:00–7:00 daily). As you ascend the broad staircase, don't miss the pointed Gothic arches sup- ported by delicately carved slim stone columns. At the top of the stone staircase the wooden beams of the gallery's ceil- ing are beautifully painted and decorated with inlaid wood in

Moorish style. Opposite the staircase is the door to the **Chapel San Jorge** which is decorated with Flemish tapestries and a beautiful altar piece. Go through an arch from the gallery into a large enchanting patio planted with orange trees and dominated by a pinacled tower. On the left of the patio, the state council of Catalonia meets in an ornate council chamber with gilded ceiling, huge Venetian glass chandelier and fifteenth-century tapestry on the wall. (The concierge at the entrance to the building will take you to visit the Chapel and Council Chamber.)

On your return to the Plaza de San Jaime, you may feel like taking a turn on the **Calle Fernando** to your right. This is old Barcelona's main shopping street and continues for a few blocks to the **Rambla.** Before you leave Barcelona you should walk along the colorful Rambla—the traditional promenade—from the Plaza de Cataluña to the **statue of Columbus** opposite the docks. Along the Rambla and on the streets just off it you'll see everything from sailors' cafés to the covered **markets of San José,** a small edition of Les Halles in Paris.

The **Town Hall** (open 9:00–2:00 daily incl. Sunday) is the imposing neoclassic building directly opposite the Diputación. Go to the concierge's office in the beautiful courtyard and ask for a *maceros* (guard) to show you the elaborate salons. The **Salon de Ciento,** named for the municipal councillors' meeting place, dates from 1373 and is distinguished for its Gothic arches, Renaissance doorway, and highly decorative Mudejar ceiling. You should also see the **Salon de Sert** where the great Catalonian artist José Maria Sert depicted the history of Catalonia in spectacular murals and ceiling frescoes.

Turn right from the Town Hall into the **Calle de Jaime I.** As you pass the first through cross street, look left for views of the Cathedral tower rising above the old buildings in this part of the city.

In a few moments you will be in the **Plaza del Angel.** Cross the square and after turning right into the Via Layetana, bear left along the **Calle Platería.** When you walk along this street (named for the silversmiths whose shops used to line it) you will pass little alleys and narrow passageways, the heart of medieval Barcelona. Wander into one of these if you feel like exploring what lies beneath the wrought-iron balconies and ancient doorways with their coats of arms. Washing is stretched across the tiny alleys from house to house in this slum area.

Shortly you will reach the fourteenth-century **Church of Santa Maria del Mar,** old Barcelona's finest Gothic church after the Cathedral. Despite the fire of 1936, you will see several interesting chapels and fine fifteenth-century stained glass. The door at the back of the church opens on to the **Paseo del Borne,** a lively and amusing market place with flower stalls and food shops.

A few yards beyond the rear of the church turn sharply to the left into the narrow **Calle de Moncada**—a fascinating old street with many fine mansions. Their huge doorways, iron grill balconies, overhanging roofs, and gargoyles recall the days when Spanish nobility and wealthy merchants made these palaces and fine homes centers of cultural and ostentatious living. You will want to wander in and out of these ancient doorways, admire lovely flower-filled patios and stroll past ancient lampposts that protrude over the narrow street. Stop at No. 20 on the left, the **Palacio de Dalmases,** to see the elaborately sculptured stone ballustrade and fine arches. Or look into the recently renovated patio at No. 18. At No. 19 there is an imposing staircase with iron railing and attractive palms in the patio.

No. 15, on the right, is the wonderful **Picasso Museum** (open 10:00–2:00 daily incl. Sunday), formerly the fourteenth-century Aguilar palace. This recently opened exhibit of Picasso's paintings and drawings is an extensive and intensely interesting collection of his early and blue periods as well as his later works, including his ceramics. The old palace has been excellently restored. You will admire the fine stone stairways, Gothic arches and roof beams in the patio as well as the modern lighting of the salons. You start on the top floor of this magnificent Gothic building. Here you look out over the tiled roofs of the old quarter or look down from the little cloistered walk into the attractive patio. Visit the exhibition rooms as you descend to the ground floor. The great Spanish artist may leave much of his personal collection to be shown after his death against this background of Catalonian antiquity in the city where his artistic genius first flowered.

From the Calle Moncada you cross the busy Calle de Princesa and in fifty yards you will come to the little Romanesque **Chapel of Marcus** in the tiny square of the same name. Turn left along the Calle de Carders and then through the **Plaza de Lana,** where the wool traders used to be located. A few minutes more along the Calle de la Borla and you will be back in the Plaza del Angel. Turn right on the Calle Layetana to the nearby **Plaza de Berengues el Grande.** Just across the square are the Roman walls—only minutes along the Calle Tapineria from the Cathedral.

XVIII MADRID

THE OLD TOWN

Plaza Mayor to Rastro

Old Madrid is the most interesting and fascinating part of Spain's capital city, a metropolis of two and a half million people. Most of the city is modern and reflects the great expansion that took place first in the late nineteenth century and again after the Civil War in 1936. Although you will include the world-renowned Prado art gallery and the Royal Palace in another walk around Madrid, you will get a better feel of the city by starting in the old section. Here you will sense Madrid's historical background. While wandering in these narrow streets and artistic squares, you will be carried back to earlier times—especially the glorious days of seventeenth century Spain. If you are only visiting Madrid and will not have the chance to tour other cities that are more typical of pre-industrial Spain, the old part of Madrid will at least give you some of the romantic flavor of those days.

Old Madrid is very accessible—right in the center of the city. You'll find that it is concentrated, does not cover a large area, and is quite an easy walk. In fact, you can see it properly only on foot. There are many little turnings, passageways and patios off the narrow streets that you would miss in a car. When you are strolling, you have and therefore take time to look more carefully at the details of the buildings and churches that you pass.

Start at the **Puerta del Sol**—the historic heart of Madrid and still the center of the city's life. It is only a few yards away from the old section. Nine streets meet in this bustling, traffic crowded, commercial square. Its name, Puerta del Sol,

PASEO DE CALVO SOTELO

PLAZA DE LA INDEPENDENCIA

PLAZA DE LA CIBELES

ALCALÁ

POST OFFICE

MUSEUM

CALLE DE

DEL PRADO

RETIRO

ALFONSO XII

San Jerónimo

CORTES

PLAZA DE LA LEALTAD

MUSEUM

CALLE DE

FINISH 3

PASEO

PRADO

MADRID

ROUTE 1 ‑ ‑ ‑ ‑▶
ROUTE 2 ‑·‑·‑▶
ROUTE 3 ••••••••▶

100 50 0   100   200   300 YARDS

comes from the fact that a sun was painted over the door of a chapel which used to stand here by an ancient gate in the city wall.

The large building in the French style facing the square is the **Ministry of the Interior.** Both time and distance in Spain are set at this spot. The clock in the tower is the country's official timepiece and the marker on the pavement is the measuring point to major cities throughout the country.

If you are facing the Ministry, walk a few yards to the right and you will be in the **Calle Mayor.** Almost at once bear left along the **Calle de Esparteros** and in a couple of minutes you will come to the **Plaza de Santa Cruz.** Directly in front of you across the square stands the elegant red-brick seventeenth-century building of the **Ministry of Foreign Affairs.** The slated square towers with peaked cupolas, typical of this part of Spain, reflect the Austrian influence of the Hapsburgs.

Turn right from the Plaza de Santa Cruz on the Calle de Gerona and go under a lofty arch to enter the splendid **Plaza Mayor.** Philip III built this large square in 1619 and his statue dominates it. This was the center of life under the Hapsburg monarchs. Here fiestas, religious plays, autoś-da-fe during the Inquisition, political and criminal executions, bull fights, and public festivals took place. The famous Spanish riding school also performed in this square. On the north side you will see the twin towers of the **Panadería.** The king presided over these public occasions from the center balcony.

Arcades run beneath the five-storied brown stucco buildings with their iron grill balconies and French windows. Pause for a few moments in the center near one of the four lampposts, similar to those in the Place Vendôme in Paris, and glance around the square. As you face the baroque Panadería, you can imagine a seventeenth-century scene when the Plaza Mayor was the brilliant center of Madrid life—the king in his royal box, thousands of citizens leaning out of the balconies and windows in the three upper stories, and the square jammed with people.

Now stroll casually around the arcades, stopping at the

little shops which sell a great variety of goods. On Sundays vendors put up stands under the arcades for the sale and exchange of stamps. Just to the right of the Arch of Gerona (where you came in) you will see several shops displaying old silverware in the **Calle de Zaragoza.** You can go in the **Casa de la Panadería** just under the center balcony with the crest above it. The bakery originally was on the ground floor. Upstairs you will see a tiled room with tapestries just off the royal balcony.

At the far left-hand corner of the square from the Arch de Gerona, you will reach a flight of steps. Just on the right there is the popular restaurant **El Pulpito,** named for a pulpit-like stair landing. When you pass you may see the chefs preparing sea food, which is their specialty. Just ahead go through one of the Plaza's great archways—the **Arco de Cuchilleros**— and down the steps to the street below. This is a popular corner of the old town, often the subject of song and verse. Just at the foot of the steps there's an old bar and wine cellar, **Las Cuevas de Luis Candelas,** built in the cellars below the Plaza. Just ahead a few yards on the left on the **Calle de Cuchilleros** is a night club, **Tablao Español,** where you can enjoy Flamenco dancing from 10:30 P.M.–3:30 A.M. A few yards further will brings you to the **Restaurant Botín,** an attractive old inn. It is fun to watch the chef roast suckling pig in a huge oven decorated with colorful tiles. University students, dressed in medieval costumes, often serenade the diners.

Return to the foot of the steps and keep to the left along the **Cava de San Miguel** beside the high walls of the buildings that face the Plaza Mayor. There were prisons and dungeons in the cellars of these buildings during the time of the Inquisition.

The **market** of San Miguel is just ahead on the left. In this hectic place you will be jostled by the people of the neighborhood doing their daily shopping. Stands display meats, chickens, eggs, Spanish sardines, and other fish, and great bowls with all kinds and varieties of olives. Young boys dash about with cuts of beef slung over their shoulders. Outside on the street are more stalls with fresh vegetables and fruits.

From the market walk a few yards to the nearest main street, the **Calle Mayor,** then go left. In about fifty yards on your left, you will reach the **Plaza de la Villa.** The red stucco and stone building with twin towers and cupolas across the square is Madrid's City Hall, the **Casas Consistoriales** or Casa Ayuntamiento. On the left of the square is the recently restored **Torre de la Lujanes.** Note the fine late Gothic doorway just beyond the tower built in mudejar style (a miniature of Moorish and Christian) where Francis I was kept prisoner in 1525. This palace, which you enter at No. 3, belongs to the Academy of Moral and Political Science. Go inside and you will find a delightful enclosed patio with a grape arbor and potted palms. Up the late fifteenth-century stairway is the reading room of the Hemeroteca Municipal, an outstanding **newspaper library** (open 9:30–1:00; 5:00–7:00 except Saturday afternoon and Sunday). On returning to the square, turn left. The large stone building on your right before you enter the narrow Calle Cordón is the **Casa de Cisneros** which has a beautiful plateresque façade and an attractive courtyard.

At the end of the short Calle Cordón you will reach the small and charming **Plaza del Cordón.** Pause for a moment at the corner of the Calle Sacramento before crossing to the plaza. Glance up at the iron grill balconies on the stone building (the Casa Cisneros) at the corner. There are some attractive ocher-colored houses opposite you along the street.

After descending a flight of steps from the plaza, turn right on the Calle del Conde. Here is the **Méson de San Janvier,** an old-style Madrid restaurant. Continue down the cobblestoned Calle del Cordón to the Calle de Segovia. A few yards on the right is a famous inn—the **Hosteria Carlos III**—over four hundred and fifty years old. You'll enjoy poking around its ancient wine cellars.

On the other side of the Calle de Segovia stands the ancient **Church of San Pedro** and its tower. Turn right just opposite the church along the Calle del Principe Anclona and continue for a couple of minutes to the medieval Plaza Comillas. At the end of the square on the left at No. 9 you will discover the stone stairway and entrance to the sixteenth-century **Capilla del Obispo.** This is a Renaissance church with the most beautiful altar in Madrid. Highly ornamental, its carved wooden panels are covered with gold.

Now go around the church to the left to the Plaza Julio Romero de Torres, then bear to the right and walk down the hill on the Carrera de San Francisco for a few minutes to the large **Church of San Francisco el Grande** (open 11:00–1:00; 4:00–7:00, closed Monday morning). Its exterior resembles the Pantheon in Rome. Its circular interior, erected in the eighteenth century, has a cupola whose diameter is greater than that of St. Paul's Cathedral in London. Be sure to see the richly carved choir stalls from El Paular near La Granja, as well as an extremely fine Goya in the chapel to the left of the altar.

Retrace your steps up the Carrera de San Francisco, then cross the large square, Puerta de Moros. Now take the street to the left that is on a lower level—the **Cava Baja** or Low Ditch, so called because it used to carry water. This is one of the most interesting streets in the old city. It is lined with posadas or old posting-house inns. Don't fail to notice the ancient signs as at No. 14 further down or the inscriptions over the entrance doors. Wander along the cobblestone street and stop on the left about one hundred yards along at the **Posada de la Merced.** Notice how the old colored tiles decorate the doorway. At No. 30 next door, the **Méson del Segoviano,** you will find old beams and an amusing painting of a donkey drawing a carriage just inside the entrance. Above the old courtyard there is an iron grill balcony from which one enters the bedrooms.

At the end of the Cava Baja you are at the **Puerta Cerrada** —the intersection of five streets—where in medieval days the country people waited in the morning for the city gates to open. If you happen to reach here at about two or two-thirty in the afternoon, why not cross over to the Calle Cuchilleros and lunch at **Restaurant Botín** only a few yards along on the right?

Otherwise turn right from the Cava Baja in the Puerta Cerrada where you will see a stone cross and after a few yards right again into the Calle de Toledo. On the left is the baroque **Cathedral of San Isidro.** Bear left at the fork into the Calle de los Estudios. In about one hundred yards the street opens up and you will see ahead a large square usually filled with parked cars. This is the **Plaza de Cascorro.**

On the far side of this elongated square you enter the **Rastro,** often called **Madrid's flea market.** It's particularly busy on Sunday mornings. Vendors at outdoor stalls shout their wares—clothing, house furnishings, leather saddles, watches, copper, and brass. As you descend the wide street, you'll feel like joining the prospective customers who are examining the goods.

In addition to the outdoor stalls, well-patronized antique dealers and curiosity shops are located in courtyards off the street.

Go into No. 12 on the right—the **Nuevos Gallerias.** This interesting stone courtyard with a little fountain in the center is crowded with antique shops both in the lower level and the gallery above. Colored tiles and potted plants decorate the patio. Wander into some of the shops. You will find old furniture, marble statues, copper and brass, as well as religious relics and figures. There are stone tubs for garden plants and old brass carriage lamps. One shop may specialize in old maps and guns, another in oriental chandeliers, a third in old furniture.

Another group of antique shops on the opposite side of the street further down is also worth visiting—the **Galerias Piquer.** The shops in these galleries usually are open until 2:00 and again at 5:00. Here you can also browse for pottery, silver and Chinese pieces.

This is a leisurely place to end this walk through old Madrid. To return to the center of town, you can pick up a taxi in the **Plaza de Cascorro.**

THE MODERN CITY

Puerta del Sol to Royal Palace

Promenading is a national custom in Spain and a particular pleasure in such an attractive city as Madrid. Visitors to Madrid often compare it to Paris, perhaps because of its wide tree-lined boulevards and many buildings erected in the early part of this century. But Madrid is a much newer city than Paris and much more compact. The main places you will want to visit, like the **Royal Palace,** the **Prado** and **Retiro Gardens,** are located in the same central part of the city.

If you have walked through old Madrid to get a feeling of the city's history and tradition, you'll now be keen to stroll along the busy thoroughfares and visit the most interesting sights in modern Madrid. So that you won't try to do too much at one time, **two walks** are suggested. Neither is long and each includes fascinating places you will want to see. In fact, these two walks and the one in old Madrid cover nearly all the major points of interest in the city.

Both of these walks also start at Madrid's Times Square, the **Puerta del Sol.** On your right as you face the clock tower, you'll find the **Calle del Arenal** at the end of the square. Stroll along this crowded street for about two hundred yards, then turn right into the Plaza del Celenque. This leads you to the Calle del Maestro Victoria. In a few yards go left on the **Calle de la Misericordia** and on your right you'll see the large stone and brick building of the **Museo de las Descalzas Reales.** (Open 10:30–1:30 daily; 4:00–6:00 Mon., Tues., Wed., Thurs.)

This is one of the most unusual museums in Madrid and has only been open to the public in recent years. It is part of a convent founded for royal nuns by Juana, daughter of Charles V, in 1564. Used by nuns today, it still has an air of seclusion and quiet, though right in the center of the city.

You are not likely to visit any other museum in Madrid with rooms and furnishings of the period of Emperor Charles V that are so well preserved. An English-speaking guide will take you on a forty-five minute tour of the fourteenth-century building and its many works of art. The convent was in effect a part of the royal palace because so many ladies of royal blood took the veil there. As a result, it acquired not only lavish religious treasures such as vestments, jeweled monstrances and magnificent altars, but also an extraordinary collection of paintings. In addition to excellent examples of Flemish primitives, including a Breughel, there are portraits by Titian and Rubens as well as Zurbarán's fine portrait of St. Francis. Be sure to see the delightful **cloister** with wooden beam roof which looks out on a large flower and vegetable garden right beneath the back wall of one of Madrid's big department stores, the **Galerias Preciados.**

On leaving the convent, turn right into the square and along the Postigo de San Martin which narrows into the **Plaza del Callao.** The tall modern building on the right is the Galerias Preciados.

At this point you might like to do a little window shopping along the **Avenida de José Antonio,** known as the **Gran Via,** one of Madrid's finest shopping streets (opened in 1918). Then cross the broad avenue and turn left along it down the hill past popular restaurants and movie theaters. In a few minutes you will come to a large square, the **Plaza de España.** Rising above it stand Madrid's skyscrapers, two of the tallest buildings in Europe. One is a 34-floor apartment house and office building, the **Torre de Madrid,** and the other the **Edificio España** contains the Plaza hotel.

Cross over to the little park, planted with sycamore trees. After looking at the monument to Cervantes, have an apéritif at the refreshment bar in the park. From the far side of the square you can get a good view of the Torre and its attractive balconies overlooking the city.

If you have time, you can take a diversion from the park that will lead you in about twenty minutes to the **Chapel of San Antonio de la Florida.** Here is the tomb of Goya but, more important, some of his greatest art. He painted a magnificent series of frescoes on the ceiling which many consider the most striking example of Goya's genius. The individual figures, so realistically portrayed, have an extraordinary dramatic quality. To reach the charming eighteenth-century chapel, you take the Paseo de Onésimo Redondo downhill at the far corner of the Plaza de España, then continue past the Estación del Norte, and keep right on the Paseo de la Florida to the little church on the right (open 10:00–1:00; 3:00–6:00 daily; 4:00–6:00 in summer; 10:00–1:00 Sundays). If you don't feel like taking this detour now, make a point of going later to see these remarkable frescoes.

From the Plaza de España cross the street and go into the **Jardines Sabatini**—the gardens opposite on the Calle de Bailén. Trimmed boxwood and tall cypress trees line the path before you descend to the lower gardens where statues are grouped around the fountains. In summer this is the locale for the "Son et Lumière" performances. From the terrace you have a fine view of the **Casa de Campo Park** on the far side of the river which flows below the palace.

A couple of minutes further along the other side of the Calle Bailén will bring you to the **Plaza de Oriente.** The equestrian statue of Philip IV is surrounded in the formal gardens by numerous others of Spanish kings and queens. The large building on the left facing the park is the **Gran Teatro** or Madrid's Opera House which was damaged by fire and has since been closed.

Now cross the Calle Bailén to visit the **Royal Palace** (open 10:00–12:45 daily and Sunday; 3:30–5:45 except Sunday; 4:00–6:30 in summer). You may wish to return for your visit to the palace. There is so much of interest that you will need an hour or more to see it.

The Royal Palace, certainly one of the finest in Europe and one of the best maintained, includes an exceptional collection of Flemish tapestries, beautiful paintings and clocks as well as the private apartments of the last royal family to rule Spain prior to the Civil War.

You enter the palace on the far right of the large courtyard.

English speaking guides are available to take you through. Be sure to buy the full ticket in order to visit the art gallery.

Located on the site of the old Alcázar, the present palace was begun in 1738 and took twenty-eight years to construct. As you go through the palace, you will be particularly impressed by the following: the magnificent main stairway of marble, the Tiepolo ceilings in the Hall of the Guards and the Throne room, the roccoco Gasperini room decorated with Chinese enamel flowers, fruit and birds, the large ornate chapel, the illuminated glass chandelier, a replica of Columbus' *Santa Maria,* and the royal library with its exquisitely bound books. It's quite an experience to be in the clock collection when all seventy clocks of every conceivable design chime the hour simultaneously.

After touring the palace, walk to the far end of the large courtyard overlooking the park (the Campo de Moro) to visit the **Royal Armory,** one of Europe's finest collections of armor, especially of the medieval period. It was started by Charles V. (Open daily 10:30–12:45; 4:00–6:00.) You may also wish to see the museum of old carriages just below the palace before leaving the grounds.

To the Prado

This walk through modern Madrid will take you to the delightful Retiro Gardens, the city's wooded park, and to the world-famous Prado art gallery.

From the **Puerta del Sol,** go left as you face the clock into the **Calle de Alcalá,** fine broad avenue and main shopping street. A few steps to the left will bring you to the **Academy of Fine Arts** (open daily 10:00–1:30; 4:00–6:30). This outstanding collection of paintings includes, in addition to Flemish and Italian works, excellent examples of Goya and Zurbarán.

Stroll a block or so further along the Alcalá, which for years was the glamorous center of Madrid life and magnet for provincial visitors until most of its famous cafés disappeared. Then imposing banks and office buildings replaced them. But it still has much of its old-world dignity and atmosphere. There's a fine vista down the Alcalá at the junction of the Gran Via. From **Dolar's café** at this corner you look down the hill to the artistic **fountain of the Cibeles.**

Cross over from Dolar's and walk back a block or so on the opposite side of the Alcalá to the Calle de Sevilla where you turn left for a hundred yards or so to reach another of Madrid's fashionable shopping streets, the **Calle de San Jeronimo.** Turn left down this street to the **Palacio de las Cortes,** a classic building with two bronze lions flanking the steps. This is the seat of the **Cortes Españolas** which meets from time to time to enact legislation approved by the government. The American Express is one block further on the left.

Continue two blocks to the large square, the Plaza Canovas del Castillo, then stroll to the left along the wide tree-lined Paseo to the **Plaza de la Cibeles.** This eighteenth-century fountain, a goddess driving a chariot drawn by lions, should also be seen at night under floodlights.

If you want to enjoy strolling along Madrid's spacious **Paseo** planted with trees and flowers, you can continue straight ahead for quite a distance. But perhaps you'd rather save this promenade for late in the day or the early evening.

To the right of the square stands the extraordinary and bizarre **Post Office** building. Its cathedral-like size and 230-foot tower have given it the popular nickname of "Neustra Señora de las Communicaciones" ("Our Lady of Communications").

A couple of blocks past the Post Office building on the Alcalá will bring you to the **Plaza de la Independenza,** a large square dominated by the Puerta de Alcalá, a late eighteenth-century arch.

You now enter, on your right, the **Retiro,** Madrid's finest park. One of the most beautiful and largest city parks in Europe, the Retiro includes a lake, zoo, rose garden (lovely in spring and summer) as well as informal paths through shrubbery and wooded groves—the remains of a forest that used to surround Madrid. If you happen to be visiting Madrid in summer, this stroll through the cool shaded Retiro will be a welcome change from the sunny streets. In many ways the formal and informal landscaping of the Retiro will remind you of the Bois de Boulogne in Paris. Also, you'll find many baroque statues in odd places. Although the park dates from the fifteenth century, when it was a forest park attached to Philip II's palace, it was replanted about a hundred years ago.

If you walk along the **Avenida de Mexico** through the gate from the Plaza de la Independenza, you will soon come to the large artificial lake surmounted by a huge, ornate monument to Alphonso XII. You can turn right at the far end of the lake and leave the Retiro by the Puerta de Felipe IV.

After crossing the **Calle de Alphonso XII** which runs along the Retiro, you will be in the Calle Felipe IV. In a moment you will see on your right a red brick building, the **Army Museum,** built on the remains of the old royal palace of Buen Retiro. Now it houses a vast military collection of guns, models of forts, and weapons from the fifteenth century to the Spanish Civil War. This museum (open 10:00–1:00 except Saturdays; 10:00–2:00 Sundays and holidays) has a particular appeal for boys. Almost opposite the entrance and facing the broader part of the Calle de Felipe IV stands the **Casón de Felipe Cuatro,** a classic building with stone pillars, the last remaining part of the old Retiro Palace and now used for special exhibits.

One block along the Calle de Felipe IV and another to the left will bring you to the Gothic **Church of San Jeronimo el Real** where heirs to the Spanish throne took the oath of allegiance.

From the front of this church it's only a short block to the main entrance of the **Prado,** Spain's national collection of painting and sculpture and **one of the world's greatest art galleries** (open 10:00–5:00 daily; 10:00–2:00 Sunday). You should allow at least a couple of hours to view the superb works of art exhibited here. Although the museum specializes in the great Spanish masters with an unrivaled collection of Goya, Velasquez, and El Greco, you will also want to see the unusual selection of Flemish and Italian paintings as well as the famous Greco-Iberian statue, the Dama de Elche. The Prado is so vast that you should organize your tour according to the artists and schools you most want to see.

There is no more delightful place in Madrid to end a walk than in this marvelous art museum.

XIX TOLEDO

THE SPIRIT OF EL GRECO

From Cathedral to Alcázar

Toledo is so much the essence of Spain that the entire city has been declared a National Monument. The most characteristic of all Spanish cities, Toledo embodies the country's turbulent and varied past. From the days when it was a Roman settlement, Toletum, at the beginning of the Christian era to the siege of the Alcázar in the Spanish Civil War, Toledo has figured prominently in the great movements of Spanish history. Christian and Arabic cultures are intermingled because Toledo was Moorish for three hundred years. It is a city of art treasures and was the home of El Greco for most of his life. The largest collection of the artist's works, including perhaps his finest masterpieces, are on exhibit here.

Dramatically perched on a rocky bluff, Toledo is encircled on three sides by the deep gorge of the Tagus River. It is a walled city with ancient stone gateways or puertas. There is a mysterious air of the past in its tiny, tortuous streets which wind like deep ravines beneath high buildings and walls.

Most visitors make Toledo a one-day trip by car from Madrid—a distance of forty-three miles. You should start early so you can stop en route at **Llescas** (half way) to see the five superb El Grecos (especially the painting of St. Ildefonso) in the sixteenth-century chapel of the **Caridad Hospital.** To reach the hospital, take a right turn from the main road to the largest building in the village. Go into the patio and pull the bell at the door on the left next to an entry. A nun will be glad to open the iron screen grill so that you can get close to the paintings.

302

Toledo is ideal for the walker. In fact it's the only way to explore the city. Many of the cobblestone streets are too narrow for wheeled traffic. If time permits, you should spend the night. Then you will have enough time just to wander around the old streets and poke about the squares and courtyards as well as other interesting corners that cannot be included in a one-day visit. (You can tour Toledo's outstanding historic and artistic monuments in a single day.)

In typical Moorish fashion, delightful patios are hidden behind huge wooden doors and high walls. Often the door is open so you can look inside, but the towering houses above the canyon-like streets do obstruct prominent landmarks and make it harder to find one's way.

Start your tour in the **Plaza del Ayuntamiento** in front of the magnificent **Cathedral.** It contains such a wealth of treasures that you should go there while you are fresh for at least a preliminary visit. You can return in the late afternoon to see the stained glass windows at their best. The seat of the Primate of Spain, the Cathedral dominates the city architecturally and artistically. It is certainly one of the finest in Spain and ranks among the great cathedrals of Europe. It was finished in 1493—one year after the discovery of America—is French-Gothic, and took more than two hundred and fifty years to build.

Before entering the Cathedral, you should walk to the far side of the plaza where you can view the decorative exterior and the impressive 295-foot tower, built in three main sections.

Then stroll around to the south side (on the right as you face the building) to see the **portal of the Puerta de los Leones** with its sixteenth century bronze doors, elaborate stone carving and ornamental sculpture.

Enter the **Cathedral** (open 11:30–1:00 and 3:30–5:00) through the Puerta del Mollete at the foot of the tower. The vast interior is filled with an unusual number of artistic and religious treasures in the many chapels and throughout the Cathedral. You will be struck at once by the beautiful iron

grill screen of the **Capilla Mayor.** Behind this, the massive Gothic gilded altar piece of larch wood rises to a height of ninety feet. On either side are two plateresque pulpits. The carved walnut double choir stalls opposite the main altar are considered the finest in Spain. Behind the Capilla Mayor light shines through a specially constructed rose window in the roof on a fantastic ornamental screen of baroque bronzes and marbles—known as the **Transparente.**

The sacristy possesses an unusual collection of paintings by El Greco—including *Christ Being Stripped of His Garments,* one of the artist's greatest works in Toledo. See the beautifully illuminated French thirteenth-century Bibles in the vestry next to the sacristy. The **Custodia,** a seven-foot, five-hundred pound gilded silver monstrance of the sixteenth century with highly ornamented diamonds and precious stones, is the most elaborate piece in the Cathedral's Treasure.

You should linger for a few minutes in the two-storied cloister on the way out. It is a delightful courtyard planted with flowers and trees.

From the cloister turn right past the **Palace of the Archbishop** across from the Cathedral and then go left along the Calle de la Trinidad following the signs pointing to the **Casa El Greco.** There is a convent on the right on the way up the hill. Along the narrow street are faded red brick buildings and a high bell tower, a frequent sight in Toledo.

At the end of the street stands the **Salvador Church.** Here you can see remains of the days when the Visigoths occupied the city. Visigothic sculpture on the marble columns next to the altar dates from the sixth century.

After visiting this church, bear right and follow the signs along the **Calle de Santo Tomé.** On the left is an interesting old house with big glass bay windows and on the right a pleasant little square. Further down on the left you will see the Mudejar bell tower of the **Church of Santo Tomé** (open 10:00–1:30 and 3:00–6:00). (Mudejar style is an architectural mixture of Christian and Moorish.) Inside the church is a masterpiece by El Greco, *The Burial of the Count of*

Orgaz, which hangs above the Count's tomb. The artist himself is included among the group of Toledans in this painting —another of El Greco's greatest works.

Just nearby at No. 6 you can look around a lovely Toledan patio by entering an old wooden door embellished with huge nail heads—characteristically Moorish. An ancient well head and decorative plants set off a flooring of colorful Moorish tiles. A wooden gallery with fine iron grill work overlooks the gay patio. The shop opposite the Church of Santo Tomé has an interesting collection of Toledan metal work on display. You will be interested to watch the craftsmen at work.

Straight ahead along the street leading to El Greco's house, you should stop in at No. 20 to glance at the patio of a modern house. Just to the right you can glimpse the spires of the Church of San Juan de los Reyes.

A left turn (as indicated by the marked route) leads into the **Calle de Samuel Levi.** Immediately on the left is the building known as the **house of El Greco.** Although the artist never lived here, he probably resided nearby. It was built in the fourteenth century by **Samuel Levi,** Pedro the Cruel's Jewish treasurer and chief landowner of this Jewish quarter. The house (open 10:00–2:00 and 3:30–6:00) has been restored as a sixteenth-century Toledan residence and contains an interesting collection of paintings by El Greco and other Spanish masters as well as furniture of the period. For example, you can see the original writing table shown in El Greco's painting of San Ildefonso at Llescas. The wooden gallery, sixteenth-century kitchen with large fireplace surrounded by cooking utensils and colorful pottery, as well as the fine linen fold paneling, make the house well worth visiting. Stroll around the delightful garden from which there is a striking view of terra-cotta colored roofs, ocher bell towers, and several nearby cigaralles, country houses that look out over the Tagus.

Adjoining the house is a small museum with many unusually fine paintings including El Greco's famous *View of Toledo.* Also, you should visit the chapel inside the museum decorated with ancient Moorish tiles and frieze below an artesanado ceiling (constructed of little pieces of wood artistically fitted together).

Go down the alley just a few yards from the House of El Greco to the **ancient synagogue** of the Jewish aristocracy, **El Transito.** Built in 1366 for Samuel Levi and later converted into a Christian church after the expulsion of the Jews from Spain in 1492, its interior is richly decorated. Oddly enough the Hebraic inscriptions as originally carved on the frieze remain as do some old tombs. The row of Moorish arches above the frieze and all around the building is a fine example of the ornamental Andalusian style. The original larchwood ceiling inlaid with ivory in geometric designs and the elaborately decorated front wall help to make the interior one of the most beautiful in Toledo.

Turn right outside the synagogue and follow the sign marked **Church of San Juan de los Reyes** on the street of the same name. Shortly after crossing a large square you will see the entrance to **Santa Maria la Blanca** beyond a small garden of cedars and locusts. Before being converted into a church this was the oldest **synagogue in Toledo** and was founded in 1180 (open 10:00–1:00 and 3:00–6:00). Note the lovely Moorish horseshoe arches and the carving on the stone capitals of the pillars.

Just a short distance further along the **Calle de los Reyes Católicos,** you will find on the right an interesting antique shop with an ancient cellar.

The **Church of San Juan de los Reyes** (open 10:00–6:00) on the left is, except for the Cathedral, Toledo's most elaborate church. It was originally planned by Ferdinand and Isabella as their last resting place. However, after conquering Granada, they chose to be buried there. Just before entering the church, you should notice on the outside of the apse the chains of Christians captured by the Moors and released by Ferdinand. The interior, unusually bright for a Spanish church, contains much elaborately carved stonework. But it is the double cloister that makes this church so remarkable.

In florid Gothic design, its exquisitely carved stone arches, doorways, and pillars make it one of the finest in Spain. Go up to the second story and look out over this wonderful cloister and the tall cypresses in the garden courtyard.

After visiting the church, pause on the terrace to enjoy the fine view over the old city wall, the river below and the Tagus valley beyond. The stone gateway with twin towers on the right is the **Puerta de Cambrón.**

From the terrace keep the church on your right and a few yards beyond it, opposite a school, bear left on the **Calle del Angel.** After passing a red brick gate in Moorish style the street goes up a slope and beneath an archway. Don't miss the overhanging tiled roofs. Just ahead is the **Tower of Santo Tomé.** About twenty yards before reaching the tower, look carefully on the left for a tiny alleyway, the **Callejon de la Soledad.** This is one of those fascinating corners of Toledo that makes wandering around it so delightful. Here is an old house with iron grill work and ancient lamppost which has that mysterious air of the past, so prevalent in old Toledo.

Opposite the Tower of Santo Tomé follow the narrow cobblestone street, **Calle de la Campaña.** Have a look at some of the tiled patios on either side. At the top bear right, then left on **Calle Alfonso XII.** On the right side of a tree-planted square facing the **Church of San Ildefonso** take a narrow street—**Callejon del Nuncio Viejo** down a slope. At some places this street is only three or four feet wide. After about fifty yards turn right and shortly you will come out on the Cathedral square.

It is only about a ten-minute walk from the Cathedral to Toledo's main square, the **Plaza de la Zocodover,** where you can find hotels and restaurants for a late lunch following Spanish custom.

From the Cathedral turn right beyond the cloister into the narrow **Calle del Hombre de Palo.** Have a look at the alleys on the right and left. Just ahead several little streets meet in a small square, the Plaza de las Cuatro Calles. Straight ahead is Toledo's main shopping street, the **Calle del Comercio.** A few yards further along it on the left beyond the little Plaza del Solarejo you will see a strange building in nineteenth-century style. Five stories high, its long glass windows seem out of place in Toledo.

Note the decorative street sign on the left at the next little square—**Calle Toledo de Ohio**—in honor of the long connection between the two cities.

The three-cornered Plaza de Zocodover just ahead is the center of Toledan life and was the scene of bull fights, autos-da-fe, etcetera, in past centuries. Iron grill balconies decorate the buildings around the square. It is amusing to wander down the two arcades and stop in at one of the crowded cafés.

If you want to lunch in Toledo's best hotel, take the **Calle Barrio del Rey** almost opposite the clock tower and bear left past a church tower for about 25 yards to the **Hotel Charles V** on the right.

After lunch, you can complete the short remainder of this walk. On returning to the Plaza de Zocodover stop on the left at the **Plaza del Corral de Don Diego.** In the courtyard, outdoor dramatic performances took place in the seventeenth century.

Leaving the main square, go through the high archway beneath the clock—the **Arco de la Sangre**—of Moorish design. The home of Cervantes, the great Spanish novelist, used to stand a few yards from the bottom of the steps below the arch before its destruction during the Spanish Civil War.

The **Hospital of Santa Cruz** on the left is Toledo's most interesting museum and art gallery (open 10:30–1:30; 3:30–7:00). Founded as a hospital during the sixteenth century, and built in the form of a Greek cross, it is considered one of Spain's finest Renaissance buildings. The entrance façade is particularly elegant. In addition to an archaeological section in its spacious and richly decorated halls, there is, on the second floor, a wing of fine paintings by El Greco.

After visiting the museum, you will be enchanted by the magnificent two-story plateresque cloister which is adjacent and its ornamental marble stairway. Stand for a moment in an archway and watch the tall cypress in the patio silhouetted against the terra cotta roof.

Climb the flight of steps opposite the hospital, pass through a gate and continue up the hill to the **Alcázar,** Toledo's historic citadel. There is a wonderful view over the Tagus and the surrounding countryside from the terrace.

The Alcázar (open 9:30–1:30; 3:30–6:30) located on the highest point in the city—at one time the site of a Roman camp—is perhaps the most famous fortress in Spain. Ever since the days of Ferdinand the Great and Charles V. the Alcázar has been the scene of battle. Burned three times, its last great siege was during the Spanish Civil War in 1936. (It is now being reconstructed.) Stop at the impressive monument just below the terrace in memory of those who died here in the Civil War.

From the Alcázar it takes only a few minutes down the **Cuesta del Alcázar** to return to the Plaza de Zocodover.

Before returning to Madrid you should be sure to see the dramatic views of Toledo from overlooks on the road that circles the hillside on the opposite side of the river. Cross the Tagus on the new bridge below the Alcázar and return to the Madrid road by the thirteenth-century bridge of San Martin.

XX SEGOVIA

A WHIFF OF MEDIEVAL SPAIN

From Alcázar to Aqueduct

An excursion to **Segovia** will take you back several centuries to the days of medieval Spain. Only an hour and a half by car from Madrid, Segovia can be visited in a one-day trip.

The fairyland quality of the turrets and towers of Segovia's **Alcázar** expresses the romantic, enchanting mood that pervades Segovia.

It is a quiet town—not crowded with tourists like Toledo. Aside from the Alcázar, there isn't too much intensive sightseeing to do. Rather it's the kind of place where you feel transported into the past. As you wander around the crowded, narrow streets and into the little squares, where so often you will discover a magnificent Romanesque church and quaint houses, you will sense the atmosphere of the Spanish Middle Ages. You feel little has changed in Segovia for it seems relatively untouched by modern civilization.

Perched on a long, narrow, rocky eminence, Segovia is surrounded by ancient walls dating from Roman times. At various points there are striking vistas over the countryside and the valley beneath the town.

You will find walking delightful in Segovia. At every turn you encounter an artistic scene. There is little motor traffic to disturb you; many of the streets are too narrow for cars, and the city is quite small and compact. The soft and clear light, for which Segovia is noted, casts a special aura over the ocher-colored buildings.

Begin your stroll through Segovia at the Alcázar—its most dramatic building architecturally and most interesting his-

312

torically. Before you cross the drawbridge over the moat, walk along the curving terrace, the **Paseo de Ronda,** to get a full view of the castle. From here you will see the round turrets with their steeply sloping slate roofs and the battlemented central tower rising above.

The Alcázar (open 10:30–7:30 daily) is one of the most famous fortress-castles in Spain. Founded in the eleventh century, the present building dates mostly from the thirteenth and fourteenth centuries. You will notice both Gothic and Moorish influences in the great halls and magnificent chambers. Lovely Romanesque arches, elaborate gold-leaf ceilings and mudejar friezes in plaster are among the Alcázar's artistic attractions. Isabelle was proclaimed Queen of **Castile** in its throne room; Columbus made his will here in 1505, six months before his death, and his king, Ferdinand, acted as a witness.

Walk out on the battlemented terrace both to look up at the Alcázar's towers and for a wonderful panorama of the valley. Before you leave Segovia, for the finest view of the castle, drive to the bridge at the confluence of the two streams you see below the rocky buttress. From this point the rocky promontory on which the castle stands appears like a prow of a ship. Here you will sense that fairy-like quality that is so characteristic of the Alcázar.

In the small **armory** you will find a collection of medieval artillery including one of the first cannons in Spain—a fourteenth-century piece. On your way out pause for a few minutes in Clock Court—a charming patio.

After leaving the Plaza del Alcázar, you should bear to the right along the narrow **Calle de Daoiz.** Segovians call it the Canonjia de Velarde because the tiny houses with iron grill work and tile roofs belonged to the canons of the Cathedral. Stop in on the left at the patio of No. 32 to look at the flowers, plants, and trees on the terrace. Note the crests carved in stone over the Romanesque doorways. In a moment you will pass the arch of the Puerta de la Claustra—once the gateway to the canons' quarters.

CALLE DE SAN AUGUSTIN

AQUEDUCT

PLAZA DEL
AZOGUEJO

C. DE SAN FRANCISCO

FINISH

PL. DE
SN. NICOLAS

PL. LOS
HUERTOS

ARIAS
DAVILA

LOZOYA

CALLE REAL

AVDA. DE FERNANDEZ LADREDA

S. MARTIN

ALPUENTE

S. MIGUEL

S. MILLAN

CALLE REAL

PLAZA
MAYOR

SAN FRUTOS

CATEDRAL

HOYOS

SEGOVIA

ROUTE ------>

100 50 0 100 YARDS 200

Just beyond the **Plaza de la Merced** you will be in the **Calle de Marqués de Arco.** At No. 6, on the left, you should step inside to see the attractive patio belonging to the palace of the Marqués de Arco.

The **Cathedral** (open 9:00–1:00; 3:30–6:00) is a fine example of sixteenth-century Castilian Gothic architecture. You will be impressed by a feeling of light and space in its beautifully proportioned interior which is further distinguished by graceful vaulting and fine stained-glass windows. The baroque wrought-iron gates of the chapels and the carved choir stalls are examples of most artistic workmanship. Before leaving, stroll around the Gothic cloisters.

The **Plaza Franco,** Segovia's main square, faces the Cathedral. Wander under the colonnades to the **Church of San Miguel** on the far side. On the way you will pass some interesting old streets that radiate off the square. From the church's steps you can see the towers, buttresses and pinnacles of the Cathedral.

Now take the **Calle del 4 de Agosto** at the same end of the square. Bear to the left for about ten yards, then right on the Calle de la Trinidad beneath a high wall. In a few moments you will come to the Romanesque **church of Santo Trinidad.** The graceful arches of its porch, its bell tower and beautifully restored interior make it among the most beautiful churches in Segovia.

As you continue along the **Calle de la Trinidad,** you will pass attractive gardens and tall cedar trees. In the **Plaza de Guevara** there is, on the left, a fine building with massive wooden doors. If you go into the patio, you will come upon a bubbling fountain and a superb iron grill gate.

Now follow the **Calle de Doctor Laguna** just opposite, into the Plaza del Doctor Laguna. On the far side of the little park you will see the battlemented tower of the **Arias-Dávila palace**—the finest of its kind in Segovia. After passing the tower, a few yards further and down some steps will bring you to the **Church of San Martin.**

Here is Segovia's finest Romanesque church. Its exterior

galleries, portal and porch are quite exceptional. You should study this magnificent church from different angles. The outer porticos, which distinguish so many of Segovia's Romanesque churches, are a regional characteristic. They offer protection from the sun in summer and on cold, clear winter days are often warmer than the church's interior.

Just below the church is the little square of los Sirenas. The high square-topped tower rising behind the **statue of Juan Bravo,** leader of the revolt against Charles V, is the fifteenth century **Casa de Lozoya,** one of the finest residences in Segovia.

At this point you should stroll along the **Calle Real** for a few moments towards the Plaza Franco. A turn to the left just before you reach the square will bring you to the **Convent of Corpus Christi** (open 10:00–12:00; 4:00–6:00). Before 1410 this was the **leading synagogue** of Segovia's important Jewish community.

Retrace your steps to the square of las Sirenas. On the right you will find several interesting and fine Segovian residences. One, the **Casa del Siglo XV,** is on the Calle Real. Another, the Gothic palace of the **Conde Alpuente,** is located a few yards down a little lane. The third one you should notice is the **Casa de Tordesilla** at No. 3 on the Calle Real—a house with a decorative façade and graceful aches above the portal.

A little further on the left, along the Calle Real, you will come to the fortress-like façade of the **Casa de los Picos.** It was built in about 1500, but a hundred years earlier had been a fortified mansion to defend this gate of the city.

From here continue down the Calle Real and shortly you will see ahead the majestic arches of the great **Aqueduct.** Dating from the days of Trajan, this remarkable construction is one of the best preserved Roman aqueducts in Europe. It is hard to realize that these tremendous blocks of granite have stood for two thousand years without any mortar to hold them together. As you look up at the highest of its arches (ninety-three feet), you will be impressed by the well proportioned tapering pillars which give an extraordinary effect of lightness and slenderness to the entire structure. The conduit above the double tier of arches is about half a mile long and still carries water to the city.

When you reach the **Plaza del Azoguejo,** walk under the arches for a short distance in order to see the Aqueduct from beneath, and from a different angle on the other side. It is particularly effective to stand on the side away from the sun to see the design created by the light and shade.

By now you are probably ready for a late lunch. The **Méson del Candido** in the Plaza del Azoguejo, an attractive medieval house full of Castilian atmosphere, is the best restaurant in Segovia.

After lunch you should stroll around the square and then take the **Avenida de Fernandez Ladreda,** which is on your right as you face the Méson del Candido. Keep right at the fork and walk under the arcades on the right-hand side of the street for a short distance to the **Church of San Millán.** The exterior of this pure Romanesque church is particularly beautiful, especially the arcaded gallery, portal and apse. Go inside to see the mudejar carved roof and carved columns of the nave.

Before going to the **bridge below the Alcázar,** as suggested earlier, stroll back to the Aqueduct. These two monuments, each so extraordinarily dramatic and thrilling and yet so completely different, provide the two poles for a delightful and interesting walk through medieval Segovia.

About the Author

George W. Oakes, the ambient author of TURN RIGHT AT THE FOUNTAIN, took up walking shortly after he was born in 1909, and has been traveling ever since. Along the way he has acquired an education at Princeton and Oxford, a London-born wife, a daughter and a son, as well as a considerable reputation as a journalist. His knowledge of British affairs and European travel has led to numerous articles in the New York *Times,* the Washington *Star,* the Louisville *Courier-Journal,* and many other publications. A specialist on the subject of the Federal government's relationship to education, he was assigned to prepare a policy statement on aid to education for John F. Kennedy's 1960 presidential campaign. Mr. Oakes has been traveling in Europe since 1925, and resided in London from 1955 to 1957. When not traveling, he makes his home in Washington, D.C.